# EDUCATION TODAY

# EDUCATION TODAY

## By JOHN DEWEY

*Edited and with a Foreword by*

JOSEPH RATNER

*What the best and wisest parent
wants for his own child, that must
the community want for all its children. Any other ideal for our schools
is narrow and unlovely; acted upon it
destroys our democracy.*—JOHN DEWEY

GREENWOOD PRESS, PUBLISHERS
NEW YORK

# FOREWORD

JOHN DEWEY is not one of those who required a world crisis to make them realize that the maintenance and development of a democratic society and way of life is not an easy but a difficult thing. He has been teaching this truth for close to half a century. More thoroughly than any other leader of American thought, he has explored the problems of democracy and has, with tireless persistency, revealed the obstacles that must be continually overcome if our democratic society is not to be just a promise but a living and flourishing reality.

Education has always occupied the central place in Dewey's philosophy of democracy. Representative government, universal franchise, the freedoms guaranteed in the Bill of Rights, provide the necessary framework within which the democratic social processes can go on. They are necessary but not everything. They constitute the essential structure, the skeletal form of the social-political body. They are not, however, its flesh and blood. The flesh and blood are the attitudes, dispositions and habits, the beliefs and customs, the ways of thinking and doing—in sum, the intellectual and moral characters of the people. As Dewey wrote in 1897: "Education is the fundamental method of social progress and reform. All reforms which rest simply upon the enactment of law, or the threatening of certain penalties, or upon changes in mechanical and outward arrangements, are transitory and futile." Democracy as a way of life, as Dewey conceives it, is essentially a life of social progress and reform.

Some educators, in recent years, have asked whether the

school *dare* build a new social order. Dewey's answer to this basic question the reader will find written throughout *Education Today*. It is that no social order, least of all the democratic, can be securely built unless the school is an active participant in the building of it.

If the importance of the school in the life of society were at any time a matter of speculative theory, it is so no longer. The totalitarian states have made the school's importance plain enough for even the blind to see. The totalitarian dictatorships have destroyed many institutions, but upon no institution they inherited have they concentrated their destructive powers more fiercely than upon the educational. With systematic thoroughness, they have changed the content and method of education so that not a vestige of freedom remains, for teacher and student alike. Totalitarianism cannot tolerate an educational system that is even partially devoted to cultivating individual differences or that in any way encourages the development of independence of mind and the integrity of character that grows out of the exercise of free intelligence. The dictators know that they dare not try to build a totalitarian order of society without transforming the school, from top to bottom, into a supporter and agent of totalitarianism.

The rapidity with which the totalitarian dictatorships have achieved their domestic transformations has sometimes, indeed far too often, been taken as a challenge for democratic societies to accomplish their ends with similar dispatch. But a democratic society cannot, without committing suicide, use the methods of the totalitarians, and it is by their methods that they make such speed. It takes relatively no time at all to burn books and to kill, exile, and terrorize teachers and students. It is a long, slow, and difficult process to create a democratic educational system.

During the past forty years—the period covered by *Education Today*—great strides have been made in the direction of developing a genuinely American education. On the physical side, on the side of providing the *outward arrangements" of education, the work begun a little over a century ago has been carried further, perhaps, than the pioneers for free public schools dared even to dream of as possible. Not that even this aspect of the work has been satisfactorily completed and we may now rest complacently on our national oars. There are many areas in the United States where the physical educational facilities are miserably poor in quality and woefully inadequate in extent. However, more than the abstract principle of tax-supported education has been vindicated. The existence of free schools from kindergarten to university in many of the states of the Union is effective and living demonstration on the part of democratic society of its obligation to provide for the education of its young.

On the educational side, on the side of transforming the "inner arrangements" of the school, notable advances have also been made during the same period. The history of the progressive education movement is not a seamless series of successes. It is a history marked by failures and frustrations, some of them due to old traditions it could not overcome, some to new oppositions it could not foresee, and some caused by its own defects of understanding and practice. But, when all allowances are made and all that can legitimately be discounted is taken off the books of progressive education, there is left a net gain for American education, impressive and encouraging.

John Dewey is the most important single force in the progressive education movement. Building on various sporadic reforms that had been initiated, he developed a new psychology of learning and logic of thinking and laid down the comprehensive philosophical foundations that made it possible for the new education to develop and prosper.

Basic to Dewey's philosophy of education is his conception of learning as a social process. Traditional education, institutionalized in the grade school, with its system of credits, promotions, and physical, vindictive punishment, conceived of education as a one-way procedure of handing down from above to below. In the sixties, one American educator summed up the basic principles in the following words:

The teacher's authority as absolute, must be imperative, rather than deliberative or demonstrative. His requirements and decisions, in whatever form presented, whether that of request, demand or mandate, must be unargued. What he resolves upon and pronounces law, should be simply and steadily insisted upon as right *per se,* and should be promptly and fully accepted by the pupil as right, on the one ground that the teacher, as such, is governor.

Reform movements had partially broken down this extreme "ideal" of education by the time Dewey entered the field in the nineties. But it cannot be said even now that this "ideal" has been entirely uprooted from the minds of all educators and completely eliminated from the practice of all schools.

This authoritarian, pipe-line theory of education has a long and involved history, psychological, moral, social, religious, and intellectual. Some have traced its intellectual origins as far back as Alexandria. The controlling idea of this theory is that the pupil is the empty vessel at the lower end and the teacher (by optimistic convention) the full vessel at the upper end. Education consists in transmitting or piping the information, knowledge or "truth" from the full into the empty vessel. The flow down the pipes was not free and uninterrupted. Many obstructions and blockages occurred. These were due to the presence within the empty vessel of recalcitrant traits of character, obdurate resistances to education, to innate and acquired perversities of nature. The young were inherently opposed to education. The discipline of the birch was the basic means for remedying this depravity of native human nature.

The pipe-line theory is not in its origins unnatural as its persistence to this day amply testifies. From point of view of adults who are accustomed to imposing their will on others, who have a vested interest in their possessions and achievements, and who can conceive of nothing better than to have their own ways perpetuated unchanged, it is the most natural

thing in the world to see education as a matter of transmitting, of authoritatively handing down, the "heritage" from
one generation to the next. Such conception of education is
as natural as the ancient law of primogeniture and serves a
similar function.

The difficulty traditional education had in holding attention, in maintaining the interest and effort of the pupil, is
conclusive evidence that from point of view of the young
and growing, education has a radically different significance.
From the day of birth, the young are active, exploring agents,
not passive recipients. As living and growing creatures they
are interacting with the environment, adjusting to it, actively
appropriating and gaining mastery over it. The curiosity of
the young is proverbial. Curiosity is not an innate psychic
power, secreted in some prenatally acquired self. It is a
quality of the behavior of a plastic creature freely interacting with a novel environment. Traditional education, instead
of fostering and utilizing the plasticity of the young, did its
best to destroy it by imposing a system of rigid, routine habits. Its cut and dried organization of subject matter and
dictatorial teaching methods forced the pupil passively to
accept what was given and as given. Instead of creating an
educational environment within which the natural dispositions of the young would be directed, not thwarted, strength-
ened not crushed, the traditional school built up obstacle
walls to learning. Had the deliberate design been to dull
sensibility and kill curiosity, the natural outgoing learning
activity, traditional education could hardly have done a better job.

The wisdom of traditional education is summed up in two
of its favorite maxims. "Education is a preparation for life"
epitomizes its conception of the content or subject matter of
education in relation to the pupil. "Spare the rod and spoil
the child" embodies its fundamental conception of the methods of teaching and of the way in which desirable character
is formed.

For Dewey, education is not a preparation *for* life. It *is* life or growth. "Education is a process of living and not a preparation for future living." Each phase of a growing life has its own distinctive needs, qualities, and powers. The organization of study and the methods of teaching must for each phase be such that the process of learning will satisfy the needs, enrich the qualities, and mature the powers of the individual. "Education must be carried on in forms worth living for their own sake." The good life is not a vision to be held before the pupil as a distant reward for enduring and suffering the hardships of education. The qualities of the good life should be inherent qualities of the educative process.

When society moved from century to century substantially unchanged, there was some practical sense to the idea of education as transmission. You can "prepare for life" if the "life" will be there after the period of preparation is over. Whether education *should* ever be of this kind is another question, since such education is one way of ensuring social and cultural stagnation. However, in a static, stratified society "preparation for life" on the traditional model is a practicable if not desirable educational ideal. But in modern American society, the adults are not preserving the *status quo*. American social and cultural conditions are constantly changing. "With the advent of democracy and modern industrial conditions," Dewey wrote in 1897, "it is impossible to foretell definitely just what civilization will be twenty years from now. Hence it is impossible to prepare the child for any precise set of conditions." When adult society is undergoing rapid reconstruction, traditional education becomes a deliberate miseducation of the young, a program for unfitting them for life. In a changing society, "to prepare [the child] for future life means to give him command of himself, it means so to train him that he will have the full and ready use of all his capacities."

To train the child in this way, the educational experience must be one in which the qualities of self-directing activity are given ample opportunity and material for developing.

This does not mean that the child is to be left to his own devices, so that he may unfold according to the inner dictates of his own nature. This blossoming-flower theory of education Dewey has always opposed. It is based on the false idea that the self is an original entity, its characters embryonically encysted in it at birth. For Dewey, the self is a product, a consequence of interacting in a social environment, of participating in social life and action. The school is a form of community life. The kind of self the child develops, the qualities of his mind and character, will depend upon the kind of community the school is, and upon the richness or poverty of the materials for growth it affords. To make and maintain the school as a genuine educational environment requires all the skill, all the art and knowledge that adults possess. The Deweyan education requires infinitely more thought and effort on the part of teachers than traditional education ever did. And it requires teachers who have alert, informed, sensitive, and disciplined minds.

In educational literature, the term "experimentation" has been the focus of a great deal of controversy. To list all the claims and counterclaims that have been made would take a long time. In Dewey's educational philosophy, "experimentation" is not a loose term used to denote any kind of novel, spontaneous, or random departure from habitual ways. For him it is a precise term, denoting the way of thinking and doing that is exemplified, in its most highly developed form, in modern science. Within science, experimentation is not a blind reaction against the old or habitual, against the knowledge and techniques that have already been developed. It is a way of creatively reconstructing the old. Every scientific experiment is based upon and utilizes the experience of the past for the purpose of solving new problems and discovering new truth. It is poles apart from random or impulsive behavior. Every experiment involves careful selection and organization of materials, a thinking through of the relations of means to consequences, and a control of the whole undertaking by ideas.

The method of scientific experimentation also exhibits the way in which the social heritage and individual variation and initiative can interact with each other to the benefit and enrichment of both. The advance of science depends upon the creative intelligence of individual scientists; their power to create in turn depends upon the social resources, the funded scientific knowledge at their command. Within the domain of scientific inquiry, the welfare of the individual is not attained at the sacrifice of the social or common scientific welfare, nor is the welfare of the scientific society attained by sacrificing the welfare, the individuality of its members. The welfare of both is inextricably and mutually interwoven. There is also, within the scientific domain, no ineluctable opposition between "tradition" and "progress." The richer the scientific tradition, the greater are the possibilities for progress.

Scientific experimentation, as pursued in the great laboratories, is a mature art and only highly educated adults can meet its demands. However, the general pattern of scientific experimentation, the general method exemplified in its procedures, defines, for Dewey, what the educative process is on any level or at any stage of growth. Scientific method is not a peculiar secret of an esoteric group—an attitude toward science which is to be found in more places than the popular and which is inherited from the days of the "magicians." Scientific method is the method of learning, the form that learning takes when intelligence is fully freed.

Science has already transformed our material culture, but it has as yet made only the slightest inroads on our non-material or spiritual culture. In all domains outside the sphere of making and using scientific inventions, we still think and act in ways that antedate by millenia the discovery of science. This is as true in the schools as in the general community. Science is taught, for the most part, the way the three R's were taught: it is another subject added to the old curriculum. The spiritual values of science, its values as intellectual and moral discipline, are ignored. The controlling idea both of Dewey's educational and social philosophy (which are inherently interrelated) can be stated as having for its end making the spiritual values of science an integral part of our cultural life. When science is interpreted in broad terms of human values, it is what Dewey calls "freed intelligence."

It is not likely that American democracy, in the immediate future, will realize the ideal of freed intelligence, that it will in the conduct of its affairs reach the intelligent development already attained in the restricted area of scientific inquiry. A democracy that studied and solved all its problems by the free and disciplined method of experimental intelligence would be pretty close to perfect, if not actually in that final state. But, if American democracy means anything serious and permanent in the organization of human life, it means that it has as its working ideal the purpose of creating an intelligent society, the members of which will all have an active part in shaping and directing the common life. The comprehensive purpose of education in a democracy is so to develop its young that they will be able to fulfill the intelligent functions of free individuals living in and working for a free society.

Forty-three years ago—when Dewey wrote *My Pedagogic Creed*—America was on the threshold of its period of great expansion. If it was not then bliss for everyone to be alive, there was at least buoyant confidence and the sense of promise throughout the land. Today, the immediate prospect is far different. No man knows nor can confidently foresee the nature of the epoch upon which we are entering. But we can know now that the life ahead of us is not fatally preordained, that it will not happen regardless of what we may do. The future of American democracy will depend upon the effort and intelligence with which we attack our present problems. *Education Today*, by the perspective it gives on the development of American culture, and by the searching light that it throws on the key problems of a democratic society, can immeasurably help us to shape events in the direction that enlightened America wants to go.

JOSEPH RATNER

The College of the City of New York

## ACKNOWLEDGMENTS

Grateful thanks for permission to reprint are due the editors of: *The American Teacher, The Barnwell Bulletin, Current History, Educational Method, Educational Review, Elementary School Teacher, Ethical Culture Society, Forum, Journal of Education, Journal of Home Economics, Manual Training Magazine, The New Era, The New Republic, School and Society, Science Education,* and *The Social Frontier.*

# CONTENTS

|  |  | PAGE |
|---|---|---|
| FOREWORD |  | v |
| ACKNOWLEDGMENTS |  | xiv |

CHAPTER

| 1. | My Pedagogic Creed | 3 |
| 2. | The Primary-Education Fetich | 18 |
| 3. | The People and the Schools | 36 |
| 4. | The Place of Manual Training in the Elementary Course of Study | 53 |
| 5. | Democracy in Education | 62 |
| 6. | Religion and Our Schools | 74 |
| 7. | Our Educational Ideal in Wartime | 87 |
| 8. | Universal Service as Education | 92 |
| 9. | The Schools and Social Preparedness | 101 |
| 10. | American Education and Culture | 106 |
| 11. | Nationalizing Education | 112 |
| 12. | Experiment in Education | 122 |
| 13. | Learning to Earn | 126 |
| 14. | Public Education on Trial | 133 |
| 15. | Education and Social Direction | 139 |
| 16. | Education as Religion | 144 |

| CHAPTER | | PAGE |
|---|---|---|
| 17. | Education as Engineering | 150 |
| 18. | Education as Politics | 157 |
| 19. | Mediocrity and Individuality | 164 |
| 20. | Individuality, Equality and Superiority | 171 |
| 21. | Culture and Professionalism in Education | 178 |
| 22. | The Prospects of the Liberal College | 184 |
| 23. | The Liberal College and Its Enemies | 190 |
| 24. | The Direction of Education | 198 |
| 25. | General Principles of Educational Articulation | 203 |
| 26. | How Much Freedom in New Schools? | 216 |
| 27. | The Duties and Responsibilities of the Teaching Profession | 224 |
| 28. | Monastery, Bargain Counter or Laboratory in Education? | 230 |
| 29. | Political Interference in Higher Education and Research | 244 |
| 30. | Education and Our Present Social Problems | 250 |
| 31. | The Economic Situation: A Challenge to Education | 260 |
| 32. | Why Have Progressive Schools? | 269 |
| 33. | The Supreme Intellectual Obligation | 282 |
| 34. | The Need for a Philosophy of Education | 288 |
| 35. | The Teacher and His World | 300 |
| 36. | The Teacher and the Public | 303 |
| 37. | Youth in a Confused World | 308 |
| 38. | Toward a National System of Education | 311 |
| 39. | Liberty and Social Control | 316 |
| 40. | The Social Significance of Academic Freedom | 320 |

# CONTENTS

| CHAPTER | | PAGE |
|---|---|---|
| 41. | Class Struggle and the Democratic Way | 325 |
| 42. | Rationality in Education | 331 |
| 43. | Democracy and Educational Administration | 337 |
| 44. | Education and Social Change | 348 |
| 45. | Democracy and Education in the World of Today | 359 |
| | INDEX | 371 |

# EDUCATION TODAY

# 1

## MY PEDAGOGIC CREED *

### ARTICLE I—*What Education Is*

*I Believe that*

—all education proceeds by the participation of the individual in the social consciousness of the race. This process begins unconsciously almost at birth, and is continually shaping the individual's powers, saturating his consciousness, forming his habits, training his ideas, and arousing his feelings and emotions. Through this unconscious education the individual gradually comes to share in the intellectual and moral resources which humanity has succeeded in getting together. He becomes an inheritor of the funded capital of civilization. The most formal and technical education in the world cannot safely depart from this general process. It can only organize it or differentiate it in some particular direction.

—the only true education comes through the stimulation of the child's powers by the demands of the social situations in which he finds himself. Through these demands he is stimulated to act as a member of a unity, to emerge from his original narrowness of action and feeling, and to conceive of himself from the standpoint of the welfare of the group to which he belongs. Through the responses which others make to his own activities he comes to know what these mean in social terms. The value which they have is reflected back into them. For

* Originally published 1897.

instance, through the response which is made to the child's instinctive babblings the child comes to know what those babblings mean; they are transformed into articulate language, and thus the child is introduced into the consolidated wealth of ideas and emotions which are now summed up in language.

—this educational process has two sides—one psychological and one sociological—and that neither can be subordinated to the other, or neglected, without evil results following. Of these two sides, the psychological is the basis. The child's own instincts and powers furnish the material and give the starting-point for all education. Save as the efforts of the educator connect with some activity which the child is carrying on of his own initiative independent of the educator, education becomes reduced to a pressure from without. It may, indeed, give certain external results, but cannot truly be called educative. Without insight into the psychological structure and activities of the individual, the educative process will, therefore, be haphazard and arbitrary. If it chances to coincide with the child's activity it will get a leverage; if it does not, it will result in friction, or disintegration, or arrest of the child nature.

—knowledge of social conditions, of the present state of civilization, is necessary in order properly to interpret the child's powers. The child has his own instincts and tendencies, but we do not know what these mean until we can translate them into their social equivalents. We must be able to carry them back into a social past and see them as the inheritance of previous race activities. We must also be able to project them into the future to see what their outcome and end will be. In the illustration just used, it is the ability to see in the child's babblings the promise and potency of a future social intercourse and conversation which enables one to deal in the proper way with that instinct.

—the psychological and social sides are organically related, and that education cannot be regarded as a compromise between the two, or a superimposition of one upon the other. We are told that the psychological definition of education is barren and formal—that it gives us only the idea of a development of all the mental powers without giving us any idea of the use to which these powers are put. On the other hand, it is urged that the social definition of education, as getting adjusted to civilization, makes of it a forced and external process, and results in subordinating the freedom of the individual to a preconceived social and political status.

—each of these objections is true when urged against one side isolated from the other. In order to know what a power really is we must know what its end, use, or function is, and this we cannot know save as we con-ceive of the individual as active in social relationships. But, on the other hand, the only possible adjustment which we can give to the child under existing conditions is that which arises through putting him in complete possession of all his powers. With the advent of democracy and modern industrial conditions, it is impossible to foretell definitely just what civilization will be twenty years from now. Hence it is impossible to prepare the child for any precise set of conditions. To prepare him for the future life means to give him command of himself; it means so to train him that he will have the full and ready use of all his capacities; that his eye and ear and hand may be tools ready to command, that his judgment may be capable of grasping the conditions under which it has to work, and the executive forces be trained to act economically and efficiently. It is impossible to reach this sort of adjustment save as constant regard is had to the individual's own powers, tastes, and interests—that is, as education is continually converted into psychological terms.

In sum, I believe that the individual who is to be educated is a social individual, and that society is an organic union of individuals. If we eliminate the social factor from the child we are left only with an abstraction; if we eliminate the individual factor from society, we are left only with an inert and lifeless mass. Education, therefore, must begin with a psychological insight into the child's capacities, interests, and habits. It must be controlled at every point by reference to these same considerations. These powers, interests, and habits must be continually interpreted—we must know what they mean. They must be translated into terms of their social equivalents—into terms of what they are capable of in the way of social service.

### ARTICLE II—*What the School Is*

*I Believe that*

—the school is primarily a social institution. Education being a social process, the school is simply that form of community life in which all those agencies are concentrated that will be most effective in bringing the child to share in the inherited resources of the race, and to use his own powers for social ends.

—education, therefore, is a process of living and not a preparation for future living.

—the school must represent present life—life as real and vital to the child as that which he carries on in the home, in the neighborhood, or on the playground.

—that education which does not occur through forms of life, forms that are worth living for their own sake, is always a poor substitute for the genuine reality, and tends to cramp and to deaden.

—the school, as an institution, should simplify existing social life; should reduce it, as it were, to an embryonic form. Existing life is so complex that the child cannot be brought into contact with it without either confusion or distraction; he is either overwhelmed by the multiplicity of activities which are going on, so that he loses his own power of orderly reaction, or he is so stimulated by these various activities that his powers are prematurely called into play and he becomes either unduly specialized or else disintegrated.

—as such simplified social life, the school life should grow gradually out of the home life; that it should take up and continue the activities with which the child is already familiar in the home.

—it should exhibit these activities to the child, and reproduce them in such ways that the child will gradually learn the meaning of them, and be capable of playing his own part in relation to them.

—this is a psychological necessity, because it is the only way of securing continuity in the child's growth, the only way of giving a background of past experience to the new ideas given in school.

—it is also a social necessity because the home is the form of social life in which the child has been nurtured and in connection with which he has had his moral training. It is the business of the school to deepen and extend his sense of the values bound up in his home life.

—much of present education fails because it neglects this fundamental principle of the school as a form of community life. It conceives the school as a place where certain information is to be given, where certain lessons are to be learned, or where certain habits are to be formed. The value of these is conceived as lying largely in the remote future; the child must do these things for the sake of something else he is to do; they are mere preparations. As a result they do not become a part of the life experience of the child and so are not truly educative.

—the moral education centers upon this conception of the school as a mode of social life, that the best and deepest moral training is precisely that which one gets through having to enter into proper relations with others in a unity of work and thought. The present educational systems, so far as they destroy or neglect this unity, render it difficult or impossible to get any genuine, regular moral training.

—the child should be stimulated and controlled in his work through the life of the community.

—under existing conditions far too much of the stimulus and control proceeds from the teacher, because of neglect of the idea of the school as a form of social life.

—the teacher's place and work in the school is to be interpreted from this same basis. The teacher is not in the school to impose certain ideas or to form certain habits in the child, but is there as a member of the community to select the influences which shall affect the child and to assist him in properly responding to these influences.

—the discipline of the school should proceed from the life of the school as a whole and not directly from the teacher.

—the teacher's business is simply to determine, on the basis of larger experience and riper wisdom, how the discipline of life shall come to the child.

—all questions of the grading of the child and his promotion should be determined by reference to the same standard. Examinations are of use only so far as they test the child's fitness for social life and reveal the place in which he can be of the most service and where he can receive the most help.

### ARTICLE III—*The Subject-Matter of Education*

*I Believe that*

—the social life of the child is the basis of concentration, or correlation, in all his training or growth. The social life gives the unconscious unity and the background of all his efforts and of all his attainments.

—the subject-matter of the school curriculum should mark a gradual differentiation out of the primitive unconscious unity of social life.

—we violate the child's nature and render difficult the best ethical results by introducing the child too abruptly to a number of special studies, of reading, writing, geography, etc., out of relation to this social life.

—the true center of correlation on the school subjects is not science, nor literature, nor history, nor geography, but the child's own social activities.

—education cannot be unified in the study of science, or so-called nature study, because apart from human activity, nature itself is not a unity; nature in itself is a number of diverse objects in space and time, and to attempt to make it the center of work by itself is to introduce a principle of radiation rather than one of concentration.

—literature is the reflex expression and interpretation of social experience; that hence it must follow upon and not precede such experience. It, therefore, cannot be made the basis, although it may be made the summary of unification.

—once more that history is of educative value in so far as it presents phases of social life and growth. It must be controlled by reference to social life. When taken simply as history it is thrown into the distant past and becomes dead and inert. Taken as the record of man's social life and progress it becomes full of meaning. I believe, however, that it cannot be so taken excepting as the child is also introduced directly into social life.

—the primary basis of education is in the child's powers at work along the same general constructive lines as those which have brought civilization into being.

—the only way to make the child conscious of his social heritage is to enable him to perform those fundamental types of activity which make civilization what it is.

—the so-called expressive or constructive activities are the center of correlation.

—this gives the standard for the place of cooking, sewing, manual training, etc., in the school.

—they are not special studies which are to be introduced over and above a lot of others in the way of relaxation or relief, or as additional accomplishments. I believe rather that they represent, as types, fundamental forms of social activity; and that it is possible and desirable that the child's introduction into the more formal subjects of the curriculum be through the medium of these activities.

—the study of science is educational in so far as it brings out the materials and processes which make social life what it is.

—one of the greatest difficulties in the present teaching of science is that the material is presented in purely objective form, or is treated as a new peculiar kind of experience which the child can add to that which he has already had. In reality, science is of value because it gives the ability to interpret and control the experience already had. It should be introduced, not as so much new subject-matter, but as showing the factors already involved in previous experience and as furnishing tools by which that experience can be more easily and effectively regulated.

—at present we lose much of the value of literature and language studies because of our elimination of the social element. Language is almost always treated in the books of pedagogy simply as the expression of thought. It is true that language is a logical instrument, but it is fundamentally and primarily a social instrument. Language is the device for communication; it is the tool through which one individual comes to share the ideas and feelings of others. When treated simply as a way of getting individual information, or as a means of showing off what one has learned, it loses its social motive and end.

—there is, therefore, no succession of studies in the ideal school curriculum. If education is life, all life has, from the outset, a scientific aspect, an aspect of art and culture, and an aspect of communication. It cannot, therefore, be true that the proper studies for one grade are mere reading and writing, and that at a later grade, reading, or literature, or science, may be introduced. The progress is not in the succession of studies, but in the development of new attitudes towards, and new interests in, experience.

—education must be conceived as a continuing reconstruction of experience; that the process and the goal of education are one and the same thing.

—to set up any end outside of education, as furnishing its goal and standard, is to deprive the educational process of much of its meaning, and tends to make us rely upon false and external stimuli in dealing with the child.

### Article IV—*The Nature of Method*

*I Believe that*

—the question of method is ultimately reducible to the question of the order of development of the child's powers and interests. The law for presenting and treating material is the law implicit within the child's own nature. Because this is so I believe the following statements are of supreme importance as determining the spirit in which education is carried on:

—the active side precedes the passive in the development of the child-nature; that expression comes before conscious impression; that the muscular development precedes the sensory; that movements come before conscious sensations; I believe that consciousness is essentially motor or impulsive; that conscious states tend to project themselves in action.

—the neglect of this principle is the cause of a large part of the waste of time and strength in school work. The child is thrown into a passive, receptive, or absorbing attitude. The conditions are such that he is not permitted to follow the law of his nature; the result is friction and waste.

—ideas (intellectual and rational processes) also result from action and devolve for the sake of the better control of action. What we term reason is primarily the law of orderly or effective action. To attempt to develop the reasoning powers, the powers of judgment, without reference to the selection and arrangement of means in action, is the fundamental fallacy in our present methods of dealing with this matter. As a result we present the child with arbitrary symbols. Symbols are a necessity in mental development, but they have their place as tools for economizing effort; presented by themselves they are a mass of meaningless and arbitrary ideas imposed from without.

—the image is the great instrument of instruction. What a child gets out of any subject presented to him is simply the images which he himself forms with regard to it.

—if nine-tenths of the energy at present directed towards making the child learn certain things were spent in seeing to it that the child was forming proper images, the work of instruction would be indefinitely facilitated.

—much of the time and attention now given to the preparation and presentation of lessons might be more wisely and profitably expended in training the child's power of imagery and in seeing to it that he was continually forming definite, vivid, and growing images of the various subjects with which he comes in contact in his experience.

—interests are the signs and symptoms of growing power. I believe that they represent dawning capacities. Accordingly the constant and careful observation of interests is of the utmost importance for the educator.

—these interests are to be observed as showing the state of development which the child has reached.

—they prophesy the stage upon which he is about to enter.

—only through the continual and sympathetic observation of childhood's interests can the adult enter into the child's life and see what it is ready for, and upon what material it could work most readily and fruitfully.

—these interests are neither to be humored nor repressed. To repress interest is to substitute the adult for the child, and so to weaken intellectual curiosity and alertness, to suppress initiative, and to deaden interest. To humor the interests is to substitute the transient for the permanent. The interest is always the sign of some power below; the important thing is to discover this power. To humor the interest is to fail to penetrate below the surface, and its sure result is to substitute caprice and whim for genuine interest.

—the emotions are the reflex of actions.

—to endeavor to stimulate or arouse the emotions apart from their corresponding activities is to introduce an unhealthy and morbid state of mind.

—if we can only secure right habits of action and thought, with reference to the good, the true, and the beautiful, the emotions will for the most part take care of themselves.

—next to deadness and dullness, formalism and routine, our education is threatened with no greater evil than sentimentalism.

—this sentimentalism is the necessary result of the attempt to divorce feeling from action.

## ARTICLE V—*The School and Social Progress*

*I Believe that*

—education is the fundamental method of social progress and reform.

—all reforms which rest simply upon the enactment of law, or the threatening of certain penalties, or upon changes in mechanical or outward arrangements, are transitory and futile.

—education is a regulation of the process of coming to share in the social consciousness; and that the adjustment of individual activity on the basis of this social consciousness is the only sure method of social reconstruction.

—this conception has due regard for both the individualistic and socialistic ideals. It is duly individual because it recognizes the formation of a certain character as the only genuine basis of right living. It is socialistic because it recognizes that this right character is not to be formed by merely individual precept, example, or exhortation, but rather by the influence of a certain form of institutional or community life upon the individual, and that the social organism through the school, as its organ, may determine ethical results.

—in the ideal school we have the reconciliation of the individualistic and the institutional ideals.

—the community's duty to education is, therefore, its paramount moral duty. By law and punishment, by social agitation and discussion, society can regulate and form itself in a more or less haphazard and chance way. But through education society can formulate its own purposes, can organize its own means and resources, and thus shape itself with definiteness and economy in the direction in which it wishes to move.

—when society once recognizes the possibilities in this direction, and the obligations which these possibilities impose, it is impossible to conceive of the resources of time, attention, and money which will be put at the disposal of the educator.

—it is the business of every one interested in education to insist upon the school as the primary and most effective instrument of social progress and reform in order that society may be awakened to realize what the school stands for, and aroused to the necessity of endowing the educator with sufficient equipment properly to perform his task.

—education thus conceived marks the most perfect and intimate union of science and art conceivable in human experience.

—the art of thus giving shape to human powers and adapting them to social service is the supreme art; one calling into its service the best of artists; that no insight, sympathy, tact, executive power, is too great for such service.

—with the growth of psychological service, giving added insight into individual structure and laws of growth; and with growth of social science, adding to our knowledge of the right organization of individuals, all scientific resources can be utilized for the purposes of education.

—when science and art thus join hands the most commanding motive for human action will be reached, the most genuine springs of human conduct aroused, and the best service that human nature is capable of guaranteed.

—the teacher is engaged, not simply in the training of individuals, but in the formation of the proper social life.

—every teacher should realize the dignity of his calling; that he is a social servant set apart for the maintenance of proper social order and the securing of the right social growth.

—in this way the teacher always is the prophet of the true God and the usherer in of the true kingdom of God.

## 2

## THE PRIMARY-EDUCATION FETICH *

IT IS some years since the educational world was more or
less agitated by an attack upon the place occupied by
Greek in the educational scheme. If, however, Greek occupies the place of a fetich, its worshippers are comparatively
few in number, and its influence is relatively slight. There is,
however, a false educational god whose idolaters are legion,
and whose cult influences the entire educational system.
This is language-study—the study not of foreign language,
but of English; not in higher, but in primary education. It is
almost an unquestioned assumption, of educational theory
and practice both, that the first three years of a child's
school-life shall be mainly taken up with learning to read
and write his own language. If we add to this the learning
of a certain amount of numerical combinations, we have the
pivot about which primary education swings. Other subjects
may be taught; but they are introduced in strict subordination.

The very fact that this procedure, as part of the natural
and established course of education, is assumed as inevitable,—opposition being regarded as captious and revolutionary,—indicates that, historically, there are good reasons
for the position assigned to these studies. It does not follow,
however, that because this course was once wise it is so any
longer. On the contrary, the fact, that this mode of education was adapted to past conditions, is in itself a reason why
it should no longer hold supreme sway. The present has its
claims. It is in education, if anywhere, that the claims of the
present should be controlling. To educate on the basis of

* From *The Forum*, May, 1898.

past surroundings is like adapting an organism to an environment which no longer exists. The individual is stultified, if not disintegrated; and the course of progress is blocked. My proposition is, that conditions—social, industrial, and intellectual—have undergone such a radical change, that the time has come for a thoroughgoing examination of the emphasis put upon linguistic work in elementary instruction.

The existing status was developed in a period when ability to read was practically the sole avenue to knowledge, when it was the only tool which insured control over the accumulated spiritual resources of civilization. Scientific methods of observation, experimentation, and testing were either unknown or confined to a few specialists at the upper end of the educational ladder. Because these methods were not free, were not capable of anything like general use, it was not possible to permit the pupil to begin his school career in direct contact with the materials of nature and of life. The only guarantee, the only criterion of values, was found in the ways in which the great minds of the past had assimilated and interpreted such materials. To avoid intellectual chaos and confusion, it was necessary reverently to retrace the steps of the fathers. The *régime* of intellectual authority and tradition, in matters of politics, morals, and culture, was a necessity, where methods of scientific investigation and verification had not been developed, or were in the hands of the few. We often fail to see that the dominant position occupied by book-learning in school education is simply a corollary and relic of this epoch of intellectual development.

Ordinary social conditions were congruent with this intellectual status. While it cannot be said that, in the formative period of our educational system in America, authority and tradition were the ultimate sources of knowledge and belief, it must be remembered that the immediate surroundings of our ancestors were crude and undeveloped. Newspapers, magazines, libraries, art-galleries, and all the daily play of intellectual intercourse and reaction which is effective today were non-existent. If any escape existed from the poverty of the intellectual environment, or any road to richer and wider mental life, the exit was through the gateway of books. In presenting the attainments of the past, these maintained the bonds of spiritual continuity, and kept our forefathers from falling to the crude level of their material surroundings.

When ability to read and write marked the distinction between the educated and the uneducated man, not simply in the scholastic sense, but in the sense of one who is enslaved by his environment and one who is able to take advantage of and rise above it, corresponding importance attached to acquiring these capacities. Reading and writing were obviously what they are still so often called—the open doors to learning and to success in life. All the meaning that belongs to these ends naturally transferred itself to the means through which alone they could be realized. The intensity and ardor with which our forefathers set themselves to master reading and writing, the difficulties overcome, the interest attached in the ordinary routine of school-life to what now seems barren,—the curriculum of the three R's,—all testify to the motive-power these studies possessed. To learn to read and write was an interesting, even exciting, thing: it made such a difference in life.

It is hardly necessary to say that the conditions, intellectual as well as social, have changed. There are undoubtedly rural regions where the old state of things still persists. With reference to these, what I am saying has no particular meaning. But, upon the whole, the advent of quick and cheap mails, of easy and continuous travel and transportation, of the telegraph and telephone, the establishment of libraries, art-galleries, literary clubs, the universal diffusion of cheap reading-matter, newspapers and magazines of all kinds and grades,—all these have worked a tremendous change in the immediate intellectual environment. The values of life and of civilization, instead of being far away and correspondingly inaccessible, press upon the individual—at least in cities—with only too much urgency and stimulating force.

We are more likely to be surfeited than starved: there is more congestion than lack of intellectual nutriment.

The capital handed down from past generations, and upon whose transmission the integrity of civilization depends, is no longer amassed in those banks termed books, but is in active and general circulation, at an extremely low rate of interest. It is futile to try to conceal from ourselves the fact that this great change in the intellectual atmosphere —this great change in the relation of the individual to accumulated knowledge—demands a corresponding ʿeducational readjustment. The significance attaching to reading and writing, as primary and fundamental instruments of culture, has shrunk proportionately as the immanent intellectual life of society has quickened and multiplied. The result is that these studies lose their motive and motor force. They have become mechanical and formal, and out of relation—when made dominant—to the rest of life.

They are regarded as more or less arbitrary tasks which must be submitted to because one is going to that mysterious thing called a school, or else are covered up and sugarcoated with all manner of pretty devices and tricks in order that the child may absorb them unawares. The complaint made by some, that the school curriculum of today does not have the disciplinary value of the old-fashioned three R's, has a certain validity. But this is not because the old ideal has been abandoned. It is because it has been retained in spite of the change of conditions. Instead of frankly facing the situation, and asking ourselves what studies can be organized which shall do for today what language-study did for former generations, we have retained that as the center and core of our course of study, and dressed it out with a variety of pretty pictures, objects, and games, and a smattering of science.

Along with this change in the relation of intellectual material and stimulus to the individual there has been an equally great change in the method and make-up of knowledge itself. Science and art have become free. The simplest processes and methods of knowing and doing have been worked out to such a point that they are no longer the monopolistic possessions of any class or guild. They are, in idea, and should be in deed, part of the social commonwealth. It is possible to initiate the child from the first in a direct, not abstract or symbolical, way, into the operations by which society maintains its existence, material and spiritual.

The process of production, transportation, consumption, etc., by which society keeps up its material continuity, are conducted on such a large and public scale that they are obvious and objective. Their reproduction in embryonic form through a variety of modes of industrial training is entirely within the bounds of possibility. Moreover, methods of the discovery and communication of truth—upon which the spiritual unity of society depends—have become direct and independent, instead of remote and tied to the intervention of teacher or book. It is not simply that children can acquire a certain amount of scientific information about things organic and inorganic: if that were all, the plea for the study of the history and literature of the past, as more humanistic, would be unanswerable. No; the significant thing is that it is possible for the child at an early day to become acquainted with, and to use, in a personal and yet relatively controlled fashion, the methods by which truth is discovered and communicated, and to make his own speech a channel for the expression and communication of truth; thus putting the linguistic side where it belongs—subordinate to the appropriation and conveyance of what is genuinely and personally experienced.

A similar modification, almost revolution, has taken place in the relation which the intellectual activities bear to the ordinary practical occupations of life. While the child of bygone days was getting an intellectual discipline whose significance he appreciated in the school, in his home life he was securing acquaintance in a direct fashion with the chief lines of social and industrial activity. Life was in the main rural. The child came into contact with the scenes of nature, and was familiarized with the care of domestic animals, the cultivation of the soil, and the raising of crops. The factory system being undeveloped, the home was the center of industry. Spinning, weaving, the making of clothes, etc., were all carried on there. As there was little accumulation of wealth, the child had to take part in these, as well as to participate in the usual round of household occupations. Only those who have passed through such training, and, later on, have seen children reared in city environments, can adequately realize the amount of training, mental and moral, involved in this extra-school life. That our successful men have come so largely from the country, is an indication of the educational value bound up with participation in this practical life. It was not only an adequate substitute for what we now term manual training, in the development of hand and eye, in the acquisition of skill and deftness; but it was initiation into self-reliance, independence of judgment and action, and was the best stimulus to habits of regular and continuous work.

In the urban and suburban life of the child of today this is simply a memory. The invention of machinery, the institution of the factory system, the division of labor, have changed the home from a workshop into a simple dwelling-place. The crowding into cities and the increase of servants have deprived the child of an opportunity to take part in those occupations which still remain. Just at the time when a child is subjected to a great increase in stimulus and pressure from his environment, he loses the practical and motor training necessary to balance his intellectual development. Facility in acquiring information is gained: the power of using it is lost. While need of the more formal intellectual training in the school has decreased, there arises an urgent demand for the introduction of methods of manual and industrial discipline which shall give the child what he formerly obtained in his home and social life.

Here we have at least a *prima facie* case for a reconsideration of the whole question of the relative importance of learning to read and write in primary education. Hence the necessity of meeting the question at closer quarters. What can be said against giving up the greater portion of the first two years of school life to the mastery of linguistic form? In the first place, physiologists are coming to believe that the sense organs and connected nerve and motor apparatus of the child are not at this period best adapted to the confining and analytic work of learning to read and write. There is an order in which sensory and motor centers develop,—an order expressed, in a general way, by saying that the line of progress is from the larger, coarser adjustments having to do with the bodily system as a whole (those nearest the trunk of the body) to the finer and accurate adjustments having to do with the periphery and extremities of the organism. The oculist tells us that the vision of the child is essentially that of the savage; being adapted to seeing large and somewhat remote objects in the mass, not near-by objects in detail. To violate this law means undue nervous strain: it means putting the greatest tension upon the centers least able to do the work. At the same time, the lines of activity which are hungering and thirsting for action are left, unused, to atrophy. The act of writing—especially in the barbarous fashion, long current in the school, of compelling the child to write on ruled lines in a small hand and with the utmost attainable degree of accuracy—involves a nicety and complexity of adjustments of muscular activity which can be definitely appreciated only by the specialist. As the principal of a Chicago school has wittily remarked in this connection, "the pen is literally mightier than the sword." Forcing children at a premature age to devote their entire attention to these refined and cramped adjustments has left behind it a sad record of injured nervous systems and of muscular disorders and distortions. While there are undoubted exceptions, present physiological knowledge points to the age of about eight years as early enough for anything more than an incidental attention to visual and written language-form.

We must not forget that these forms are symbols. I am far from depreciating the value of symbols in our intellectual life. It is hardly too much to say that all progress in civilization upon the intellectual side has depended upon increasing invention and control of symbols of one sort or another. Nor do I join in the undiscriminating cry of those who condemn the study of language as having to do with mere words, not with realities. Such a position is one-sided, and is as crude as the view against which it is a reaction. But there is an important question here: Is the child of six or seven years ready for symbols to such an extent that the stress of educational life can be thrown upon them? If we were to look at the question independently of the existing school system, in the light of the child's natural needs and interests at this period, I doubt if there could be found anyone who would say that the urgent call of the child of six and seven is for this sort of nutriment, instead of for more direct introduction into the wealth of natural and social forms that surrounds him. No doubt the skillful teacher often succeeds in awakening an interest in these matters; but the interest has to be excited in a more or less artificial way, and, when excited, is somewhat factitious, and independent of other interests of child-life. At this point the wedge is introduced and driven in which marks the growing divorce between school and outside interests and occupations.

We cannot recur too often in educational matters to the conception of John Fiske, that advance in civilization is an accompaniment of the prolongation of infancy. Anything which, at this period, develops to a high degree any set of organs and centers at the expense of others means premature specialization, and the arrest of an equable and all-round development. Many educators are already convinced that premature facility and glibness in the matter of numerical combinations tend toward an arrested development of certain higher spiritual capacities. The same thing is true in the matter of verbal symbols. Only the trained psychologist is aware of the amount of analysis and abstraction demanded by the visual recognition of a verbal form. Many suppose that abstraction is found only where more or less complex reasoning exists. But as a matter of fact the essence of abstraction is found in compelling attention to rest upon elements which are more or less cut off from direct channels of interest and action. To require a child to turn away from the rich material which is all about him, to which he spontaneously attends, and which is his natural, unconscious food, is to compel the premature use of analytic and abstract powers. It is willfully to deprive the child of that synthetic life, that unconscious union with his environment, which is his birthright and privilege. There is every reason to suppose that a premature demand upon the abstract intellectual capacity stands in its own way. It cripples rather than furthers later intellectual development. We are not yet in a position to know how much of the inertia and seeming paralysis of mental powers in later periods is the direct outcome of excessive and too early appeal to isolated intellectual capacity. We must trust to the development of physiology and psychology to make these matters so clear that school authorities and the public opinion which controls them shall have no option. Only then can we hope to escape that deadening of the childish activities which led Jowett to call education "the grave of the mind."

Were the matter not so serious it would be ludicrous, when we reflect how all this time and effort fail to reach the end to which they are specially consecrated. It is a common saying among intelligent educators that they can go into a school-room and select the children who picked up reading at home: they read so much more naturally and intelligently. The stilted, mechanical, droning, and sing-song ways of reading which prevail in many of our schools are simply the reflex of the lack of motive. Reading is made an isolated accomplishment. There are no aims in the child's mind which he feels he can serve by reading; there is no mental hunger to be satisfied; there are no conscious problems with reference to which he uses books. The book is a reading-lesson. He learns to read not for the sake of what he reads, but for the mere sake of reading. When the bare process of reading is thus made an end in itself, it is a psychological impossibility for reading to be other than lifeless.

It is quite true that all better teachers now claim that the formal act of reading should be made subordinate to the sense of what is read,—that the child has first to grasp the idea, and then to express his mental realization. But, under present conditions, this profession cannot be carried out. The following paragraph from the report of the Committee of Fifteen on elementary education states clearly enough the reason why; though, as it seems to me, without any consciousness of the real inference which should be drawn from the facts set forth:—

"The first three years' work of the child is occupied mainly with the mastery of the printed and written forms of the words of his colloquial vocabulary—words that he is already familiar enough with as sounds addressed to the ear. He has to become familiar with the new forms addressed to the eye; and it would be an unwise method to require him to learn many new words at the same time that he is learning to recognize his old words in their new shape. But as soon as he has acquired (before three years) some facility in reading what is printed in the colloquial style, he may go on to selections from standard authors."

The material of the reading-lesson is thus found wholly in the region of familiar words and ideas. It is out of the question for the child to find anything in the ideas themselves to arouse and hold attention. His mind is fixed upon the mere recognition and utterance of the forms. Thus begins that fatal divorce between the substance and the form of expression, which, fatal to reading as an art, reduces it to a mechanical action. The utter triviality of the contents of our school "Primers" and "First Readers" shows the inevitable outcome of forcing the mastery of external language-forms upon the child at a premature period. Take up the first half-dozen or dozen such books you meet with, and ask yourself how much there is in the ideas presented worthy of respect from any intelligent child of six years.

Methods for learning to read come and go across the educational arena, like the march of supernumeraries upon the stage. Each is heralded as the final solution of the problem of learning to read; but each in turn gives way to some later discovery. The simple fact is, that they all lack the essential of any well-grounded method, namely, relevancy to the child's mental needs. No scheme for learning to read can supply this want. Only a new motive—putting the child into a vital relation to the materials to be read—can be of service here. It is evident that this condition cannot be met, unless learning to read be postponed to a period when the child's intellectual appetite is more consciously active, and when he is mature enough to deal more rapidly and effectively with the formal and mechanical difficulties.

The endless drill, with its continual repetitions, is another instance of the same evil. Even when the attempt is made to select material with some literary or historic worth of its own, the practical outcome is much like making "Paradise Lost" the basis of parsing-lessons, or Caesar's "Gallic Wars" an introduction to Latin syntax. So much attention has to be given to the formal side that the spiritual value evanesces. No one can estimate the benumbing and hardening effect of this continued drill upon mere form. Another even more serious evil is the consequent emptiness of mind induced. The mental room is swept and garnished—and that is all. The moral result is even more deplorable than the intellectual. At this plastic period, when images which take hold of the mind exercise such suggestive motor force, nothing but husks are provided. Under the circumstances, our schools are doing great things for the moral education of children; but all efforts in this direction must necessarily be hampered and discounted until the school-teacher shall be perfectly free to find the bulk of the material of instruction for the early school-years in something which has intrinsic value,—

something whose introduction into consciousness is so vital as to be personal and reconstructive.

It should be obvious that what I have in mind is not a Philistine attack upon books and reading. The question is not how to get rid of them, but how to get their value,— how to use them to their capacity as servants of the intellectual and moral life. The plea for the predominance of learning to read in early school-life because of the great importance attaching to literature seems to me a perversion. Just because literature is so important, it is desirable to postpone the child's introduction to printed speech until he is capable of appreciating and dealing with its genuine meaning. Now, the child learns to read as a mechanical tool, and gets very little conception of what is worth reading. The result is, that, after he has mastered the art and wishes to use it, he has no standard by which to direct it. He is about as likely to use it in one way as in another. It would be ungrateful not to recognize the faithfulness and relative success with which teachers, for the last ten or fifteen years, have devoted themselves to raising the general tone of reading with their pupils. But, after all, they are working against great odds. Our ideal should be that the child should have a personal interest in what is read, a personal hunger for it, and a personal power of satisfying this appetite. The adequate realization of this ideal is impossible until the child comes to the reading-material with a certain background of experience which makes him appreciate the difference between the trivial, the merely amusing and exciting, and that which has permanent and serious meaning. This is impossible so long as the child has not been trained in the habit of dealing with material outside of books, and has formed, through contact with the realities of experience, habits of recognizing and dealing with problems in the direct personal way. The isolation of material found in books, from the material which the child experiences in life itself—the forcing of the former upon the child before he has well-organized powers of dealing with the latter—is an unnatural divorce which cannot have any other result than defective standards of appreciation, and a tendency to elevate the sensational and transiently interesting above the valuable and the permanent.

Two results of our wrong methods are so apparent in higher education that they are worth special mention. They are exhibited in the paradox of the combination of slavish dependence upon books with real inability to use them effectively. The famous complaint of Agassiz, that students could not see for themselves, is still repeated by every teacher of science in our high schools and colleges. How many teachers of science will tell you, for example, that, when their students are instructed to find out something about an object, their first demand is for a book in which they can read about it; their first reaction, one of helplessness, when they are told that they must go to the object itself and let it tell its own story? It is not exaggerating to say that the book habit is so firmly fixed that very many pupils, otherwise intelligent, have a positive aversion to directing their attention to things themselves,—it seems so much simpler to occupy the mind with what someone else has said about these things. While it is mere stupidity not to make judicious use of the discoveries and attainments of others, the substitution of the seeing of others for the use of one's own eyes is such a self-contradictory principle as to require no criticism. We only need recognize the extent to which it actually obtains.

On the other hand, we have the relative incapacity of students to use easily and economically these very tools—books—to which most of their energies have been directed. It is a common experience with, I will not say only the teachers of undergraduate students, but of graduate students, —candidates for advanced degrees,—to find that in every special subject a large amount of time and energy has to be spent in learning how to use the books. To take a book and present an adequate, condensed synopsis of its points of view and course of argument, is an exercise not merely in reading, but in thinking. To know how to turn quickly to a

number of books bearing upon a given topic, to choose what
is needed, and to find out what is characteristic of the author
and important in the subject, are matters which the majority
of even graduate students have to learn over again for themselves. If such be the case,—and yet attention to books has
been the dominant note of all previous education,—we are
surely within bounds in asking if there is not something
radically wrong in the way in which books have been used.
It is a truism to say that the value of books consists in their
relation to life, in the keenness and range which they impart
to powers of penetration and interpretation. It is no truism
~~to say that the~~ premature and unrelated use of books stands

used.

Just a word about the corresponding evils. We have to
take into account not simply the results produced by forcing
language-work unduly, but also the defects in development
due to the crowding out of other objects. Every respectable
authority insists that the period of childhood, lying between
the years of four and eight or nine, is the plastic period in
sense and emotional life. What are we doing to shape these
capacities? What are we doing to feed this hunger? If one
compares the powers and needs of the child in these directions with what is actually supplied in the regimen of the
three R's, the contrast is pitiful, tragic. This epoch is also
the budding-time for the formation of efficient and orderly
habits on the motor side: it is pre-eminently the time when
the child wishes to do things, and when his interest in doing
can be turned to educative account. No one can clearly set
before himself the vivacity and persistency of the child's
motor instincts at this period, and then call to mind the
continued grind of reading and writing, without feeling that
the justification of our present curriculum is psychologically
impossible. It is simply a superstition: it is a remnant of an
outgrown period of history.

All this might be true, and yet there might be no subject-
matter sufficiently organized for introduction into the school

curriculum, since this demands, above all things, a certain definiteness of presentation and of development. But we are not in this unfortunate plight. There are subjects which are as well fitted to meet the child's dominant needs as they are to prepare him for the civilization in which he has to play his part. There is art in a variety of modes—music, drawing, painting, modeling, etc. These *media* not only afford a regulated outlet in which the child may project his inner impulses and feelings in outward form, and come to consciousness of himself, but are necessities in existing social life. The child must be protected against some of the hard and over-utilitarian aspects of modern civilization: positively, they are needed, because some degree of artistic and creative power is necessary to take the future worker out of the ranks of unskilled labor, and to feed his consciousness in his hours of contact with purely mechanical things.

Those modes of simple scientific observation and experiment which go under the name of "nature-study" are calculated to appeal to and keep active the keenness of the child's interest in the world about him, and to introduce him gradually to those methods of discovery and verification which are the essential characteristics of modern intellectual life. On the social side, they give the child an acquaintance with his environment—an acquaintance more and more necessary, under existing conditions, for the maintenance of personal and social health, for understanding and conducting business pursuits, and for the administration of civic affairs. What is crudely termed manual training—the variety of constructive activities, which, begun in the Kindergarten, ought never to be given up—is equally adapted to the characteristic needs of the child and to the present demands of associated life. These activities afford discipline in continuous and orderly application of powers, strengthen habits of attention and industry, and beget self-reliant and ingenious judgment. As preparation for future social life, they furnish insight into the mechanical and industrial occupations upon which our civilization depends, and keep alive that sense of the dignity of work essential to democracy. History and literature, once more, provide food for the eager imagination of the child. While giving it worthy material, they may check its morbid and chaotic exercise. They present to the child typical conditions of social life, they exhibit the struggles which have brought it into being, and picture the spiritual products in which it has culminated. Due place cannot be given to literature and history until the teacher is free to select them for their own intrinsic value, and not from the standpoint of the child's ability to recognize written and printed verbal symbols.

Here we have the controlling factors in the primary curriculum of the future—manual training, science, nature-study, art, and history. These keep alive the child's positive and creative impulses, and direct them in such ways as to discipline them into the habits of thought and action required for effective participation in community life.

Were the attempt suddenly made to throw out, or reduce to a minimum, language-work in the early grades, the last state of our schools would undoubtedly be worse than the first. Not immediate substitution is what is required, but consideration of the whole situation, and organization of the materials and methods of science, history, and the arts, to make them adequate educational agencies. Many of our present evils are due to compromise and inconsistency. We have neither one thing nor the other—neither the systematic, all-pervasive discipline of the three R's, nor a coherent training in constructive work, history, and nature-study. We have a mixture of the two. The former is supposed to furnish the element of discipline and to constitute the standard of success; while the latter supplies the factor of interest. What is needed is a thoroughgoing reconciliation of the ideals of thoroughness, definiteness, and order, summed up in the notion of discipline, with those of appeal to individual capacities and demands, summed up in the word "interest." This is the Educational Problem, so far as it relates to the elementary school.

Change must come gradually. To force it unduly would compromise its final success by favoring a violent reaction. What is needed in the first place is, that there should be a full and frank statement of conviction with regard to the matter from physiologists and psychologists and from those school administrators who are conscious of the evils of the present *régime*. Educators should also frankly face the fact that the New Education, as it exists today, is a compromise and a transition: it employs new methods; but its controlling ideals are virtually those of the Old Education. Wherever movements looking to a solution of the problem are intelligently undertaken, they should receive encouragement, moral and financial, from the intellectual leaders of the community. There are already in existence a considerable number of educational "experiment stations," which represent the outposts of educational progress. If these schools can be adequately supported for a number of years they will perform a great vicarious service. After such schools have worked out carefully and definitely the subject-matter of a new curriculum—finding the right place for language-studies and placing them in their right perspective—the problem of the more general educational reform will be immensely simplified and facilitated. There will be clear standards, well-arranged material, and coherent methods upon which to proceed. To build up and equip such schools is, therefore, the wisest and most economical policy, in avoiding the friction and waste consequent upon casual and spasmodic attempts at educational reform.

All this amounts to saying that school reform is dependent upon a collateral wider change in the public opinion which controls school board, superintendent, and teachers. There are certain minor changes, reforms in detail, which can be effected directly within the school system itself. But the school is not an isolated institution: it is one of an organism of social forces. To secure more scientific principles of work in the school means, accordingly, clearer vision and wiser standards of thought and action in the community at large.

The Educational Problem is ultimately that society shall see clearly its own conditions and needs, and set resolutely about meeting them. If the recognition be once secured, we need have no doubts about the consequent action. Let the community once realize that it is educating upon the basis of a life which it has left behind, and it will turn, with adequate intellectual and material resources, to meet the needs of the present hour.

# 3

## THE PEOPLE AND THE SCHOOLS *

THE answer to the question, whether the schools are
doing what the people want done, depends upon the
conception of what the people want. And there is a good
deal of difficulty in finding this out; when we do find out,
we see that they want very diverse things—things so diver-
gent as to be contradictory. The school cannot really do
what the people want until there is unity, an approach to
system and organization, in the needs of the people. We
are told that when the sewing machine was first invented
and an attempt was made to introduce it, the agents had
almost to break into people's houses in order to get it into
use. If the people wanted the sewing machine, they did not
know that they wanted it. There are many things in education of which a similar thing must be said. The people
may need these things very badly, but they have not awakened to a lively consciousness of the fact.

I happen recently to have heard two gentlemen speaking
of educational matters, both of whom are in positions of
responsibility, and both marked successes in their respective
affairs. One of these men would ordinarily be called a conservative. He gave as a reason for his conservatism that he
had to conform to conditions, that it was impossible for a
successful school to be far in advance of the conditions
about it. In other words, he thought that what the people
wanted was just about what they had been accustomed to
getting. The other, of a more radical type in educational
matters, propounded as the utmost reach of his anticipations
of reform the desire that the schools should become a reflex

* From *The Educational Review,* May, 1901.

36

of existing conditions. One thought that he was limited to education of rather a routine, customary type because that is what the conditions call for, and hence what the people want; the other's highest flight of imagination regarding the reform of the school is to have an education which shall be a reflex of existing conditions, and hence what is really wanted.

The two remarks are apparently contradictory. Yet each appeals to us as possessing a certain truth. How are we to explain this state of affairs? One was thinking of what people consciously want, of what people in specific instances bring to bear in way of pressure upon the school authorities. The other had in mind what he conceived to be the meeting of the *actual* wants or necessities of the case, quite apart from their conscious recognition on the part of the people. He was thinking of breaking into people's educational houses in order to provide them with the agencies, the instrumentalities, they really want, but of the need of which they have not become aware.

I see practically no other way of answering this question. If we ask whether the schools, upon the whole, are doing what the people want—yes, certainly, if we keep in mind the more conscious and definitely formulated wants of the people growing out of the experiences and customs and expectations of the past; no, to a very considerable degree, if we mean an effective response of school aims, methods, and materials to the underlying wants which arise in the movement of modern society.

My thesis, then, is a twofold one. The schools are not doing, and cannot do, what the people want until there is more unity, more definiteness, in the community's consciousness of its own needs; but it is the business of the school to forward this conception, to help the people to a clearer and more systematic idea of what the underlying needs of modern life are, and of how they are really to be supplied.

To speak particularly of the third story of the educational edifice—the college and its relations to the needs of the people. This requires some placing of the college in connection with the elementary and secondary forms of education in order to see how its points of contact with popular needs vary from those of the other two forms, and how its methods of meeting the popular needs must also be differentiated.

The elementary school is, by the necessity of the case, in closest contact with the wants of the people at large. It is the public-school, the common-school, system. It aims at universality in its range, at including all children. It also has a universal basis, coming home to every citizen as a taxpayer. The higher institutions of learning are less under the control of immediate public opinion, with the ebb and flow of popular sentiment. They are set apart, as it were, under the control of specially selected leaders. They are dominated by a more continuous system of educational principle and policy. Their roots are in the past; they are the conservators of the wisdom, insight, and resources of bygone ages. While they may be part of the state system, yet they touch the average citizen in a much less direct way than does the elementary school. The secondary school is intermediate: it is between the upper and the nether millstone. On one side, it is subject to pressure from current public opinion; on the other, to the pressure of university tradition. While the public high school is more sensitive in the former direction, and the private academy more sensitive in the latter, neither one can be free from both influences.

The elementary school has both the advantages and the disadvantages of its more direct contact with public opinion. It is thereby more likely to respond promptly to what the people currently want. But, on the other hand, it is rendered liable to the fluctuations and confusions of the public expression of its own needs. The higher institution has the advantages and the disadvantage of its greater remoteness, its greater isolation. The advantage is in the possibility of more definite leadership by those consistently trained in continuous educational standards and methods—freedom from the meaningless and arbitrary flux and reflux of public sentiment. The disadvantages are summed up in the unfavorable connotation of the term academic, the suggestion of living in the past rather than the present, in the cloister rather than the world, in a region of abstraction rather than of practice.

The lower schools are more variable, and probably vary too easily and frequently as the various winds of public sentiment blow upon them. They are freighted with too little ballast. The traditional elementary school curriculum was so largely a formal thing, there was so little of substantial content in it, that it could not offer much resistance to external pressure. There was also less ballast in the matter of its teaching force, since the standard of requirement in scholarship and training was so much less than that demanded in the higher schools. But this in no respect detracts from their being the public, the common, schools—that in which the interests of the people are most closely and universally bound up. It only emphasizes, after all, the necessity of their being responsive to the needs of the people, and not to traditions or conventions from whatever source they arise.

The higher institutions are freighted with a definite body of tradition. Their curriculum represents the enduring experience and thought of the centuries. They are the connecting links binding us of today with the culture of Greece and Rome and medieval Europe. They are under the guidance of men who have been subjected to uniform training, who have been steeped in almost identical ideals, and with whom teaching is a profession and not an accident. In their method of administration they are much more removed from public opinion and sentiment than are the elementary schools.

Does this mean, however, that the college is relieved of the necessity of meeting public needs, of doing what the people want done; or rather, that its problem, its function with reference to this need, is a peculiar and distinctive one?

Our answer is unhesitatingly the latter. If the college derives more from the past, it is only that it may put more effectually the resources of the past at the disposition of the present. If it is more remote from immediate pressure of public demands, this should be regarded as imposing a duty, not as conferring an otiose privilege. It emphasizes the responsibility of steadying and clarifying the consciousness of the people, of rendering it less spasmodic, less vacillating, less confused; of imparting to it consistency and organization. The college has undertaken to maintain the continuity of culture. But culture should not be a protected industry, living at the expense of the freedom and completeness of present social communication and interaction. The sole reason for maintaining the continuity of culture is to make that culture operative and determining in the conditions of modern life, of daily life, of political and industrial life, if you will.

It is comparatively easy to divorce these two functions. At one end of the scale we can erect the culture college; the college which, upon the whole, in its curriculum and methods ignores the demands of the present and insists upon the well-rounded and symmetrical education of the past—an education which is well-rounded simply because the insistent demands of the present are kept from impinging upon it. At the other end of the scale is the distinctively professional technological school, which prepares specifically and definitely for the occupations of the present day; which certainly is responding in consistent and obvious ways to the needs of the people.

But, speaking for the higher institutions of learning as a whole, it is clear that both of these types of institutions solve the problem by unduly simplifying it. This is not to say that each has not its own place. It is only to say that that place is not the place of our higher institutions of learning taken in their entirety. Their problem is to join together what is here sundered, the culture factor (by which is meant acquaintance with the best that has been thought and said and done in the past) and the practical factor—or, more truly speaking, the social factor, the factor of adaptation to the present need of the people.

But what, you may ask, is the working equivalent of this proposition? What effect would the attempt to carry it out have upon the existing college curriculum and method? How does it bear, for example, upon the mooted question of the relation of the languages or the humanities to the sciences? What bearing does it have upon the mooted question of the required *versus* the elective curriculum? What bearing does it have upon the question of the method of instruction? Shall it be dogmatic and disciplinary, so as to secure to the student the advantage of a stable point of view and a coherent body of material, or shall it be stimulating and liberating, aiming at ability to inquire, judge and act for one's self?

The problem of the multiplication of studies, of the consequent congestion of the curriculum, and the conflict of various studies for a recognized place in the curriculum; the fact that one cannot get in without crowding out something else; the effort to arrange a compromise in various courses of study by throwing the entire burden upon the student of election so that he shall make out his own course of study—this problem is only a reflex of the lack of unity in the social activities themselves, and of the necessity of reaching more harmony, more system, in the direction of the people's needs. This multiplication of study is not primarily a product of the schools. The last hundred years has created a new world, has revealed a new universe, material and social. The educational problem is thus not a result of anything within our own conscious wish or intention, but of the conditions in the contemporary world.

Take, for illustration, the problem of the introduction and place of the sciences. I suppose all of us sometimes hear arguments whose implication seems to be that a certain body of self-willed men invented the sciences, and are now, because of narrowness of culture, bent upon forcing them into prominence in the college curriculum. But it needs only to make this implication explicit to realize what a travesty it is. These sciences are the outcome of all that makes our modern life what it is. They are expressions of the agencies upon which the carrying on of our civilization is completely dependent. They did not grow out of scholastic, but of human, needs. They find their serious application in the schools only because they are everywhere having their serious application in life. There is no pressing industrial question that has not arisen in some new discovery regarding the forces of nature, and whose ultimate solution does not depend upon some further insight into the truths of nature—upon some scientific advance. The revolution which is going on in industry because of the advance of natural science in turn affects all professions and occupations. It touches municipal government as well as personal hygiene; it affects the calling of the clergy as significantly as, even if more indirectly than, that of the lawyer. An intellectual and social development of such scope cannot possibly take place and not throw our educational curriculum into a state of distraction and uncertainty.

When we are asked, "Why not leave alone all these new subjects not yet well organized in themselves, and not well elaborated as material for education; why not confine ourselves to the studies which have been taught so long as to be organized for purposes of instruction?"—when these questions are put to us, we come upon a logical self-contradiction and a practical impossibility.

The logical contradiction is found in the fact that the new studies are not so isolated from the old studies as to be capable of being lopped off in this arbitrary way. In spite of confusion and conflict, the movement of the human mind is a unity. The development of the new sciences is not a mere addition of so much bulk of information to what went before. It represents a profound modification and reconstruction of all attained knowledge—a change in its quality and method. The existing conflict between the sciences and the humanities in the contemporary college curriculum would not be terminated by eliminating the sciences. Precisely the same conflict would at once reflect itself within what is left over, the languages. The scientific method has invaded this region and claims it for its own. The lines would soon be drawn between those who represent the distinctively "scientific" aspects of language—phonology, philology, the strict historical development, the analytic determinations of style, etc.—and those upholding the banner of pure literary appreciation. The point comes out more plainly by inquiring what we are to do with the modern social and historical sciences. No fact in controversy is more recurrent (or more amusing) than that while the contestants are struggling in the dark, the center of the battle somehow manages to remove itself to another point; and when the smoke clears away there is not only a new battlefield, but an entirely new point at issue. While the struggle between the classicists and the scientists has been going on, a new body of studies has been gradually making its way, and is now reaching the point of conscious insistence upon its own claims. History, sociology, political science and political economy can hardly be denied to stand for the humanities. Quite as much as any linguistic phenomena they represent fundamental values of human life. Yet they are the offspring of the scientific method. Apart from underlying biological conceptions, apart from the scientific conception of evolution, apart from that more intangible atmosphere which we call the scientific spirit, they would neither exist nor be making their way into the curriculum. The body of knowledge is indeed one; it is a spiritual organism. To attempt to chop off a member here and amputate an organ there is the veriest impossibility. The problem is not one of elimination, but of organization; not of simplification through denial and rejection, but through harmony.

The simple necessities of modern life would, however, force the college to face the problem of its entire scope even if the philosophy of the sciences did not itself compel it.

With the perspective of years, it will become clearer and clearer that the distinguishing characteristic of the nineteenth century is the development of applied science. The earlier years inherited the application to mechanics of the various uses of steam in the revolutionizing of industry. Succeeding years and decades widened the application to practically all forms of chemical and physical energy. The latter decades saw the evolution of the biological sciences to the point of application. We do not realize as yet the rapidity of the revolution which the profession of medicine is undergoing because of the ability to make application of chemistry, physiology, and bacteriology. But it is not merely medicine and public hygiene that are affected. Simple and fundamental industrial processes—agriculture, dairying, etc.—are being invaded more and more by applied science. The bacteriologist comes home to us, not only in the treatment of disease, but in the making of our butter, and cheese, and beer. The close of the century surely sees us upon the verge of an analogous translation on the part of political and moral sciences into terms of application.

Now it is absurd to the point of fatuity to say, under such circumstances, that we will restrict our curriculum to a certain group of studies; that we will not introduce others because they have not been part of the classic curriculum of the past, and consequently are not yet well organized for educational purposes. The problem which the college has to face is not one which has grown up within the college walls, nor which is confined there. The ferment happily going on in the college is due to the fact that the leaven of all modern life is at work. There seems a certain lack of perspective, a certain lack of sanity and balance in those arguments regarding the college curriculum that assume that the subjects are already in a settled condition, that there are ready-made standards by which to measure their various claims, and that it only remains to pick out just so much of this and so much of that and put an end to all this confusion and conflict which is troubling us. Until the various branches of human learning have attained something like a philosophic organization, until the various modes of their application to life have been so definitely and completely worked out as to put even the common affairs of life under scientific direction, confusion and conflict are bound to continue. When we have an adequate industrial and political organization it will be quite time to assume that there is some offhand and short-cut solution to the problem of educational organization. In the meantime it is somewhat ridiculous to argue as if there were somewhere a definite set of specific educational recipes which the managers of the collegiate institutions might fall back on, and then serve out just such and such an intellectual diet to those eager for the intellectual feast.

I have been speaking, thus far, of the problem as it presents itself on the side of the curriculum—on the side of the multiplication and conflict of studies. When we turn to the matter of aims and methods, the moral end and the fundamental intellectual attitude involved, we do not find the state of things much changed. We talk, to be sure, about character, and information, and discipline, and culture as setting our aims and controlling our methods. We speak as if each of these terms had a perfectly definite and well-recognized meaning attaching to it; we appear to believe that some sort of mathematical ratio is possible—that by taking such a per cent of culture, such a per cent of training, such a per cent of useful information, we may get a well-rounded education. Or, to take the problem in its more burning form, we may assume that we have just such and such a ratio between the authoritative determination of material for the student and his own personal choice—thus assuming that there is a certain ratio between external discipline and the play of individuality in the determination of character. All our universities are face to face, moreover, with the problem of the adjustment of what is ordinarily regarded as the strictly disciplinary and culture element in the curriculum to the professional element—the preparation for law, medicine, theology, or whatever. The common expedient, the device which works well on the practical side, is to allow the last year of the college course to count on both sides—for the degree which stands for general culture and discipline and also for the degree that stands for specific professional training. Turn from the matter of practical expediency and success to that of the philosophy of education, and what does this compromise mean? In terms of fundamental values, what is the relation between general culture and professional ability?

When we go below the surface, most of us, I think, would admit that we are in very great doubt as to what all these terms really mean in themselves, to say nothing of their definite relationship to each other. What do we mean by character as a supreme end, or even incidental end, of college education? The topic lends itself gracefully to purposes of oration in which no cross-examination is permitted; but suppose one of us had to answer, honestly and definitely, what he took to be the exact connection between each of the studies of the college course, and each daily lesson in each study, and the attainment of a right character—what would the answer be? Indeed, just exactly what is the character at which we are aiming, or ought to aim, under modern conditions? Character involves not only right intentions, but a certain degree of efficiency. Now efficiency, as biologists have made us very well aware, is a problem of adaptation, of adjustment to the control of conditions. Are the conditions of modern life so clear and so settled that we know exactly what organs, what moral habits and methods, are necessary in order to get the maximum of efficiency? Do we know how to adjust our teaching to securing this maximum?

Great as the difficulties would be in reaching an adequate definition of what we mean by character and its relation to education, the problem is slight compared with what meets us when we ask about the significance of the terms discipline and culture.

What is discipline? I find the same persons who, in one

connection, emphasize the necessity of conducting education so as to give training, are often also the persons who, in
another connection, object to a certain kind of work on the
very ground that it gives too much and too specific training.
He who upholds mental training in classics or mathematics,
when it comes to the training of a man for the profession of
a teacher or investigator, will often be found to condemn a
school of commerce, or technology, or even of medicine, in
the university on the ground that it is too professional in
character—that it smacks of the utilitarian and commercial.
The kind of discipline which enables a man to pursue one
vocation is lauded; the kind of training that fits him for
another is condemned. Why this invidious distinction? The
only clew to an answer that I have ever been able to get is
the assumption of some mysterious difference between a
general training and a special training—as if the training that
the man got in the study of Latin and Greek were somehow
distinctively the training appropriate to man as man, while
the training which he gets in the application of, say, mathematics and physics to engineering, or of history, geography,
and political economy to commerce, only touches some narrow segment or fraction of the man. Whence the justification
of any such assumption? Is not the whole man required in
the calling of an engineer or a captain of industry? If the
whole man does not at present find opportunity and outlet
for himself in these callings, is it not one of the main duties
of the university to bring about precisely this result? The
assumption that a training is general just in the degree in
which it is good for nothing in particular is one for which
it would be difficult to find any adequate philosophic
ground. Training, discipline, must finally be measured in
terms of application, of availability. To be trained is to be
trained to something and for somewhat.

This brings me to the question of culture. Doubtless, the
current implication is that general culture and professional
utility are quite independent of each other. The notion of
absolute antagonism is, doubtless, wearing away. Like the

similar conception of a fixed and obvious gulf between the
elect and the unregenerated, it cannot stand the pressure of
the interaction of modern life. It is no longer possible to hug
complacently the ideal that the academic teacher is perforce
devoted to high spiritual ideals, while the doctor, lawyer,
and man of business are engaged in the mercenary pursuit
of vulgar utilities. But we have hardly reconstructed our
theory of the whole matter. Our conception of culture is
still tainted with inheritance from the period of the aristocratic seclusion of a leisure class—leisure meaning relief
from participation in the work of a workaday world. If I
were to venture into what might appear to you the metaphysical field, I think I could also show that the current
idea of culture belongs to the pre-biological period—it is a
survival of the time when mind was conceived as an independent entity living in an elegant isolation from its environment.

We come back here to the root of the whole matter. To
very many the idea of culture covers adequately and completely that for which the college stands. Even to suggest
that the college should do what the people want is to lay
unholy hands on the sanctity of the college ideal. The people, the mob, the majority, want anything but culture—
indeed they are capable of anything but culture. The college
stands for the remnant. It is the fortress of the few who are
capable of upholding high ideals against the utilitarian
clamor of the many. To ask that the colleges do what the
people want is to surrender or compromise the idea of culture by requiring the introduction of the professional factor
—a preparation for specific callings in life.

All this I say frankly and emphatically I regard as a survival from a dualistic past—from a society which was dualistic practically and politically, drawing fixed lines between
classes, and dualistic intellectually, with its rigid separation
between the things of matter and of mind—between the
affairs of the world and of the spirit. Social democracy means
an abandonment of this dualism. It means a common her-

itage, a common work, and a common destiny. It is flat
hostility to the ethic of modern life to suppose that there
are two different ends of life located on different planes;
that the few who are educated are to live on a plane of
exclusive and isolated culture, while the many toil below
on the level of practical endeavor directed at material com-
modity. The problem of our modern life is precisely to do
away with all the barriers that keep up this division. If the
university cannot accommodate itself to this movement, so
much the worse for it. Nay, more; it is doomed to helpless
failure unless it does more than accommodate itself; unless
it becomes one of the chief agencies for bridging the gap,
and bringing about an effective interaction of all callings in
society.

This may seem pretty abstract, rather remote, in its
actual bearing upon college affairs, but there is a definite
body of fact which gives this general statement sufficient
concreteness.

I have already referred to the fact that we are living in a
period of applied science. What this means for present purposes is that the professions, the practical occupations of
men, are becoming less and less empirical routines, or
technical facilities acquired through unintelligent apprenticeship. They are more and more infused with reason; more
and more illuminated by the spirit of inquiry and reason.
They are dependent upon science, in a word. To decline to
recognize this intimate connection of professions in modern
life with the discipline and culture that come from the
pursuit of truth for its own sake, is to be at least one century
behind the times. I do not say that the engineer, the doctor,
or lawyer, or even the clergyman, or much less the average
man of commerce, has as yet awakened to the full necessity
of this interdependence of theory and practice, to the full
significance of the extent in which his activities are already
dependent upon knowledge of the truth and the right attitude toward truth. I do not say that the professional classes
are as yet fully aware of the dignity and elevation that thus

come to their practical callings in life. But this very absence of clear and complete consciousness only makes the duty of the university the clearer. It is so to order its affairs that the availability of truth for life, and the dependence of the professional occupation upon science—upon insight into an ordered body of fact, and the possession of the right attitude of inquiry—shall become patent to all men.

I thus come back to the original question: is the college doing what the people want? No; for the people do not know what they want. They need illumination, and it is the business of the university to reveal them unto themselves. Yes; for what the people need is the union of that expert knowledge and skilled discipline which the college alone can supply, with the direction of the professions, the businesses of life; and all the forces and tendencies of college instruction and administration are tending irresistibly, even if blindly, in this direction. To say that the reality of the present university is professional training would perhaps give little less than material for misunderstanding. It would seem to mean that what most would regard as the important and essential feature of the university was a mere preliminary or incident, and that the reality is located in the schools of medicine, law, engineering, etc. This, of course, is not what is meant. I do mean, however, that the business of the university is coming to be more and more the supplying of that specific knowledge and that specific training which shall fit the individual for his calling in life. Just how the tendency shall work itself out on the formal and external side is a matter of comparatively little moment. The fact is sure that the intellectual and moral lines, dividing the university courses in science and letters from those of the professional ·schools, are gradually relaxing and are bound finally to fade away. And this is what the people want—it is the answer to their deepest needs.

What is termed general training and general culture is to be the function of the secondary school. A recent writer has stated that the college is threatened with attack from two sources: the high school on one side, the professional school on the other. This exactly states the situation to my mind—excepting that I should not regard these instrumentalities as foes, but rather as the twofold differentiation of function which the old-time amorphous college is assuming. Formally, the first two years of college work may perhaps belong to the secondary period. I am not speaking, however, of externals, but of the educational substance. This is not the place or time to go into the question of what is meant by general training and its relation to secondary-school work. It certainly means, however, that the pupil shall be touched, shall be stimulated, on all sides; that he shall be given a survey, at least, of the universe in its manifold phases. Through this survey, through this elaboration, coming to know both himself and the universe, he may get his orientation—his placing of himself in the larger world. With proper economy and instruction, and harmonious organization instead of blind confusion in the curriculum, this result should certainly be attained by the time the average student is twenty or twenty-one.

Having found himself, a student would then be prepared to enter upon that special training which is needed to equip him for the particular calling in life which he finds adapted to the freest and most effective expression of his own powers. This, by whatever name called, is professional training. The extent to which our larger universities have already moved in this direction is concealed, first, by the fact that they still retain considerable secondary work in the earlier years of their course; and secondly, by the fact that training for the calling of teaching, or of special research, is marked off in the public mind from training for the calling of doctor, lawyer, or engineer. In reality, the kind of training which students receive to make them professors or directors of laboratories is, of course, as professional as that of the school of technology or medicine.

There is still, however, a great deal of reconstructive work to be done. There is still a good deal of so-called higher college or university work which is thoroughly anomalous in character. It is neither one thing nor the other. It gives neither that kind of education which awakens the student to a sense of his own powers and their relation to the world of action, nor does it afford specific training for any particular walk in life. It is aimed in the air, with the pious hope that something will come of it in some direction or other.

The movement, however, is steady, and I believe inevitable, in one direction: the demarcation of secondary work as the period of general training and culture, thus restoring to it freshness and vitality by making it what it should be, the renaissance of the individual mind, the period of self-consciousness in the true sense, of knowledge of self in relation to the larger meanings of life; and the reservation of the higher institution for specific training, for gaining control of the particular body of knowledge and methods of research and verification which fit the individual to apply truth to the guidance of his own special calling in life. All of us have callings, occupations—only the luxuriously idle and the submerged idle, only the leisure class of fashion and of pauperism, violate this law. When education ceases to ignore this fact, when it recognizes it frankly and fully, and adapts its curriculum and methods to it, the university will be coherent in itself and also doing what the people really want done.

# 4

## THE PLACE OF MANUAL TRAINING IN THE ELEMENTARY COURSE OF STUDY *

AS a matter of convenience, the studies of the elementary curriculum may be placed under three heads; this arrangement is also, I think, of some philosophic value. We have, first, the studies which are not so much studies as active pursuits or occupations—modes of activity which appeal to the child for their own sake, and yet lend themselves to educative ends. Secondly, there is the subject-matter which gives us the background of social life. I include here both geography and history; history as the record of what has made present forms of associated life what they are; geography as the statement of the physical conditions and theater of man's social activities. At more advanced stages of education it may be desirable to specialize these subjects in such a way that they lose this direct relationship to social life. But in elementary education, of which I am speaking, I conceive that they are valuable just in the degree in which they are treated as furnishing social background. Thirdly, we have the studies which give the pupil command of the forms and methods of intellectual communication and inquiry. Such studies as reading, grammar, and the more technical modes of arithmetic are the instrumentalities which the race has worked out as best adapted to further its distinctively intellectual interests. The child's need of command of these, so that, using them freely for himself, he can appropriate the intellectual products of civilization, is so obvious that they constitute the bulk of the traditional curriculum.

* From *Manual Training Magazine,* July, 1901.

Looking along the line of these three groups, we see a movement away from direct personal and social interest to its indirect and remote forms. The first group presents to the child the same sort of activities that occupy him directly in his daily life; and re-presents to him modes of social occupation with which he is thoroughly familiar in his everyday surroundings. The second group is still social, but gives us the background rather than the direct reality of associated life. The third is social, but rather in its ultimate motives and effects—in maintaining the intellectual continuity of civilization—than in itself or in any of its more immediate suggestions and associations.

Manual training, constructive work (or whatever name we may care to employ), clearly belongs in the first group and makes up a very large part of it. Physical activity, the use of the bodily organs, is necessarily a phase of whatever directly occupies and absorbs the child. Plays and games obviously come here. So also do a variety of school resources that we might not at first sight put under this head: such as outdoor excursions, much of the more active observation and experimental work in nature study, etc. In this experimental work it is not so much the objective facts, much less the scientific laws, that concern the child, as it is the direct manipulation of materials, and the application of simple forms of energy to produce interesting results. Much of the meaning of art work with little children would also be lost, if we eliminated this aspect of the direct output of physical energy in realizing ideas. School gardens belong here, too. But it is of the manual training, the work with cardboard, wood, bent iron, the cooking, sewing, weaving, etc., that we have more directly to do. They so obviously involve modes of physical activity that the name used to designate them, "manual training," has been selected on this basis alone. No one any longer doubts the thorough training of hand and eye, and (what is of greater importance) of the hand and eye co-ordination, which is gained through these agencies. Recent psychology has made it unnecessary any longer to argue the fact that this training of hand and eye is also directly and indirectly a training of attention, constructive and reproductive imagination, and power of judgment. The manual-training movement has been greatly facilitated by its happy coincidence with the growing importance attached in psychological theory to the motor element. The old emphasis upon the strictly intellectual elements, sensations and ideas, has given way to the recognition that a motor factor is so closely bound up with the entire mental development that the latter cannot be intelligently discussed apart from the former.

I do not propose to repeat these arguments, but rather to assume them as both established in themselves and reasonably familiar to the reader, and go on to inquire whether there is not also something peculiarly appropriate, upon the *social* side, in demanding a considerable part in elementary education for this group of activities.

The idea of formal discipline, of the value of isolated and independent training of the so-called faculties of observation, memory, and reasoning, has invaded both physical culture and manual training. Here also we have been led to believe that there is a positive inherent value in the formal training of hand and eye quite apart from the actual content of such training—apart from its social relations and suggestions. Now, we ought to go deeper than this in our conception of the educational position of the constructive activities. We ought to see where and how they not only give formal training of hand and eye, but lay hold of the entire physical and mental organism; give play to fundamental aptitudes and instincts, and meet fundamental organic necessities. It is not enough to recognize that they develop hand and eye, and that this development reacts favorably into physical and mental development. We should see what social needs they spring out of, and what social values, what intellectual and emotional nutriment, they bring to the child which cannot be conveyed as well in any other way. And to carry the matter to this point, to recognize the substantial value of the educative material of which they are vehicles, is to connect them with social life; it is to conceive them from the standpoint of the social meaning they realize in child life.

The culture-epoch theory in education, and the recapitulation theory in biology, have made us familiar with the notion that the development of life in the individual corresponds to the development of life in the race—that the child achieves, in short years and months, that for which life upon the earth has required the slow ages. In spite of absurd pedagogical conclusions that have been drawn from this doctrine (through overlooking the fact that education is meant to accelerate and enrich this recapitulation instead of retarding and prolonging it), no one, I suppose, would deny to it a certain and important element of truth.

This element of truth, rightly apprehended, has, to my mind, a significant bearing upon the question of the place of manual training in education. The point is that the child, with his untried powers, his paucity of experience, is in much the same attitude toward the world and toward life as was early man. That the child should recapitulate the exact external conditions, performances, and blunders of primitive man is a ludicrous proposition. That he should assume a similar *attitude* is almost inevitable. The former conception leads to the notion that, since the race had to advance out of the errors of an animistic interpretation of nature to the truth as made known in science, the child must be kept in the mist of a sentimental and myth-enwrapped nature study before he can deal in any direct and truthful way with things and forces about him. The second conception means that it is the business of education to get hold of the essential underlying attitude which the child has in common with primitive man, in order to give it such play and expression as to avoid the errors and wanderings of his forefathers, and to come to the ends and realities toward which, after all, primitive man was struggling.

However, even admitting that this is the proper educational interpretation of the doctrine of recapitulation, what has it got to do with the place of manual training? Just this: both primitive man and the child are decidedly motor in their activity. Both are interested in objects and materials, not from a contemplative or theoretical standpoint, but from the standpoint of what can be done with them, and what can be got out of them. It needs no argument to show that primitive man must have mainly occupied himself with the direct problems of life—questions of getting food, fuel, shelter, protection. His concerns were the utensils, tools, instrumentalities that secured him a constantly improving life. His interest in nature was based upon its direct and indispensable relation to his own needs and activities. His nature-myths, his conception of natural forces as hostile and favorable, his interpretation of the events of his daily life, grew out of this industrial basis. His modes of associated life, family relations, political control, etc., were intimately dependent upon his industrial occupations.

Now, if there is anything at all in the doctrine of recapitulation, it indicates the probability, first, that we shall find the child a reservoir of motor energy, urgent for discharge upon his environment; and, second, that this will be likely to take forms akin to that of the social occupations through which humanity has maintained and developed itself.

In one important respect, however, there is a fundamental difference between the child and primitive man. Necessity, the pressure of getting a living, was upon the savage. The child is, or should be, protected against economic stress and strain. The expression of energy takes in his case a form of play—play which is not amusement, but the intrinsic exhibition of inherent powers so as to exercise and develop them. Accordingly, while the value of the motor activities of the savage was found chiefly in the external result—in the game that was killed or the fish that was caught—and only incidentally in a gain of skill and insight, with the child the exact reverse is the case. With him the external result is only a sign, a token; it is just a proof and exhibition to himself of his own capacities. In it he comes to consciousness of his own impulses. He learns to know them through seeing what they can effect. But the primary interest and the ultimate value remain in precisely the culture of the powers of action which is obtained in and through their being put to effective use.

If there be any measure of truth in these conceptions, then the forms of occupation, constructive work, manual training (whatever name be given them), which are employed in the school, must be assigned a central position. They, more than any other one study, more than reading or geography, story-telling or myth, evoke and direct what is most fundamental and vital in the child; that in which he is the heir of all the ages, and through which he recapitulates the progress of the race. It was certainly a gain for educational theory and practice when appeal to personal and immediate sense-perception displaced reliance upon symbols and abstract ideas. But, after all, to have sensations, to receive impressions through sight or hearing, is not the ultimate thing. To do, to perform, to execute, to make, to control and direct activity—it is for the sake of such things that perceptions and impressions exist. Indeed, to see and to hear is more than to have impressions; to see and to hear is to do, to do in co-operation with head, arm, hand, and leg. It must remain part of the imperishable renown of Froebel that he first of all educational reformers seized upon the primordial significance of this phase of child nature, and insisted upon modes of education which should give it outlet. What his exercises did for the kindergarten, that, and more, constructive and occupation work of various sorts must do for the elementary school.

Hence manual training can never take its proper place in the elementary curriculum as long as its chief aim is measured either by the actual result produced or by the gain in technical skill that comes to the producer. These have their place, but this place is not large enough to cover the territory to be rightfully assigned. The first consideration must be to give play to the deep-lying motor instincts and demands of the child; to enable him to become conscious of his powers through the variety of uses to which he can put them; and thus to become aware of their social values. To give play, to give expression to his motor instincts, and to do this in such a way that the child shall be brought to know the larger aims and processes of living, is the problem. The saw, hammer, and plane, the wood and clay, the needle and cloth, and the processes by which these are manipulated, are not ends in themselves; they are rather agencies through which the child may be initiated into the typical problems which require human effort, into the laws of human production and achievement, and into the methods by which man gains control of nature, and makes good in life his ideals. Out of this larger human significance must grow gradually the interest in the technical problems and processes of manual training. When the interest becomes of the purely technical sort, then of necessity manual training no longer occupies a central position; it belongs upon the level where all other forms of special technique are found.

When manual training is so interpreted, there is a necessary correlation between it and history and science. Just as man came originally to know nature in its variety of forms and forces through the active dealings which he had with it, through his attempts to modify it to meet his needs, so the child who in orderly fashion directs his motor powers to recapitulate social industries comes to know typical materials and the typical causal forces upon which the outward facts depend. In reassuming the motor attitude of the race, he recapitulates also the motives which induced the race to study nature and find out its laws. He takes the position from which the facts and truths of science are most easily accessible, and from which they have the most vital significance. Correlation of manual training with science is likely to be a rather external and artificial matter where the manual training itself is conducted for technical ends—for ends which lie within itself. But when it is treated as a means of organizing the powers of the child in social directions, its scope is necessarily broadened to take in salient facts of geography, physics, chemistry, botany, mathematics, etc.

Thus we return to the notion of the three groups of studies with which I set out. If I have made myself clear in what I have said, it is evident that manual training, properly conceived, is an inevitable and indispensable introduction to the studies of the second group, to history and geography, as the background of social endeavor. It projects, it ramifies, into these inevitably. It only remains for the teacher to be alert to these connections and to take advantage of them. It is the conception of formal discipline or a merely specific benefit to be derived from these studies which limits them to any narrower position. The restriction is due, not to their own nature, but to the failure to take a large view of them— failure to see them in their proper perspective. The connection with the third group of studies, those which have to do with the symbols and forms of distinctive intellectual advance, is equally important, even if more indirect. In number work it cannot even be said to be more indirect. Measurement, the application of number to limit form and arrange matters of shape and size, is a necessity. The child not only gets expertness in recognizing and handling certain number facts and relations, but, what is even more important, he gets a "number sense": he gets to be aware of the use and meaning of number; it becomes a reality to him, so that there is a vital motive in his own experience for pursuing it farther. Doubtless an ingenious and wideawake teacher will find natural connections also with the matter of reading and writing, but there is no need of forcing matters in this direction. Upon the whole, the connection here is indirect. But we may be sure that the training of the general intelligence which the child gets, his sense of reality, will arouse an interest in these matters. He will feel their necessity, even if he does not always have immediate motive for using them supplied by the constructive work. These tools of learning have been so integrally associated with productive work in the whole progress of humanity that the momentum which is secured from the pursuit of the latter will surely reflect itself, with increased effect, in devotion to the other.

If the term "primary" in the phrase "primary education" denotes anything more than merely a time element, if it means quality, if it means what is fundamental and basic, then the constructive arts and manual occupations have a claim to be considered distinguishing and characteristic features of primary education.

## 5

## DEMOCRACY IN EDUCATION *

MODERN life means democracy, democracy means freeing intelligence for independent effectiveness—the emancipation of mind as an individual organ to do its own work. We naturally associate democracy, to be sure, with freedom of action, but freedom of action without freed capacity of thought behind it is only chaos. If external authority in action is given up, it must be because internal authority of truth, discovered and known to reason, is substituted.

How does the school stand with reference to this matter? Does the school as an accredited representative exhibit this trait of democracy as a spiritual force? Does it lead and direct the movement? Does it lag behind and work at cross-purpose? I find the fundamental need of the school today dependent upon its limited recognition of the principle of freedom of intelligence. This limitation appears to me to affect both of the elements of school life: teacher and pupil. As to both, the school has lagged behind the general contemporary social movement; and much that is unsatisfactory, much of conflict and of defect, comes from the discrepancy between the relatively undemocratic organization of the school, as it affects the mind of both teacher and pupil, and the growth and extension of the democratic principle in life beyond school doors.

The effort of the last two-thirds of a century has been successful in building up the machinery of a democracy of mind. It has provided the ways and means for housing and equipping intelligence. What remains is that the thought-

* From *The Elementary School Teacher*, December, 1903.

activity of the individual, whether teacher or student, be permitted and encouraged to take working possession of this machinery: to substitute its rightful lordship for an inherited servility. In truth, our public-school system is but two-thirds of a century old. It dates, so far as such matters can be dated at all, from 1837, the year that Horace Mann became secretary of the state board of Massachusetts; and from 1843, when Henry Barnard began a similar work in Connecticut. At this time began that growing and finally successful warfare against all the influences, social and sectarian, which would prevent or mitigate the sway of public influence over private ecclesiastical and class interests. Between 1837 and 1850 grew up all the most characteristic features of the American public-school system: from this time date state normal schools, city training schools, county and state institutes, teachers' associations, teachers' journals, the institution of city superintendencies, supervisory officers, and the development of state universities as the crown of the public-school system of the commonwealth. From this time date the striving for better schoolhouses and grounds, improved text-books, adequate material equipment in maps, globes, scientific apparatus, etc. As an outcome of the forces thus set in motion, democracy has in principle, subject to relative local restrictions, developed an organized machinery of public education. But when we turn to the aim and method which this magnificent institution serves, we find that our democracy is not yet conscious of the ethical principle upon which it rests—the responsibility and freedom of mind in discovery and proof—and consequently we find confusion where there should be order, darkness where there should be light. The teacher has not the power of initiation and constructive endeavor which is necessary to the fulfillment of the function of teaching. The learner finds conditions antagonistic (or at least lacking) to the development of individual mental power and to adequate responsibility for its use.

1. *As to the teacher.*—If there is a single public-school system in the United States where there is official and constitutional provision made for submitting questions of methods of discipline and teaching, and the questions of the curriculum, text-books, etc., to the discussion and decision of those actually engaged in the work of teaching, that fact has escaped my notice. Indeed, the opposite situation is so common that it seems, as a rule, to be absolutely taken for granted as the normal and final condition of affairs. The number of persons to whom any other course has occurred as desirable, or even possible—to say nothing of necessary—is apparently very limited. But until the public-school system is organized in such a way that every teacher has some regular and representative way in which he or she can register judgment upon matters of educational importance, with the assurance that this judgment will somehow affect the school system, the assertion that the present system is not, from the internal standpoint, democratic seems to be justified. Either we come here upon some fixed and inherent limitation of the democratic principle, or else we find in this fact an obvious discrepancy between the conduct of the school and the conduct of social life—a discrepancy so great as to demand immediate and persistent effort at reform.

The more enlightened portions of the public have, indeed, become aware of one aspect of this discrepancy. Many reformers are contending against the conditions which place the direction of school affairs, including the selection of text-books, etc., in the hands of a body of men who are outside the school system itself, who have not necessarily any expert knowledge of education and who are moved by non-educational motives. Unfortunately, those who have noted this undemocratic condition of affairs, and who have striven to change it, have, as a rule, conceived of but one remedy, namely, the transfer of authority to the school superintendent. In their zeal to place the center of gravity inside the school system, in their zeal to decrease the prerogatives of a non-expert school board, and to lessen the opportunities for corruption and private pull which go with that, they have tried to remedy one of the evils of democracy by adopting the principle of autocracy. For no matter how wise, expert, or benevolent the head of the school system, the one-man principle is autocracy.

The logic of the argument goes farther, very much farther, than the reformer of this type sees. The logic which commits him to the idea that the management of the school system must be in the hands of an expert commits him also to the idea that every member of the school system, from the first-grade teacher to the principal of the high school, must have some share in the exercise of educational power. The remedy is not to have one expert dictating educational methods and subject-matter to a body of passive, recipient teachers, but the adoption of intellectual initiative, discussion, and decision throughout the entire school corps. The remedy of the partial evils of democracy, the implication of the school system in municipal politics, is in appeal to a more thorough-going democracy.

The dictation, in theory at least, of the subject-matter to be taught, to the teacher who is to engage in the actual work of instruction, and frequently, under the name of close supervision, the attempt to determine the methods which are to be used in teaching, mean nothing more or less than the deliberate restriction of intelligence, the imprisoning of the spirit. Every well graded system of schools in this country rejoices in a course of study. It is no uncommon thing to find methods of teaching such subjects as reading, writing, spelling, and arithmetic officially laid down; outline topics in history and geography are provided ready-made for the teacher; gems of literature are fitted to the successive ages of boys and girls. Even the domain of art, songs and methods of singing, subject-matter and technique of drawing and painting, come within the region on which an outside authority lays its sacrilegious hands.

I have stated the theory, which is also true of the practice to a certain extent and in certain places. We may thank our heavens, however, that the practice is rarely as bad as the theory would require. Superintendents and principals often encourage individuality and thoughtfulness in the invention and adoption of methods of teaching; and they wink at departures from the printed manual of study. It remains true, however, that this great advance is personal and informal. It depends upon the wisdom and tact of the individual supervisory official; he may withdraw his concession at any moment; or it may be ruthlessly thrown aside by his successor who has formed a high ideal of "system."

I know it will be said that this state of things, while an evil, is a necessary one; that without it confusion and chaos would reign; that such regulations are the inevitable accompaniments of any graded system. It is said that the average teacher is incompetent to take any part in laying out the course of study or in initiating methods of instruction or discipline. Is not this the type of argument which has been used from time immemorial, and in every department of life, against the advance of democracy? What does democracy mean save that the individual is to have a share in determining the conditions and the aims of his own work; and that, upon the whole, through the free and mutual harmonizing of different individuals, the work of the world is better done than when planned, arranged, and directed by a few, no matter how wise or of how good intent that few? How can we justify our belief in the democratic principle elsewhere, and then go back entirely upon it when we come to education?

Moreover, the argument proves too much. The more it is asserted that the existing corps of teachers is unfit to have voice in the settlement of important educational matters, and their unfitness to exercise intellectual initiative and to assume the responsibility for constructive work is emphasized, the more their unfitness to attempt the much more difficult and delicate task of guiding souls appears. If this body is so unfit, how can it be trusted to carry out the recommendations or the dictations of the wisest body of experts? If teachers are incapable of the intellectual responsibility which goes with the determination of the methods they are to use in teaching, how can they employ methods when dictated by others, in other than a mechanical, capricious, and clumsy manner? The argument, I say, proves too much.

Moreover, if the teaching force is as inept and unintelligent and irresponsible as the argument assumes, surely the primary problem is that of their improvement. Only by sharing in some responsible task does there come a fitness to share in it. The argument that we must wait until men and women are fully ready to assume intellectual and social responsibilities would have defeated every step in the democratic direction that has ever been taken. The prevalence of methods of authority and of external dictation and direction tends automatically to perpetuate the very conditions of inefficiency, lack of interest, inability to assume positions of self-determination, which constitute the reasons that are depended upon to justify the régime of authority.

The system which makes no great demands upon originality, upon invention, upon the continuous expression of individuality, works automatically to put and to keep the more incompetent teachers in the school. It puts them there because, by a natural law of spiritual gravitation, the best minds are drawn to the places where they can work most effectively. The best minds are not especially likely to be drawn where there is danger that they may have to submit to conditions which no self-respecting intelligence likes to put up with; and where their time and energy are likely to be so occupied with details of external conformity that they have no opportunity for free and full play of their own vigor.

I have dwelt at length upon the problem of the recognition of the intellectual and spiritual individuality of the teacher. I have but one excuse. All other reforms are conditioned upon reform in the quality and character of those who engage in the teaching profession. The doctrine of the man behind the gun has become familiar enough, in recent discussion, in every sphere of life. Just because education is the most personal, the most intimate, of all human affairs, there, more than anywhere else, the sole ultimate reliance and final source of power are in the training, character, and intelligence of the individual. If any scheme could be devised which would draw to the calling of teaching persons of force of character, of sympathy with children, and consequent interest in the problems of teaching and of scholarship, no one need be troubled for a moment about other educational reforms, or the solution of other educational problems. But as long as a school organization which is undemocratic in principle tends to repel from all but the higher portions of the school system those of independent force, of intellectual initiative, and of inventive ability, or tends to hamper them in their work after they find their way into the schoolroom, so long all other reforms are compromised at their source and postponed indefinitely for fruition.

2. *As to the learner.*—The undemocratic suppression of the individuality of the teacher goes naturally with the improper restriction of the intelligence of the mind of the child. The mind, to be sure, is that of a child, and yet, after all, it is mind. To subject mind to an outside and ready-made material is a denial of the ideal of democracy, which roots itself ultimately in the principle of moral, self-directing individuality. Misunderstanding regarding the nature of the freedom that is demanded for the child is so common that it may be necessary to emphasize the fact that it is primarily intellectual freedom, free play of mental attitude, and operation which are sought. If individuality were simply a matter of feelings, impulses, and outward acts independent of intelligence, it would be more than a dubious matter to urge a greater degree of freedom for the child in the school. In that case much, and almost exclusive, force would attach to the objections that the principle of individuality is realized

in the more exaggerated parts of Rousseau's doctrines: sentimental idealization of the child's immaturity, irrational denial of superior worth in the knowledge and mature experience of the adult, deliberate denial of the worth of the ends and instruments embodied in social organization. Deification of childish whim, unripened fancy, and arbitrary emotion is certainly a piece of pure romanticism. The would-be reformers who emphasize out of due proportion and perspective these aspects of the principle of individualism betray their own cause. But the heart of the matter lies not there. Reform of education in the direction of greater play for the individuality of the child means the securing of conditions which will give outlet, and hence direction, to a growing intelligence. It is true that this freed power of mind with reference to its own further growth cannot be obtained without a certain leeway, a certain flexibility, in the expression of even immature feelings and fancies. But it is equally true that it is not a riotous loosening of these traits which is needed, but just that kind and degree of freedom from repression which are found to be necessary to secure the full operation of intelligence.

Now, no one need doubt as to what mental activity or the freed expression of intelligence means. No one need doubt as to the conditions which are conducive to it. We do not have to fall back upon what some regard as the uncertain, distracting, and even distressing voice of psychology. Scientific methods, the methods pursued by the scientific inquirer, give us an exact and concrete exhibition of the path which intelligence takes when working most efficiently, under most favorable conditions.

What is primarily required for that direct inquiry which constitutes the essence of science is first-hand experience; an active and vital participation through the medium of all the bodily organs with the means and materials of building up first-hand experience. Contrast this first and most fundamental of all the demands for an effective use of mind with what we find in so many of our elementary and high schools.

There first-hand experience is at a discount; in its stead are summaries and formulas of the results of other people. Only very recently has any positive provision been made within the schoolroom for any of the modes of activity and for any of the equipment and arrangement which permit and require the extension of original experiences on the part of the child. The school has literally been dressed out with hand-me-down garments—with intellectual suits which other people have worn.

Secondly, in that freed activity of mind which we term "science" there is always a certain problem which focusses effort, which controls the collecting of facts that bear upon the question, the use of observation to get further data, the employing of memory to supply relevant facts, the calling into play of imagination, to yield fertile suggestion and construct possible solutions of the difficulty.

Turning to the school, we find too largely no counterpart to this mental activity. Just because a second-handed material has been supplied wholesale and retail, but anyway ready-made, the tendency is to reduce the activity of mind to a docile or passive taking in of the material presented— in short, to memorizing, with simply incidental use of judgment and of active research. As is frequently stated, acquiring takes the place of inquiring. It is hardly an exaggeration to say that the sort of mind-activity which is encouraged in the school is a survival from the days in which science had not made much headway; when education was mainly concerned with learning, that is to say, the preservation and handing down of the acquisitions of the past. It is true that more and more appeal is made every day in schools to judgment, reasoning, personal efficiency, and the calling up of personal, as distinct from merely book, experiences. But we have not yet got to the point of reversing the total method. The burden and the stress still fall upon learning in the sense of becoming possessed of the second-hand and ready-made material referred to. The prevailing ideal is a perfect recitation, an exhibition without mistake, of a lesson learned. Until

the emphasis changes to the conditions which make it necessary for the child to take an active share in the personal
building up of his own problems and to participate in
methods of solving them (even at the expense of experimentation and error), mind is not really freed.

In our schools we have freed individuality in many modes
of outer expression without freeing intelligence, which is the
vital spring and guarantee of all of these expressions. Consequently we give opportunity to the unconverted to point
the finger of scorn, and to clamor for a return to the good
old days when the teacher, the representative of social and
moral authority, was securely seated in the high places of
the school. But the remedy here, as in other phases of our
social democracy, is not to turn back, but to go farther—to
carry the evolution of the school to a point where it becomes
a place for getting and testing experience, as real and adequate to the child upon his existing level as all the resources
of laboratory and library afford to the scientific man upon
his level. What is needed is not any radical revolution, but
rather an organization of agencies already found in the
schools. It is hardly too much to say that not a single subject
or instrumentality is required which is not already found in
many schools of the country. All that is required is to gather
these materials and forces together and unify their operation.
Too often they are used for a multitude of diverse and often
conflicting aims. If a single purpose is provided, that of freeing the processes of mental growth, these agencies will at
once fall into their proper classes and reinforce each other.

A catalogue of the agencies already available would include at least all of the following: Taking the child out of
doors, widening and organizing his experience with reference to the world in which he lives; nature study when pursued as a vital observation of forces working under their
natural conditions, plants and animals growing in their own
homes, instead of mere discussion of dead specimens. We
have also school gardens, the introduction of elementary
agriculture, and more especially of horticulture—a move-

ment that is already making great headway in many of the western states. We have also means for the sake of studying physiographic conditions, such as may be found by rivers, ponds, or lakes, beaches, quarries, gulleys, hills, etc.

As similar agencies within the school walls, we find a very great variety of instruments for constructive work, or, as it is frequently, but somewhat unfortunately termed, "manual training." Under this head come cooking, which can be begun in its simpler form in the kindergarten; sewing, and what is of even greater educational value, weaving, including designing and the construction of simple apparatus for carrying on various processes of spinning, etc. Then there are also the various forms of tool-work directed upon cardboard, wood, and iron; in addition there are clay-modeling and a variety of ways of manipulating plastic material to gain power and larger experience.

Such matters pass readily over into the simpler forms of scientific experimentation. Every schoolroom from the lowest primary grade up should be supplied with gas, water, certain chemical substances and reagents. To experiment in the sense of trying things or to see what will happen is the most natural business of the child; it is, indeed, his chief concern. It is one which the school has largely either ignored or actually suppressed, so that it has been forced to find outlet in mischief or even in actually destructive ways. This tendency could find outlet in the construction of simple apparatus and the making of simple tests, leading constantly into more and more controlled experimentation, with greater insistence upon definiteness of intellectual result and control of logical process.

Add to these three typical modes of active experimenting, various forms of art expression, beginning with music, clay-modeling, and story-telling as foundation elements, and passing on to drawing, painting, designing in various mediums, we have a range of forces and materials which connect at every point with the child's natural needs and powers, and which supply the requisites for building up his experience upon all sides. As fast as these various agencies find their way into the schools, the center of gravity shifts, the régime changes from one of subjection of mind to an external and ready-made material, into the activity of mind directed upon the control of the subject-matter and thereby its own up-building.

Politically we have found that this country could not endure half free and half slave. We shall find equally great difficulty in encouraging freedom, independence, and initiative in every sphere of social life, while perpetuating in the school dependence upon external authority. The forces of social life are already encroaching upon the school institutions which we have inherited from the past, so that many of its mainstays are crumbling. Unless the outcome is to be chaotic, we must take hold of the organic, positive principle involved in democracy, and put that in entire possession of the spirit and work of the school.

In education meet the three most powerful motives of human activity. Here are found sympathy and affection, the going out of the emotions to the most appealing and the most rewarding object of love—a little child. Here is found also the flowering of the social and institutional motive, interest in the welfare of society and in its progress and reform by the surest and shortest means. Here, too, is found the intellectual and scientific motive, the interest in knowledge, in scholarship, in truth for its own sake, unhampered and unmixed with any alien ideal. Copartnership of these three motives—of affection, of social growth, and of scientific inquiry—must prove as nearly irresistible as anything human when they are once united. And, above all else, recognition of the spiritual basis of democracy, the efficacy and responsibility of freed intelligence, is necessary to secure this union.

# 6

## RELIGION AND OUR SCHOOLS *

### I

A LEARNED and self-conscious generation has fittingly discovered religion to be a universal tendency of human nature. Through its learning, anthropology, psychology, and comparative religion have been summoned to give this testimony. But because of its self-consciousness the generation is uneasy. As it surveys itself it is fearful lest, solitary among the ages, it should not be religious. The self-same learning which has made it aware that other times have had their life permeated with religious faith is part of the conditions which have rendered the religions of those periods impossible. The dilemma is striking and perplexing. Shall the very circumstances which convince us that religion is necessary also make it impossible? Shall the evidence that it is a universal tendency make those who are aware of this tendency the flagrant exception to its universality? We have learned so much about religious "instincts": shall we therefore lose them?

It indeed seems hard that a generation which has accumulated not only material wealth, but intellectual riches, to the extent that it is compelled to pull down its barns—its systems of philosophy and doctrine—and build greater, should be lacking in just that grace and sanction of life which ignorant and poor people have possessed as matter of course. But our learnedly self-conscious generation is also mechanical. It has a tool for everything, and almost everything has become for it a tool. Why, then, should we longer suffer

* From *The Hibbert Journal*, July, 1908.

from deficiency of religion? We have discovered our lack: let us set the machinery in motion which will supply it. We have mastered the elements of physical well-being; we can make light and heat to order, and can command the means of transportation. Let us now put a similar energy, goodwill, and thoughtfulness into the control of the things of the spiritual life. Having got so far as to search for proper machinery, the next step is easy. Education is the modern universal purveyor, and upon the schools shall rest the responsibility for seeing to it that we recover our threatened religious heritage.

I cannot expect that those who are now especially concerned with the maintenance and the spread of conscious and explicit religious instruction (for the time being one must use this question-begging epithet) will recognize their attitude or intention in what I have just said. And it has no application to those who are already committed to special dogmas of religion which are the monopoly of special ecclesiastic institutions. With respect to them, the fight for special agencies and peculiar materials and methods of education in religion is a natural part of their business: just as, however, it is the business of those who do not believe that religion is a monopoly or a protected industry to contend, in the interest both of education and of religion, for keeping the schools free from what they must regard as a false bias. Those who believe that human nature without special divine assistance is lost, who believe that they have in their charge the special channels through which the needed assistance is conveyed, must, naturally, be strenuous in keeping open these channels to the minds of men. But when the arguments for special religious education at special times and places by special means proceed from philosophic sources— from those whose primary premise is denial of any breach between man and the world and God, then a sense of unreality comes over me. The arguments perforce translate themselves ironically. They seem to say that, since religion is a universal function of life, we must particularly safeguard it lest it disappear; that since religion is the consciousness of the spiritual import of experience, we must find mechanical appliances for developing it.

Those who approach religion and education from the side of unconstrained reflection, not from the side of tradition, are of necessity aware of the tremendous transformation of intellectual attitude effected by the systematic denial of the supernatural; they are aware of the changes it imports not merely in special dogma and rites, but in the interpretation of the world, and in the projection of social, and, hence, moral life. It testifies to the current unreality of philosophy (itself probably a product of that forced idealism in which modern thought has taken refuge) that philosophers should seem to think that great intellectual generalizations may be, as it were, plastered over life to label its contents, and not imply profound practical alterations within life itself. In no other way is it easy to account for the attitude of those who are convinced of the final departure of the supernatural interpretation of the world and of man, and who yet think that agencies like the church and the school must not be thoroughly reconstructed before they can be fit organs for nurturing types of religious feeling and thought which are consistent with modern democracy and modern science.

That science has the same spiritual import as supernaturalism; that democracy translates into the same religious attitude as did feudalism; that it is only a matter of slight changes of phraseology, a development of old symbolisms into new shades of meaning—such beliefs testify to that torpor of imagination which is the uniform effect of dogmatic belief. The reconstruction of the Church is a matter which concerns, indeed, the whole community so far as its outcome is concerned; while the responsibility for its initiation belongs primarily to those within the churches. The burden of conducting the development, the reconstruction, of other educational agencies belongs, however, primarily to the community as a whole. With respect to its intellectual aspect, its philosophy, it belongs especially to those who, having become conscious in some degree of the modern ideas of nature, of man and society, are best able to forecast the direction which social changes are taking. It is lucidity, sincerity, and the sense of reality which demand that, until the non-supernatural view is more completely elaborated in all its implications and is more completely in possession of the machinery of education, the schools shall keep hands off and shall do as little as possible. This is indeed a *laissez-faire* policy. It is frankly, avowedly so. And, doubtless, *laissez-faire* policies are not in favor in self-conscious and mechanical days. One of the further ironies of our time is that, having discovered the part played by unconscious, organic, collective forces in the processes of human development, we are possessed by a great eagerness, a great uneasiness, consciously to foster and to guide these forces.

We need, however, to accept the responsibilities of living in an age marked by the greatest intellectual readjustment history records. There is undoubted loss of joy, of consolation, of some types of strength, and of some sources of inspiration in the change. There is a manifest increase of uncertainty; there is some paralysis of energy, and much excessive application of energy in materialistic directions. Yet nothing is gained by deliberate effort to return to ideas which have become incredible, and to symbols which have been emptied of their content of obvious meaning. Nothing can be gained by moves which will increase confusion and obscurity, which tend to an emotional hypocrisy and to a phrasemongering or formulae which seem to mean one thing and really import the opposite. Bearing the losses and inconveniences of our time as best we may, it is the part of men to labor persistently and patiently for the clarification and development of the positive creed of life implicit in democracy and in science, and to work for the transformation of all practical instrumentalities of education till they are in harmony with these ideas. Till these ends are further along than we can honestly claim them to be at present, it is better that our schools should do nothing than that they should do wrong things. It is better for them to confine themselves to their obviously urgent tasks than that they should, under the name of spiritual culture, form habits of mind which are at war with the habits of mind congruous with democracy and with science. It is not laziness nor cynicism which calls for the *laissez-faire* policy; it is honesty, courage, sobriety, and faith.

If one inquires why the American tradition is so strong against any connection of State and Church, why it dreads even the rudiments of religious teaching in state-maintained schools, the immediate and superficial answer is not far to seek. The cause was not, mainly, religious indifference, much less hostility to Christianity, although the eighteenth century deism played an important rôle. The cause lay largely in the diversity and vitality of the various denominations, each fairly sure that, with a fair field and no favor, it could make its own way; and each animated by a jealous fear that, if any connection of State and Church were permitted, some rival denomination would get an unfair advantage. But there was a deeper and by no means wholly unconscious influence at work. The United States became a nation late enough in the history of the world to profit by the growth of that modern (although Greek) thing—the state consciousness. This nation was born under conditions which enabled it to share in and to appropriate the idea that the state life, the vitality of the social whole, is of more importance than the flourishing of any segment or class. So far as church institutions were concerned, the doctrine of popular sovereignty was a reality, not a literary or legal fiction. Upon the economic side, the nation was born too soon to learn the full force of the state idea as against the class idea. Our fathers naïvely dreamed of the continuation of pioneer conditions and the free opportunity of every individual, and took none of the precautions to maintain the supremacy of the state over that of the class which newer commonwealths are taking. For that lack of foresight we are paying dearly, and are like to pay more dearly. But the lesson of the two and a half centuries lying between the Protestant revolt and the formation of the nation was well learned as respected the necessity of maintaining the integrity of the state as against all divisive ecclesiastical divisions. Doubtless many of our ancestors would have been somewhat shocked to realize the full logic of their own attitude with respect to the subordination of churches to the state (falsely termed the *separation* of Church and State); but the state idea was inherently of such vitality and constructive force as to carry the practical result, with or without conscious perception of its philosophy. And any general agitation in the United States of the question of religious instruction in the schools could have but one explanation. It would mean that, from economic segregation and unassimilated immigration, the state-consciousness of the country had been sapped by the growth of social factions.

## II

As I recall, some of the Platonic dialogues discuss the question whether virtue can be taught, and all of them contain overtones or reminiscences of the topic. For the discussion led a long way. What is virtue? That is not an altogether easy question; and since to answer it we must know virtue and not merely have opinions about it, it will be well to find out what knowledge is. Moreover, teaching implies learning, and learning is coming to know, or knowledge in process of learning. What, then, is the connection of the becoming of knowledge with the being of knowledge? And since the teaching of virtue means, not getting knowledge "about" virtue, but the conversion of character to the good, what, after all, is the relation between becoming good and that becoming wise which is the result of learning?

Somehow, I am more aware that Plato discusses all these questions than I am certain of any final answer to the question whether virtue may be taught. Yet I seem to recall some hypothetical suggestions for an answer. If, as we have reason to believe, the soul of man is naturally akin to good—if, indeed, it truly *is* only through participation in the good—then may various objects, also in their measure expressions of good, serve to remind the soul of its own or original nature. If these various reminders may be organized into a comprehensive scheme, continuous and continual in operation—if, in other words, there may be found a state organized in righteousness—then may the soul be finally brought to the apprehension of its own being or good; and this coming to know and to be we may term learning. But, if I remember rightly, Plato always classed endeavors to teach virtue apart from an accompanying thorough reorganization of social life and of science as a piece of confused and self-contradictory thinking—as a case, that is, of sophistic.

Have we any reason for taking the present problem of teaching religion to be simpler in conception or easier in execution? The contemporary problem appears, indeed, to be more intricate and difficult. Varied and conflicting as were the views of Plato's Greek contemporaries as to what things should be included and taught under the head of virtues, the question of just what concretely comes under the caption of religion today is as much harder to decide as our social life is more heterogeneous in origin and composition than was the Athenian. We certainly cannot teach religion as an abstract essence. We have got to teach *something* as religion, and that means practically *some* religion. Which? In America, at least, the answer cannot be summarily given even as Christianity in general. Our Jewish fellow-citizens not only have the same "hands, organs, dimensions, senses, affections, passions" as the Christians, but, like them, they pay taxes, vote, and serve on school boards. But we should not be very much better off even if it were a question of Christianity alone. *Which* Christianity? Oriental in its origin, it has been since Latinized and Germanized, and there are even those who have dreamed of humanizing it.

The problem of today is more complex as respects also the process of learning, of coming to know. In the day of Plato, art and science, skilled practice and theory, were only beginning to be separated. Just as a man learned shoemaking in process of becoming a shoemaker, so might a man learn virtue in becoming a member of a good state—if such a thing could be found. Today knowledge is something specialized, and learning does not consist in intelligent mastery of an activity, but in acquiring a diversity of information about things, and control over technical methods for instituting symbolic references to things. Knowledge to Plato was the sort of thing that the forefathers of some of us called "getting religion." It was a personal experiencing and a vital realization. But what shall knowledge of religion as an outcome of instruction mean today? Shall it mean the conversion of character into spirituality? Shall it mean the accumulation of information *about* religion? Or are there those who still believe in some magic power resident in memorized words, phrases, and facts of transmuting themselves into personal insight, the development of fundamental mood and the formation of permanent attitudes towards experience?

When we consider knowledge from the side of its method and from the standpoint of what it takes to get something really worthy to be called knowledge, the problem increases in difficulty. As yet, the standpoint of science, its spirit, has not of course leavened very adequately our methods of teaching. From the standpoint of those methods of inquiry and testing which we call science, much, perhaps most, of what passes for knowledge is in reality what Plato called opinion. Our science is still an outward garb more or less awkwardly worn rather than a habit of mind. But none the less the scientific norm of mental activity presses daily closer upon life and upon the schools. We are getting daily further away from the conditions in which one subject more or less taught by dogmatic, catechetical, and memoriter methods was of slight consequence. We are becoming aware of the absurdity implied in calling things which happen to be studied and learned in school "knowledge," when they have been acquired by methods frequently at odds with those necessary to give science. Can those who take the philosophic and historic view of religion as a flower and fruition of the human spirit in a congenial atmosphere tolerate the incongruity involved in "teaching" such an intimate and originally vital matter by external and formal methods? And can those who hold that true religion is something externally imported tolerate any other methods? Is it not confusion to seek a reconciliation of two such disparate ideas?

Already the spirit of our schooling is permeated with the feeling that every subject, every topic, every fact, every professed truth must submit to a certain publicity and impartiality. All proffered samples of learning must go to the same assay-room and be subjected to common tests. It is the essence of all dogmatic faiths to hold that any such "showdown" is sacrilegious and perverse. The characteristic of religion, from their point of view, is that it is—intellectually —secret, not public; peculiarly revealed, not generally known; authoritatively declared, not communicated and tested in ordinary ways. What is to be done about this increasing antinomy between the standard for coming to know in other subjects of the school, and coming to know in religious matters? I am far from saying that the antinomy is an inherent one, or that the day may not come when religion will be so thoroughly naturalized in the hearts and minds of men that it can be considered publicly, openly, and by common tests, even among religious people. But it is pertinent to point out that, as long as religion is conceived as it now is conceived by the great majority of professed religionists, there is something self-contradictory in speaking of education in religion in the same sense in which we speak of education in topics where the method of free inquiry has made its way. The "religious" would be the last to be willing that either the history or the content of religion should be taught in this spirit; while those to whom the scientific standpoint is not a merely technical device, but is the embodiment of integrity of mind, must protest against its being taught in any other spirit.

As Plato brought out with reference to the teaching of virtue, there is one other factor in coming to know—the teachers. Plato was quite sure that, whether or no virtue might be taught, it might not be taught by its professed teachers—the sophists. I express my appreciation of Plato rather than my lack of appreciation of the professional teachers of our own day, when I say that if Plato were to return to take part in the current discussion, he would raise questions about those who were to teach religion analogous to those he brought up about the teachers of his own time. It is not that those into whose hands the giving of instruction would fall are so irreligious or so non-religious as to be unfitted for the task. The sophists were doubtless superior rather than inferior in personal virtues to their average neighbor. It is one thing to be fairly or even exceptionally virtuous; it is another thing to command the conditions and the qualifications for successful importation of virtue to others. Where are the experts in religion? and where are the authoritative teachers? There are theologians; do we want theology taught? There are historians, but I fear the day has not come when the history of religion can be taught as history. Here precisely is one of those fields of clarification and criticism where much labor needs to be done, and where the professional religionist is one of the most serious obstacles to reckon with, since a wider and deeper historic knowledge would overthrow his traditional basis.

There are preachers and catechists, but, unless we are committed to some peculiar faith or institution, it is not exhortation or discipline of this sort that constitutes religious instruction. There are psychologists: but is introspection our aim? There remains, indeed, the corps of faithful, more or less well-prepared, hard-working and hard-worked teachers. This brings us to the crux of the whole matter. Is religion a thing so specialized, so technical, so "informational" that, like geography or history or grammar, it may be taught at special hours, times, and places by those who have properly "got it up," and who have been approved as persons of fit character and adequate professional training?

This question of the mode, time, and stuff of specific instruction trenches indeed upon a question in which national temper and tradition count for much. We do not find it feasible or desirable to put upon the regular teachers the burden of teaching a subject which has the nature of religion. The alternative plan of parceling out pupils among religious teachers drawn from their respective churches and denominations brings us up against exactly the matter which has done most to discredit the churches, and to discredit the cause, not perhaps of religion, but of organized and institutional religion: the multiplication of rival and competing religious bodies, each with its private inspiration and outlook. Our schools, in bringing together those of different nationalities, languages, traditions, and creeds, in assimilating them together upon the basis of what is common and public in endeavor and achievement, are performing an infinitely significant religious work. They are promoting the social unity out of which in the end genuine religious unity must grow. Shall we interfere with this work? shall we run the risk of undoing it by introducing into education a subject which can be taught only by segregating pupils and turning them over at special hours to separate representatives of rival faiths? This would be deliberately to adopt a scheme which is predicated upon the maintenance of social divisions in just the matter, religion, which is empty and futile save as it expresses the basic unities of life. An acute English critic has recently called us, with much truth, a "nation of villagers." But in this matter of education at least we have no intention or desire of letting go our hard-won state-consciousness in order to relapse into divisive provinciality. We are far, indeed, from having attained an explicit and articulated consciousness of the religious significance of democracy in education, and of education in democracy. But some underlying convictions get ingrained in unconscious habit and find expression in obscure intimation and intense labor, long before they receive consistent theoretic formulation. In such a dim, blind, but effective way the American people is conscious that its schools serve best the cause of religion in serving the cause of social unification; and that under certain conditions schools are more religious in substance and in promise without any of the conventional badges and machinery of religious instruction than they could be in cultivating these forms at the expense of a state-consciousness.

We may indeed question whether it is true that in any relative sense this is a peculiarly irreligious age. Absolutely speaking, it doubtless is so; but have superficiality, flippancy, and externality of life been such uniformly absent traits of past ages? Our historic imagination is at best slightly developed. We generalize and idealize the past egregiously. We set up little toys to stand as symbols for long centuries and the complicated lives of countless individuals. And we are still, even those who have nominally surrendered supernatural dogma, largely under the dominion of the ideas of those who have succeeded in identifying religion with the rites, symbols, and emotions associated with these dogmatic beliefs. As we see the latter disappearing, we think we are growing irreligious. For all we know, the integrity of mind which is loosening the hold of these things is potentially much more religious than all that it is displacing. It is increased knowledge of nature which has made supra-nature incredible, or at least difficult of belief. We measure the change from the standpoint of the supernatural and we call it irreligious. Possibly if we measured it from the standpoint of the natural piety it is fostering, the sense of the permanent and inevitable implication of nature and man in a common career and destiny, it would appear as the growth of religion. We take note of the decay of cohesion and influence among the religiously organized bodies of the familiar historic type, and again we conventionally judge religion to be on the decrease. But it may be that their decadence is the fruit of a broader and more catholic principle of human intercourse and association which is too religious to tolerate these pretensions to monopolize truth and to make private possessions of spiritual insight and aspiration.

It may be so; it may be that the symptoms of religious ebb as conventionally interpreted are symptoms of the coming of a fuller and deeper religion. I do not claim to know. But of one thing I am quite sure: our ordinary opinions about the rise and falling off of religion are highly conventional, based mostly upon the acceptance of a standard of religion which is the product of just those things in historic religions which are ceasing to be credible. So far as education is concerned, those who believe in religion as a natural expression of human experience must devote themselves to the development of the ideas of life which lie implicit in our still new science and our still newer democracy. They must interest themselves in the transformation of those institutions which still bear the dogmatic and the feudal stamp (and which do not?) till they are in accord with these ideas. In performing this service, it is their business to do what they can to prevent all public educational agencies from being employed in ways which inevitably impede the recognition of the spiritual import of science and of democracy, and hence of that type of religion which will be the fine flower of the modern spirit's achievement.

# 7

## OUR EDUCATIONAL IDEAL IN WARTIME *

EXTERNALLY viewed, the most obvious fact about our educational system is its inconsistency. We have repaired, patched and extended freely under the pressure of circumstance and immediate demand. Our conscious philosophy has, however, remained timid and traditional. Even when practical urgencies have made big breaches, we have done our best to conceal from ourselves the meaning of what we have done. We have stretched the intellectual mantle of tradition till it has covered the breaches from view, and have settled back to enjoy the consolations of the orthodox catchwords of culture and discipline. Man is a creature of instinct and habit. Action, overt action, is always easier than thought—a laboriously acquired art in which man is still far from at home. I would suggest to those who feel the tension of enforced inaction when all the rest of the world is hard at it, that their energies might better be directed to intellecutal scrutiny and construction than to pleas for direct action—which would be hardly more than discharge of and relief from nervous strain. And in the problem of moral and intellectual examination, the business of national education stands first.

When we look at the enlarged picture of English and German education which the war has thrown upon the screen, the lesson regarding our own educational aims appears plain. The strong and weak points revealed supplement each other, and they define our own needs. Germany has succeeded in scientific and specialized education, England, at least relatively speaking, in general and humanistic. We

* From *The New Republic,* April 15, 1916.

have worked sporadically at both, and often with so little definite intent that we have done just enough in one direction to undo our accomplishments in the other. Yet there is a sound instinct in our refusal to commit ourselves exclusively to either one or the other.

Every one who recalls the war of 1870 knows how tritely universal became the remark that the victory was the victory of the German schoolmaster. The intellectual prestige of Germany dates largely from that victory. Its meed of success in the present war is the success of technical education, an education which is everywhere technical and professional no matter what the label of the school giving it. A writer has said that while the Germans have talked much twaddle about culture, there is no doubt about their supremacy in that form of culture known as agri-culture. The same might be said about almost any one of the arts of industry. The consistent application of trained intellect to special practical problems in order to develop and employ a skilled technique has given Germany her efficiency. Her boasted idealism, so far as it has not been sentimental and romantic, has been the idealism of faith in intellect—in scientific method applied to detail, bit by bit, to what has to be done. It is silly to confine the Prussianization of Germany to the inculcation of militarism, and not recognize the educational phase of the work Prussia has done for Germany. Prussia disciplined Germany in specialization of science applied to the conduct of affairs. Let us give her credit along with the debit account.

For the two things belong together. It is impossible to train for highly specialized divisions of labor without creating an almost machine-like social automatism. Everything must fit into everything else, or hopeless confusion at once results. In the early days of the war no remark was commoner than that the Germans, trained as they were to obedience, would break down when the demand came for initiative. The remark did not take into account that their training was an intellectual training dependent upon scientific division of labor, not upon mere mechanical habituations. Only

when the whole is thrown out of gear will the parts cease to
work. That degree of strain has not been reached; it may not
be reached in this war. But the habit of mind thus formed
is as incompatible with democracy as is sheer militarism; indeed, a persistently effective militarism is hardly possible
without this scientifically organized division of labor in
which each part takes its cue from the working of the other
parts. For us to take such a system as our exclusive model
would indicate that we had already ceased to be ourselves.

What would be our weakness, because an attempt at the
impossible, has been Germany's strength—at least up to a certain point. Beyond that point it has been a weakness for Germany itself. One does not need to be competent in diplomacy
to know that Germany has failed miserably in judging other
peoples, whether belligerents or neutrals. Her White Book
was an obvious success at home; the mental temper of those
to whom it was directly addressed was gauged marvelously.
But I doubt if a single outsider who had previously refrained
from committing himself as to the justice of the cause did not
conclude that if that was all that Germany had to say for
herself, bad indeed must be her cause. The documents issued
by the intellectuals for the express purpose of impressing
neutral opinion were eloquent in the same sense. Memories
are short in these days when events tread so rapidly on one
another's heels. But I doubt if anyone can reread, say, the
Address to the Civilized World, without being again overcome by those old sensations of incredulity and amazement.
Was it possible that men to whom we had been trained to
look up could lend their names, even in a moment of patriotic fervor, to such a farrago?

It were rash to generalize from a few instances. But in the
main the failure of Germany wherever the general and
broadly human factor counted most has been as marked as
her achievements wherever it was a question of specialized
efficiency. One may be wrong about this or that item. The
neutral world can hardly be wrong about the cumulative
sum of evidence as to the inability of the German people to

judge either themselves or others. And I do not see how this blindness can be explained save upon the basis of a failure in their national education. To develop a generalized social sense is supposedly the object of a humanistic education. So judged, German education has not been humanistic.

English education has been German education upside down. Imagine a German minister gravely announcing that since it had been *recently* discovered that glycerine could be derived from soap fats, the latter would henceforth be contraband—after their importation into Germany had been permitted for months! There are surely cases where the warning not to generalize from a single instance breaks down —even in social matters. England has paid—Belgium and the world have paid—a high price for England's devotion to a literary education. To suppose that any amount of enforced military service would have given England an adequate preparedness under such conditions is to snatch at superficialities. On the other hand, in her foreign affairs England has for a long time been a citizen of the world. Even those who accuse her statesmen of a truly diabolic cunning cannot deny to them the maintenance of the externals of civilization. In connection with her long worldwide responsibilities, the humanistic education of England has accomplished something which we look for in vain in Germany's exhibition of herself to the world.

I do not know how we are to effect in this country a combination of a scientific and a humanistic education. I doubt if anyone knows. But that there lies our problem, I thoroughly believe. We must frankly recognize that the measure of a humanistic education is its results—its production of a social and socialized sense. We must surrender that superstitious tradition which identifies humanism with the interests of literary training, and which in our country, whatever it may have accomplished elsewhere, produces only a feebly pretentious snobbishness of culture. But we must employ science for flexible resourcefulness of adaptation, not for framing social organization into rigid divisions of labor.

Surely there must be something behind our tendencies toward smattering and miscellaneous generalities. Were it all the smattering and superficiality and nothing else which it sometimes seems to be, we should be infinitely incompetent. There is some power in the instinct which keeps us, with our alleged worship of efficiency and our materialism, from going in for systematized specialization. That something, I think, is the habit of mind formed by our wide and free range of human contacts. When we learn how to interpenetrate this human sense of one another with thorough training in scientific method and knowledge we shall have found ourselves educationally.

## 8

## UNIVERSAL SERVICE AS EDUCATION *

### I

IT IS our American habit if we find the foundations of our educational structure unsatisfactory to add another story or a wing. We find it easier to add a new study or course or kind of school than to reorganize existing conditions so as to meet the need. Manual training schools, trade schools, vocational schools and courses, now prevocational schools—and next year perhaps pre-prevocational and post-vocational—testify how we manage when it is seen that our system does not conform to the demands of present life. Just now we have discovered new defects and are having another addition to our educational scheme urged upon us. The defects are that our educational measures do not assimilate the foreign-born and that they do not develop public-mindedness, a sense of public service and responsibility. Some persons might think that the remedy is to improve our existing educational agencies and to make our existing public institutions —including government—more serviceable to the people so that they would arouse greater devotion. But no: let everything else be as it is, and let us add a new agency devised *ad hoc*. Let us have the school of universal and compulsory military service, and the trick is done.

It is a pleasure to acknowledge that there is an awakening to the presence in our country of large immigrant masses who may remain as much aliens as if they never entered our gateways. It is questionable, however, if there is much gain in passing at one bound from seeing nothing to seeing red.

* From *The New Republic*, April 22 and 29, 1916.

Having formerly lulled ourselves to sleep with the word "melting-pot" we have now turned to the word "hyphenate" as denoting the last thing in scares with a thrill. Casting about for some magic, universal military service is to replace the schoolhouse as the melting and brewing pot. In the words of Major General Wood, "Great portions of our population develop in racial areas, reading a dialect press and controlled in the intervening years by dialect interests. Some sort of community of service must be established in order to develop a proper and necessary appreciation of the duties and obligations of American citizenship. I believe that the best method is by some sort of a systematized military training of a universal character." Is it then axiomatic that nothing socializes the mind and enables it to think in public terms so much as a service rendered under military auspices, with the accustomed environment of military paraphernalia and by the traditional rules of military command and obedience?

A speech of Major General Wood as reported in a Philadelphia newspaper puts the matter more vividly. "It is a pretty dangerous situation to turn loose in this country all kinds of humanity seen on the docks at Ellis Island, to turn them loose with no sense of responsibility to their new land. They come in racial groups, drift through our schools in racial groups and are controlled by a dialect press. We are doing absolutely nothing to make these people understand that they are Americans, at least in the making." Then with swift intuition comes the remedy. "There is nothing like compulsory military service to accomplish this." I will not ask how much ignorance, and how much of the snobbery of those who, having been longer in the country, look with contempt and suspicion upon newcomers there may be in this view, though I suspect that it is safer to idealize with Mary Antin's "Promised Land" than it is to take after-dinner long-distance surveys of Ellis Island hordes. I will not even inquire whether inter-racialism is not a truer definition of America than that provided by even the most cultivated New England provincialism, or whether the melting-pot metaphor is not itself traitorous to the American ideal. It is enough that there is a genuine intellectual and moral problem in connection with the heterogeneously diversified factors in our population.

But the problem is not to reduce them to an anonymous and drilled homogeneity, but to see to it that all get from one another the best that each strain has to offer from its own tradition and culture. If authentic America is not to be a cross-fertilization of our various strains, it had better be a juxtaposition of alien elements than an amalgam of the barracks, an amalgam whose uniformity would hardly go deeper than the uniforms of the soldiers. Admit everything which can be said in favor of the European system of military service, admit that we ought to turn from our previous wholesale condemnation to an equally wholesale glorification, and there is yet something childishly undisciplined in supposing that we could reduplicate its merits by establishing compulsory system on American soil. We forget how largely its efficacy there is due to the prior existence of just the uniformity of tradition and outlook whose absence is the reason urged in support of it here. We forget how real and how constant in the mind of every continental European is the sense of an enemy just over the border, and how largely the sense of cohesion is a common sense of enmity. Shall we deliberately proceed to cultivate a sense of the danger of aggression, shall we conjure up enemies, in order to get this stimulus to unity among ourselves? The tendency of the upholders of the plan of enforced universal service to resort to this appeal, unconsciously gives away their case. To stir up fear and dislike of home countries as a means of securing love of an adopted country does not seem a promising procedure.

But it is not necessary to bring accusations against the policy of military service. The real point is that we find it so much easier to cry up this policy than to remedy those defects in our existing system which produce the evils in question. Any truly educative system must precede and prevent instead of following after and palliating and undoing. Until we have at least made a beginning in nationalizing our system of education, it is premature to appeal to the army, to marching and to sleeping in barrack cots, as the best way to remedy the evils of a lack of national-mindedness. When Mr. Lippmann suggested nationalizing our means of transportation and communication as a method of securing an integrated and coherent America, some of his critics intimated that his project was too materialistic. Well, the district schoolhouse of some portions of the United States—often those very portions which most deplore the foreign invasion—with its independent district control is a symptom of a spiritual localism which defies a unified America quite as much as does any racial area and dialect press. We might at least try the experiment of making our Federal Bureau of Education at Washington something more than a book-keeping and essay-writing department before we conclude that military service is the only way of effecting a common mind. When Mr. Theodore Roosevelt writes with as much vehemence about national aid to vocational education, national aid to wipe out illiteracy, and national aid for evening and continuation schools for our immigrants, as he now writes in behalf of military service, I for one shall take him more seriously as an authority on the educational advantages of setting-up exercises, firing guns and living in the camp.

I can see a vision of a national government which takes an interest at once paternal and scientific in our alien visitors, which has a definite policy about their reception, and about their distribution, which guards them even more jealously than its own sons against industrial exploitation, and which offers them at every turn educational facilities under its own charge. If every foreign illiterate had compulsory educational service to perform, if he had not only the opportunity but the obligation to learn the English language, if he found conditions of labor safeguarded in the interest of his health and his integrity as an economic agent, and if he learned to associate these things in whatever part of the country he found himself with the United States and not with the district, township or state, it would not be long before compulsory service, if it had to be discussed at all, would be discussed as a military proposition and not as an educational one. Until we have developed an independent and integral educational policy, the tendency to assume that military service will be an efficient tool of public education indicates a deplorable self-deception. I sometimes think the worst of the evils connected with militarism, in fact and in idea, is its power to create such illusions. Military service is the remedy of despair—despair of the power of intelligence.

## II

The argument for universal military service for educational purposes is much stronger when put upon general grounds than when the needs of the immigrant are conspicuous in the plea. Rear Admiral Goodrich has said: "The average American boy is neither obedient, helpful nor well-mannered. We have learned that these things cannot be taught in the homes. Something is needed and that is universal training." The indictment of the native-born and of his home life is so sweeping as to undo itself; let it pass. Statements from a broader social point of view set forth the need of training which will develop a more extensive and vital sense of responsibility than is now found. Speaking roughly, our youth of the more favored class have much done for them, and little is expected in return; there is little to foster public-mindedness. Politically they are spoiled children. The less favored youth are so preoccupied with the practical demands of the moment and the relaxations of sparse moments of relief, that the state is for them also a remote and pallid entity. Our easygoing disposition, our comfort, our size, our congested towns, the invitations of the passing hour, combine with our individualistic tradition to depress from view the claims of organized society. We are overstimulated in matters of personal success and enjoyment; we have little that teaches subordination to the public good or that secures effective capacity to work co-operatively in its behalf. No two persons would draw up the statement in quite the same terms, but a family likeness would show through any number of different statements.

Enforced military training is urged as a remedy, not with military preparedness as its main end, but as an agency of a socializing education. As in the case of the Americanization of the immigrant, I feel that the arguments for compulsory service are more effective in depicting an evil than in setting forth a remedy. There is a temptation to digress, and ask whether the emotions aroused by the war are not the real cause of idealization of the moral possibilities of military training. For a dominant emotional mood always idealizes irrespective of facts. A heroic mood is a fine mood in which to face the urgencies of imminent action, but the indicative mood is a safer mood in which to think clearly. I have an impression that many persons, stirred to an intensified loyalty, imagine that the spirit which is their voluntary attitude will somehow accrue in others as a result of compulsory training. Surely this is belief in social magic.

It is only grudgingly, then, that I yield to the tendency to pass over details, to neglect as irrelevant to our own case the various evils which have in the past accompanied universal service, and to dwell only upon its socializing possibilities. The argument seems to be born of the feelings rather than of the intelligence. But after all this is not the main point. My recognition of the need of agencies for creating a potent sense of a national ideal and of achieving habits which will make this sense a controlling power in action is not ungrudging. But the primary question is what is the national ideal, and to what kind of universal service does it stand related?

We need a new and more political Emerson to warn us against intellectual and moral imitativeness. Under the guise of a more effective Americanization of the members of our social body, we are called upon to introduce aims and methods profoundly hostile to those habitual endeavors and social relationships which alone will ever constitute us a distinctive nation in any but a territorial sense—which is always an exclusive and timid sense. If our premise is the need for that kind of universal service which will have military preparedness only as a by-product, and whose primary aim is to create devotion to the great society which bore us and which sustains us, and yet our conclusion is borrowing a system of service based upon mutual fear and the necessity of defense, our intelligence is not even hyphenated Americanism. It is unalloyed Europeanism.

We are not deeply attached to our consciously inherited social philosophy; many of us are consciously weaned from it. For the philosophy appears to be a legalistic individualism used to sanction economic inequality and industrial disorganization. Moreover, it is not indigenous; it is borrowed from a foreign tradition. But this is no adequate ground for abandoning it so as hurriedly to snatch at the methods of an opposed tradition which is equally alien to our own strivings. We need a social ideal which is truly national; one which will unify our thoughts and focus our emotions. Our consciously accepted ideal does not effect this. We may in the end well be grateful for the uneasiness and apparent disintegration of the present time if it makes us realize these facts. But only an ideal which is the conscious articulation of forces already unconsciously operating can ever be the object of unforced and intelligent service. To assume that our actual tendencies are as individualistic as is the traditional philosophy animating our legal and business codes, and then to seek correction in an ideal which has no connection with the alleged realities of the case, is to admit defeat in advance.

But nobody really believes that the case is quite so desperate. In spite of distress at the revelation of unsuspected divergencies, everybody knows that vital integrative forces are at work. We have the material for a genuinely unified ideal, much as that material requires focusing and articulation. The suggestion of some form of universal service, so far as it is not based upon fear and the cowardliness inhering in every policy of mere defense, is in fact an endeavor to forward its conscious perception. Why not eliminate, then, from the center of attention the borrowed military aspects of the case? Why not ask what form of universal service would connect with our positive capacities and endeavors so as to reinforce and consolidate our other educational instrumentalities? Why assume that universal service is required because these agencies must fail, or why just turn our backs upon our existing educational system in behalf of an added disconnected factor?

The only answer which I have heard to such questions is that beginnings always have to be made under the cover of something with which men's minds are already familiar; that the idea of compulsory military service is a sort of screen behind which may be built up a constructive social discipline. In view of the temper of the American people towards everything military, I doubt the practical wisdom of the policy. The votes in Congress regarding our army give it little support. But the serious objection is that it evinces indisposition to think out the actualities of our social life. The American people seem to be in an unusually self-deprecatory mood at present. But we are directing our scoldings in a way which itself indicates little inclination to face our real deficiency. We are castigating ourselves for lack of courage, of energy, of ability to venture and to do. But these things are our excellences—and our vices by excess. Unwillingness to sit still, to think, restiveness at critical discrimination as wasting time which might be spent in "doing something," desire to lay hold of short cuts to results—these are our weaknesses. Why urge a scheme of universal service which exemplifies rather than remedies these defects? For such any plan does which does not express an imaginative vision of our own actualities, which copies with minor modifications some piece of foreign machinery, which is not anchored in an attempt to organize the social possibilities of our existing system of public education.

There is enough sense of reality in the American nation

and there is enough achieved unity of purpose to respond to any plan of universal service which should express its own ideal; the meaning of its existing social practice and aspiration. Such a plan must, however, embody more, not less, sense of reality and unity of social trend than already inchoately exist. Apart from some military emergency, any other plan for universal service will, I am sure, leave the American people in a state of profound and unruffled inertness. If I am asked what is the nature of the plan to which the nation might respond, I can only say that ability to answer the question would signify that one had already penetrated to the depths of our unconscious practical endeavors and perceived their direction. But I am quite sure that such a plan will aim at education rather than training; that it will be directed toward industrial conquest of nature rather than to military conquest of man, and that it will be aggressive and inclusive rather than defensive. I can, for example, imagine the American people arming universally to put an end to war. I cannot imagine them doing it to defend themselves against a possible and remote danger. The American people is more idealistic and more high-spirited than its critics.

## 9

## THE SCHOOLS AND SOCIAL PREPAREDNESS *

IN the previous articles in which I have set down some thoughts on our educational situation as it appears in the light of the war, I have said little or nothing about the specific work of the schools. Yet it is back to the schools, to the teachers, the text-books, the courses of study, the schoolroom methods of teaching and discipline, that education comes, and with education the larger part of the conscious direction of our social affairs. The public school is the willing pack-horse of our social system; it is the true hero of the refrain: Let George do it. Whenever any earnest group of people want something which is threatened preserved or something which is stable altered, they unite to demand that something or other be taught in the public schools, from "temperance hygiene" to kindness to animals, and from catechetical instruction on the Constitution as a means of saving the Republic from subversion, to the biographies of classical painters as a means of diffusing artistic taste.

A few years from now our state legislatures may be besieged by ardent advocates of international peace who will guarantee the future amity of the world if all children can have a fourteen weeks' course of lessons in "peace." Just now, however, the clamorers for preparedness have the speaker's eye, and two or three hours a week of drill exercise is to be made compulsory in high schools. Those who are in favor of new burdens are organized and clamorous; the pupils, being pupils, are discreetly dumb. The mass of the public is inert, or at least inactive, and gets in its work only by an ultimate passive resistance which first moderates and then

* From *The New Republic*, May 6, 1916.

smothers in execution the schemes legislated into existence. All of this mechanical confidence in the mechanics of school programs is an ironic tribute to our national faith in the efficacy of education. Meantime it is hard on the schools. One might think it would have occurred to those interested in military preparedness that the youth between fourteen and nineteen who have left school are just those who most need physically—and in every other way—the training it is proposed to give, and that to train those who have given up school work would not put a premium on leaving school—especially as such a policy is suggested by the German method. But no; I honestly think most good Americans would shrink from the very thought as indicating a traitorous lack of faith in the public school. Consequently, overburdened schools with congested curricula, distracted teachers and pupils stand a good chance of being offered up a sacrifice on the altar of "act first and think afterwards."

I should mourn the prospect more than I do if experience had not shown that a few years' time will suffice to divert, and, then, as I have intimated, to submerge any addition which is unwelcome to both teachers and pupils. There is, fortunately an anarchy of absorption and deglutition as well as of rebellion. But all this showy and clamorous externalism of preparedness has a more enduring evil consequence. It arrests attention; it satisfies conscience; it puts effectual blinders on inquiring eyes. The significant relationships of the school to the entire question of our international policy and to the question of internal cohesion in connection with it, become salved over and hidden from sight. If long years of peace should by good chance succeed to our present conscientiously maintained nervousness, we should relapse in our school teaching into the same sentimental seclusion from the world's affairs which dominates present instruction in history and social subjects.

An earlier generation received some seepings from biblical lore. There was some intimation of a world-history prior to its real commencement in 1492; there was at least a consciousness of a blank dimly dotted with Greeks and Romans and vague "Europeans" between the end of Jewish and the beginning of American history. Today the pupil who leaves (and most of them do) before reaching the high school can only wonder at the odd selection of 1492 as the numeral for the year one, and can proceed through his course of American history with no suspicion of Europe save as a place from which discoverers set sail and colonists departed, and as the abode of men whose evil plans got good Americans into wars, and whose affairs and governments in general are such that the less Americans have to do with them the better.

As I reread what I have written I suspect myself of exaggeration. But I am still in a condition of wonder at the unconscious untruthfulness of many of my fellow Americans who hold President Wilson responsible for the moral aloofness of the United States in the present struggle. Is it possible, I ask myself, that they do not know that he has correctly reflected not only the political tradition of "no entangling alliances," but also that isolation of all thought of American history and destiny from European affairs which is even more deeply grounded in our education? A statistically minded sociologist might block off on squared paper the decreasing interest in the war, as one travels from the American seaboard, on the basis of the space allotted to it in the newspapers. We are a pacific people and in the main a kindly disposed one; we regret the loss of life, the flames of hatred in Europe. We do not, as a people, see that it is any especial affair of ours—save as something to keep out of. I have heard this state of mind attributed to sheer cowardliness, to decay of our pristine vigor, to commercialism—usually referred to, in this connection, as a canker—to deliberate selfishness, etc.

I do not believe in any of these explanations. To speak dogmatically, I know better. It is the natural fruit of our educational system. I confess that there is something in this vast provincialism which is not altogether unpleasing. There is a certain vegetative health in this self-sufficiency. But nevertheless it is dangerous. Facts have changed. In actuality we are part of the same world as that in which Europe exists and into which Asia is coming. Industry and commerce have interwoven our destinies. To maintain our older state of mind is to cultivate a dangerous illusion. A different way of teaching American history is an infinitely greater factor in national preparedness than a few hours of perfunctory drill by boys whose minds are on their hour of release. It must be taught for what it is: largely a reflection of European movements and problems—as is seen, for example, in each wave of immigration—and as a gradual development of native interests and problems which are still affected by every change in the life of Europe, and which correspond to what is going on all over the world because of the operation of world-wide forces. A generation educated in the facts of American history instead of in an American mythology would not be at a loss to find and express a unified mind in a crisis like the present, should one recur.

Professor Beard has recently denominated our school books in civics "as colorless as chalk." This tepid characterlessness is not confined to text-books in civics. It permeates the atmosphere of the school wherever any social topic comes up. Our own past history appears as a drama between the angels of light and the demons of darkness, between forces of freedom and enslavement, where victory has ever been on the side of the right. Our constitutions and institutions generally are the embodiment of the achieved and final victory of good. If children ever suspect that any evil still exists, outside of their own as yet not wholly virtuous characters, such evil has no institutional or social embodiment. It is personal, like their own faults. The whitewash of indiscriminate eulogistic language covers the things which make social life difficult, uncertain—and interesting.

We do not need courses in social slumming, but we do need some way of making intellectually clear that there never was a struggle between pure good and pure evil; and that there is now, as there always has been, a struggle between interests entrenched in law, institutions and social convention, and the requirements of further enlightenment and emancipation. A nation habituated to *think* in terms of problems and of the struggle to remedy them before it is actually in the grip of the forces which create the problems, would have an equipment for public life such as has not characterized any people.

The connection of this intellectual habit with coherent thinking in matters of foreign relations is not far to seek. We have condemned the method of taking docile direction from our rulers; we have set up as judges on our own account. Shall we then expect something called democracy in the abstract to work miracles in our behalf? Shall we always drift without a definite policy, relieving our nerves in critical periods, as we are now doing, by treating mutual recriminations as if they were a substitute for a policy? Is there any meaning in the phrase "democratic control" of social affairs save as men have been educated into an intellectual familiarity with the weak places, the dark places, the unsettled difficulties of our society before they are overwhelmed by them practically?

Our universities must indeed lead the way. But unless the methods of critical discrimination which they foster extend into our secondary schools and thence, indirectly at least, into the elementary schools, we shall find democratic control tied to a course of inert drift alternating with periods of excited explosion. To make our schools the home of serious thought on social difficulties and conflicts is the real question of academic freedom, in comparison with which the topic which we have hitherto dealt with under that head is indeed academic.

# 10

## AMERICAN EDUCATION AND CULTURE *

ONE can foretell the derision which will be awakened
in certain quarters by a statement that the central
theme of the current meeting of the National Educational
Association is cultural education. What has culture to do
with the quotidian tasks of millions of harassed pupils and
teachers preoccupied with the routine of alphabetic combinations and figuring? What bond is there between culture
and barren outlines of history and literature? So far the
scene may be called pathetic rather than an occasion for
satire. But one foresees the critics, the self-elected saving
remnant, passing on to indignant condemnation of the voluntary surrender of our educational system to utilitarian
ends, its prostitution to the demands of the passing moment
and the cry for the practical. Or possibly the selection of
cultural education as a theme of discourse will be welcome
as a sign of belated repentance, while superior critics sor-
rowingly wonder whether the return to the good old paths
is sought out too late.

To those who are in closer contact with the opinions
which hold conscious sway in the minds of the great mass
of teachers and educational leaders there is something humorous in the assumption that they are given over to worship of the vocational and industrial. The annual pilgrimage
of the teachers of the country to European cathedral and
art gallery is the authentic indication of the conscious estimate of the older ideal of culture. Nothing gets a hand so
quickly in any gathering of teachers as precisely the sort
of talk in which the critics engage. The shibboleths and the

* From *The New Republic*, July 1, 1916.

sentimentalities are held in common by critic and the workers criticized. "Culture and discipline" serve as emblems of a superiority hoped for or attained, and as catchwords to save the trouble of personal thought. Behind there appears a sense of some deficiency in our self-conscious devotion to retrospective culture. We protest too much. Our gestures betray the awkwardness of a pose maintained laboriously against odds. In contrast there is grace in the spontaneous uncouthness of barbarians whole-heartedly abandoned in their barbarism.

While the critics are all wrong about the conscious attitude and intent of those who manage our educational system, they are right about the powerful educational currents of the day. These cannot be called cultural:—not when measured by any standard drawn from the past. For these standards concern the past—what *has* been said and thought—while what is alive and compelling in our education moves toward some undiscovered future. From this contrast between our conscious ideals and our tendencies in action spring our confusion and our blind uncertainties. We think we think one thing while our deeds require us to give attention to a radically different set of considerations. This intellectual constraint is the real foe to our culture. The beginning of culture would be to cease plaintive eulogies of a past culture, eulogies which carry only a few yards before they are drowned in the noise of the day, and essay an imaginative insight into the possibilities of what is going on so assuredly although so blindly and crudely.

The disparity between actual tendency and backward-looking loyalty carries within itself the whole issue of cultural education. Measured in other terms than that of some as yet unachieved possibility of just the forces from which sequestered culture shrinks in horror, the cause of culture is doomed so far as public education is concerned. Indeed, it hardly exists anywhere outside the pages of Mr. Paul Elmer More, and his heirs and assigns. The serious question is whether we may assist the vital forces into new forms of thought and sensation. It would be cruel were it not so impotent to assess stumbling educational efforts of the day by ideas of archaic origin when the need is for an idealized interpretation of facts which will reveal mind in those concerns which the older culture thought of as purely material, and perceive human and moral issues in what seem to be the purely physical forces of industry.

The beginning of a culture stripped of egoistic illusions is the perception that we have as yet no culture: that our culture is something to achieve, to create. This perception gives the national assembly of teachers representative dignity. Our school men and women are seen as adventuring for that which is not but which may be brought to be. They are not in fact engaged in protecting a secluded culture against the fierce forays of materialistic and utilitarian America. They are endeavoring, so far as they are not rehearsing phrases whose meaning is forgot, to turn these very forces into thought and sentiment. The enterprise is of heroic dimensions. To set up as protector of a shrinking classicism requires only the accidents of a learned education, the possession of leisure and a reasonably apt memory for some phrases, and a facile pen for others. To transmute a society built on an industry which is not yet humanized into a society which wields its knowledge and its industrial power in behalf of a democratic culture requires the courage of an inspired imagination.

I am one of those who think that the only test and justification of any form of political and economic society is its contribution to art and science—to what may roundly be called culture. That America has not yet so justified itself is too obvious for even lament. The explanation that the physical conquest of a continent had first to be completed is an inversion. To settle a continent is to put it in order, and this is a work which comes after, not before, great intelligence and great art. The accomplishment of the justification is then hugely difficult. For it means nothing less than the discovery and application of a method of subduing and settling nature in the interests of a democracy, that is to say of masses who shall form a community of directed thought and emotion in spite of being the masses. That this has not yet been effected goes without saying. It has never even been attempted before. Hence the puny irrelevancy that measures our strivings with yardsticks handed down from class cultures of the past.

That the achievement is immensely difficult means that it may fail. There is no inevitable predestined success. But the failure, if it comes, will be the theme of tragedy and not of complacent lamentation nor willful satire. For while success is not predestined, there are forces at work which are like destiny in their independence of conscious choice or wish. Not conscious intent, either perverse or wise, is forcing the realistic, the practical, the industrial, into education. Not conscious deliberation causes college presidents who devote commencement day to singing the praises of pure culture to spend their working days in arranging for technical and professional schools. It is not conscious preference which leads school superintendents who deliver orations at teachers' meetings upon the blessings of old-fashioned discipline and culture to demand from their boards new equipment, new courses and studies of a more "practical" and appealing kind. Political and economic forces quite beyond their control are compelling these things. And they will remain beyond the control of any of us save as men honestly face the actualities and busy themselves with inquiring what education they impart and what culture may issue from *their* cultivation.

It is as elements in this heroic undertaking that current tendencies in American education can be appraised. Since we can neither beg nor borrow a culture without betraying both it and ourselves, nothing remains save to produce one. Those who are too feeble or too finicky to engage in the enterprise will continue their search for asylums and hospitals which they idealize into palaces. Others will either go their way still caught in the meshes of a mechanical industrialism, or will subdue the industrial machinery to human ends until the nation is endowed with soul.

Certain commonplaces must be reiterated till their import is acknowledged. The industrial revolution was born of the new science of nature. Any democracy which is more than an imitation of some archaic republican government must issue from the womb of our chaotic industrialism. Science makes democracy possible because it brings relief from depending upon massed human labor, because of the substitution it makes possible of inanimate forces for human muscular energy, and because of the resources for excess production and easy distribution which it effects. The old culture is doomed for us because it was built upon an alliance of political and spiritual powers, an equilibrium of governing and leisure classes, which no longer exists. Those who deplore the crudities and superficialities of thought and sensation which mark our day are rarely inhuman enough to wish the old regime back. They are merely unintelligent enough to want a result without the conditions which produced it, and in the face of conditions making the result no longer possible.

In short, our culture must be consonant with realistic science and with machine industry, instead of a refuge from them. And while there is no guaranty that an education which uses science and employs the controlled processes of industry as a regular part of its equipment will succeed, there is every assurance that an educational practice which sets science and industry in opposition to its ideal of culture will fail. Natural science has in its applications to economic production and exchange brought an industry and a society where quantity alone seems to count. It is for education to bring the light of science and the power of work to the aid of every soul that it may discover its quality. For in a spiritually democratic society every individual would realize distinction. Culture would then be for the first time in human history an individual achievement and not a class possession. An education fit for our ideal uses is a matter of actual forces, not of opinions.

Our public education is the potential means for effecting the transfiguration of the mechanics of modern life into sentiment and imagination. We may, I repeat, never get beyond the mechanics. We may remain burly, merely vigorous, expending energy riotously in making money, seeking pleasure and winning temporary victories over one another. Even such an estate has a virility lacking to a culture whose method is reminiscence, and whose triumph is finding a place of refuge. But it is not enough to justify a democracy as against the best of past aristocracies even though return to them is forever impossible. To bring to the consciousness of the coming generation something of the potential significance of the life of today, to transmute it from outward fact into intelligent perception, is the first step in the creation of a culture. The teachers who are facing this fact and who are trying to use the vital unspiritualized agencies of today as means of effecting the perception of a human meaning yet to be realized are sharing in the act of creation. To perpetuate in the name of culture the tradition of aloofness from realistic science and compelling industry is to give them free course in their most unenlightened form. Not chiding but sympathy and direction of understanding is what the harsh utilitarian and prosaic tendencies of present education require.

# 11

# NATIONALIZING EDUCATION *

THE words nation and national have two quite different meanings. We cannot profitably discuss the nationalizing of education unless we are clear as to the difference between the two. For one meaning indicates something desirable, something to be cultivated by education, while the other stands for something to be avoided as an evil plague. The idea which has given the movement toward nationality which has been such a feature of the last century its social vitality is the consciousness of a community of history and purpose larger than that of the family, the parish, the sect and the province. The upbuilding of national states has substituted a unity of feeling and aim, a freedom of intercourse, over wide areas for earlier local isolations, suspicions, jealousies and hatreds. It has forced men out of narrow sectionalisms into membership in a larger social unit, and created loyalty to a state which subordinates pettier and selfish interests.

One cannot say this, however, without being at once reminded that nationalism has had another side. With the possible exception of our own country the national states of the modern world have been built up through conflict. The development of a sense of unity within a charmed area has been accompanied by dislike, by hostility, to all without. Skillful politicians and other self-seekers have always known how to play cleverly upon patriotism, and upon ignorance of other peoples, to identify nationalism with latent hatred of other nations. Without exaggeration, the present world war may be said to be the outcome of this aspect of

* From *Journal of Education*, November 2, 1916.

nationalism, and to present it in its naked unloveliness. In the past, our geographical isolation has largely protected us from the harsh, selfish and exclusive aspect of nationalism. The absence from pressure from without, the absence of active and urgent rivalry and hostility of powerful neighbors, has perhaps played a part in failure to develop an adequate unity of sentiment and idea for the country as a whole. Individualism of a go-as-you-please type has had too full swing. We have an inherited jealousy of any strong national governing agencies, and we have been inclined to let things drift rather than to think out a central, controlling policy. But the effect of the war has been to make us aware that the days of geographical isolation are at an end, and also to make us conscious that we are lacking in an integrated social sense and policy for our country as a whole, irrespective of classes and sections.

We are now faced by the difficulty of developing the good aspect of nationalism without its evil side; of developing a nationalism which is the friend and not the foe of internationalism. Since this is a matter of ideas, of emotions, of intellectual and moral disposition and outlook, it depends for its accomplishment upon educational agencies, not upon outward machinery. Among these educational agencies, the public school takes first rank. When sometime in the remote future the tale is summed up and the public as distinct from the private and merely personal achievement of the common school is recorded, the question which will have to be answered is what the American public school has done for subordinating a local, provincial, sectarian and partisan spirit of mind to aims and interests which are common to all the men and women of the country—to what extent it taught men to think and feel in ideas broad enough to be inclusive of the purposes and happiness of all sections and classes. For unless the agencies which form the mind and morals of the community can prevent the operation of those forces which are always making for a division of interests, class and sectional ideas and feelings will become dominant, and our democracy will fall to pieces.

Unfortunately at the present time one result of the excitement which the war has produced is that many influential and well-meaning persons attempt to foster the growth of an inclusive nationalism by appeal to our fears, our suspicions, our jealousies and our latent hatreds. They would make the measure of our national preparedness our readiness to meet other nations in destructive war rather than our fitness to co-operate with them in the constructive tasks of peace. They are so disturbed by what has been revealed of internal division, of lack of complete national integration, that they have lost faith in the slow policies of education. They would kindle a sense of our dependence upon one another by making us afraid of peoples outside of our border; they would bring about unity within by laying stress upon our separateness from others. The situation makes it all the more necessary that those concerned with education should withstand popular clamor for a nationalism based upon hysterical excitedness or mechanical drill, or a combination of the two. We must ask what a real nationalism, a real Americanism, is like. For unless we know our own character and purpose we are not likely to be intelligent in our selection of the means to further them.

I want to mention only two elements in the nationalism which our education should cultivate. The first is that the American nation is itself complex and compound. Strictly speaking it is inter-racial and inter-national in its make-up. It is composed of a multitude of peoples speaking different tongues, inheriting diverse traditions, cherishing varying ideals of life. This fact is basic to *our* nationalism as distinct from that of other peoples. Our national motto, "One from Many," cuts deep and extends far. It denotes a fact which doubtless adds to the difficulty of getting a genuine unity. But it also immensely enriches the possibilities of the result to be attained. No matter how loudly anyone proclaims his Americanism, if he assumes that any one racial strain, any one component culture, no matter how early settled it was in our territory, or how effective it has proved in its own land, is to furnish a pattern to which all other strains and cultures are to conform, he is a traitor to an American nationalism. Our unity cannot be a homogeneous thing like that of the separate states of Europe from which our population is drawn; it must be a unity, created by drawing out and composing into a harmonious whole the best, the most characteristic which each contributing race and people has to offer.

I find that many who talk the loudest about the need of a supreme and unified Americanism of spirit really mean some special code or tradition to which they happen to be attached. They have some pet tradition which they would impose upon all. In thus measuring the scope of Americanism by some single element which enters into it they are themselves false to the spirit of America. Neither Englandism nor New-Englandism, neither Puritan nor Cavalier any more than Teuton or Slav, can do anything but furnish one note in a vast symphony. The way to deal with hyphenism, in other words, is to welcome it, but to welcome it in the sense of extracting from it its special good, so that it shall surrender into a common fund of wisdom and experience what it especially has to contribute. All of these surrenders and contributions taken together create the national spirit of America. The dangerous thing is for each factor to isolate itself, to try to live off from its past, and then attempt to impose itself upon other elements, or at least to keep itself intact and thus refuse to accept what other cultures have to offer, and thereby become transmuted into authentic Americanism.

In what is rightly objected to as hyphenism the hyphen has become something which separates one people from other peoples—and thereby prevents American nationalism. Such terms as Irish-American or Hebrew-American or German-American are false terms because they seem to assume something which is already in existence called America to which the other factor may be externally hitched on. The fact is the genuine American, the typical American, is himself a hyphenated character. This does not mean that he is part American, and that some foreign ingredient is then added. It means that, as I have said, he is international and inter-racial in his make-up. He is not American plus Pole or German. But the American is himself Pole-German-English-French-Italian-Greek-Irish-Scandinavian-Bohemian-Jew-and so on. The point is to see to it that the hyphen connects instead of separating. And this means at least that our public schools shall teach each factor to respect every other, and shall take pains to enlighten all as to the great past contributions of every strain in our composite make-up. I wish our teaching of American history in the schools took more account of the great waves of migration by which our land for over three centuries has been continuously built up, and made every pupil conscious of the rich breadth of our national make-up. When every pupil recognizes all the factors which have gone into our being, he will continue to prize and reverence that coming from his own past, but he will think of it as honored in being simply one factor in forming a future whole nobler and finer than itself.

In short, unless our education is nationalized in a way which recognizes that the peculiarity of *our* nationalism is its internationalism, we shall breed enmity and division in our frantic efforts to secure unity. The teachers of the country know this fact much better than many of its politicians seem to do. While too often politicians have been fostering a vicious hyphenatedism and sectionalism as a bid for votes, teachers have been engaged in transmuting beliefs and feelings once divided and opposed into a new thing under the sun—a national spirit inclusive not exclusive, friendly not jealous. This they have done by the influence of personal contact, co-operative intercourse and sharing in common tasks and hopes. The teacher who has been an active agent in furthering the common struggle of native-born, African, Jew, Italian, and perhaps a score of other peoples to attain emancipation and enlightenment will never become a party to a conception of America as a nation which conceives of its history and its hopes as less broad than those of humanity —let politicians clamor for their own ends as they will.

The other point in the constitution of a genuine American nationalism to which I invite attention is that we have been occupied for the most of our history in subduing nature, not one another or other peoples. I once heard two foreign visitors coming from different countries discuss what had been impressed upon them as the chief trait of the American people. One said vigor, youthful and buoyant energy. The other said it was kindness, the disposition to live and let live, the absence of envy at the success of others. I like to think that while both of these ascribed traits have the same cause back of them, the latter statement went deeper. Not that we have more virtue, native or acquired, than others, but that we have had more room, more opportunity. Consequently the same conditions which have put a premium upon active and hopeful energy, have permitted the kindlier instincts of man to express themselves. The spaciousness of a continent not previously monopolized by man has both stimulated vigor and diverted activity from struggle against fellow man into struggle against nature. When men make their gains by fighting in common a wilderness, they have not the motive for mutual distrust which comes when they get ahead only by fighting one another. I recently heard a story which seems to me to have something typical about it. Some manufacturers were discussing the problem of labor; they were loud in their complaints. They were bitter against the exactions of unions, and full of tales of an efficiency which seemed to them calculated. Then one of them said: "Oh, well, poor devils. They haven't much of a chance and have to do what they can to hold their own. If we were in their place, we should be just the same." And the others nodded assent and the conversation lapsed. I call this characteristic, for if there wasn't an ardent sympathy, there was at least a spirit of toleration and passive recognition.

But with respect to this point as well as with respect to our composite make-up, the situation is changing. We no longer have a large unoccupied continent. Pioneer days are past, and natural resources are possessed. There is danger that the same causes which have set the hand of man against his neighbor in other countries will have the same effect here. Instead of sharing in a common fight against nature, we are already starting to fight against one another, class against class, haves against have-nots. The change puts a definite responsibility upon the schools to sustain our true national spirit. The virtues of mutual esteem, of human forbearance and well-wishing which in our earlier days were the unconscious products of circumstances, must now be the conscious fruit of an education which forms the deepest springs of character.

Teachers above all others have occasion to be distressed when earlier idealism of welcome to the oppressed is treated as a weak sentimentalism, when sympathy for the unfortunate and those who have not had a fair chance is regarded as a weak indulgence fatal to efficiency. Our traditional disposition in these respects must now become a central motive in public education, not as a matter of condescension or patronizing, but as essential to the maintenance of a truly American spirit. All this puts a responsibility upon the schools which can be met only by widening the scope of educational facilities. The schools have now to make up to the disinherited masses by conscious instruction, by the development of personal power and skill, ability and initiative, for the loss of external opportunities consequent upon the departure of our pioneer days. Otherwise power is likely to pass more and more into the hands of the wealthy, and we shall end with this same alliance between intellectual and artistic culture and the economic power due to riches which has been the curse of every civilization in the past, and which our fathers in their democratic idealism thought this nation was to put an end to.

Since the idea of the nation is equal opportunity for all, to nationalize education means to use the schools as a means of making this idea effective. There was a time when this could be done more or less well simply by providing school-houses, desks, blackboards, and perhaps books. But that day has passed. Opportunities can be equalized only as the schools make it their active serious business to enable all alike to become masters of their own industrial fate. That growing movement which is called industrial or vocational education now hangs in the scales. If it is so construed in practice as to produce merely more competent hands for subordinate clerical and shop positions, if its purpose is shaped to drill boys and girls into certain forms of auto-matic skill which will make them useful in carrying out the plans of others, it means that instead of nationalizing edu-cation in the spirit of our nation, we have given up the battle, and decided to refeudalize education.

I have said nothing about the point which my title "Na-tionalizing Education" most naturally suggests—changes in administrative methods which will put the resources of the whole nation at the disposition of the more backward and less fortunate portions, meaning by resources not only money but expert advice and guidance of every sort. I have no doubt that we shall move in the future away from a merely regional control of the public schools in the direction of a more central regulation. But I say nothing about this phase of the matter at this time not only because it brings up technical questions, but because this side of the matter is but the body, the mechanism of a nationalized education. To nationalize American education is to use education to promote our national idea,—which is the idea of democracy. This is the soul, the spirit, of a nationalized education, and unless the administrative changes are executed so as to em-body this soul, they will mean simply the development of red tape, a mechanical uniformity and a deadening supervision from above.

Just because the circumstances of the war have brought the idea of the nation and the national to the foreground of everyone's thoughts, the most important thing is to bear in mind that there are nations and nations, this kind of nationalism and that. Unless I am mistaken there are some now using the cry of an American nationalism, of an intensified national patriotism, to further ideas which characterize the European nations, especially those most active in the war, but which are treasonable to the ideal of *our* nation. Therefore, I have taken this part of your time to remind you of the fact that our nation and democracy are equivalent terms; that our democracy means amity and good will to all humanity (including those beyond our border) and equal opportunity for all within. Since as a nation we are composed of representatives of all nations who have come here to live in peace with one another and to escape the enmities and jealousies which characterize old-world nations, to nationalize our education means to make it an instrument in the active and constant suppression of the war spirit, and in the positive cultivation of sentiments of respect and friendship for all men and women wherever they live. Since our democracy means the substitution of equal opportunity for all for the old world ideal of unequal opportunity of different classes and the limitation of the individual by the class to which he belongs, to nationalize our education is to make the public school an energetic and willing instrument in developing initiative, courage, power and personal ability in each individual. If we can get our education nationalized in spirit in these directions, the nationalizing of the administrative machinery will in the end take care of itself. So I appeal to the teachers in the face of every hysterical wave of emotion, and of every subtle appeal of sinister class interest to remember that they above all are the consecrated servants of the democratic ideas in which alone this country is truly a distinctive nation—friendly and helpful intercourse between all and the equipment of every individual to serve the community by his own best powers and in his own best way.

## 12

## EXPERIMENT IN EDUCATION *

I DO not know whether the important similarities between modern publicity and ancient magic have been sufficiently noted. The daily newspapers have recently furnished an exemplification of one point of identity—the efficacy of names. What nothing else could do, the magic name of Rockefeller accomplished. It put the idea of experimentation in education on the front page of the newspaper along with world peace, and the leak in the stock market. Such a feat tempts one away from the main theme of educational experiment. To yield to the temptation is, however, too obviously to follow the lead of the newspapers themselves. It were better to rescue if possible the idea from the mass of sensational topics out of which it barely thrusts its submerged head.

Some heroism is required from such a rescuing party. One must resolutely refuse to note that a certain number of editorials are even now deploring the fact that the Rockefeller millions, having debauched university education, have engaged in an insidious attempt to capture elementary education, and thus complete the ruin of the country. One must even strive to forget some of the quasi-official statements which have been put forth, if the idea of experiment in education is to be recovered. One must be sufficiently unimpressed by the word modern in the phrase "modern school" to remember that archaeology is a distinctly modern undertaking; the ancients doubtless dug up things when they made holes in the ground, but they most definitely did not "excavate." But the real job comes when one tries to

* From *The New Republic*, February 3, 1917.

cut the expedition loose from the accumulated baggage labeled culture and discipline, vocational and utilitarian, etc. For all these things not only divert the mind from the thought of educational experiment almost as successfully as the newspapers concealed it, but contradict it. For they belong to just that atmosphere of opinion to which experimentation is fatal. I would not speak lightly of the debates which center about these notions. They not only deserve the respect due to the aged, but they still furnish channels through which things needful to say find outlet. But just in the degree in which they insinuate themselves, the tender plant of experiment is first beclouded and then, withering, droops.

All such terms are large, gross terms; they express goals, ideals, streams of tendency taken *en masse*. They are precisely the kind of terms which flourish in any subject before science, that is to say before experiment, enters. The first care of experiment is to break such large things into small and specific elements and problems. When they are so discriminated, the conceptions embodied in familiar catch-phrases, labels and party cries tend to evaporate. It is in a non-experimental environment that for example the question of language versus science flourishes. Carried into a medium of experiment, the question becomes just what does a language do and just *how* is it done? Not what in general is the educational worth of science, but how does this specific phase of a particular science become effective in the lives of individuals of this particular age who have this particular natural and industrial background? No one educational experiment station can possibly attack any very extensive portion of the field; and in view of the comparatively little which has been done in acclimating science in elementary and secondary instruction, the announced intention to make natural science central in the new scheme is a well-advised one. But this intention does not represent a dogmatic solution of an educational problem; it represents a field in which discovery of appropriate subject-matter and method is still to take place. And he knows little of present schooling who is not aware that such a search at once plunges educators into a large number of specific, difficult, harrowingly perplexing problems.

This fact illustrates, to my mind, just the significance, the typical significance, of any sincere endeavor to incarnate an experimental attitude in the conduct of a school. It substitutes detailed analyses for wholesale assertions, specific inquiries for temperamental convictions, small facts for opinions whose size is in precise ratio to their vagueness. It is within the social sciences, in morals, politics and education, that thinking still goes on by large antitheses, by theatrical oppositions of order and freedom, individualism and socialism, culture and utility, spontaneity and discipline, actuality and tradition. The field of the physical sciences was once occupied by similar "total" views, whose emotional appeal was inversely as to their intellectual clarity. But with the advance of the experimental method, the question has ceased to be which one of two rival claimants has a right to the field. It has become a question of clearing up a confused subject matter by attacking it bit by bit. I do not know a case where the final result was anything like victory for one or another among the pre-experimental notions. All of them disappeared because they became increasingly irrelevant to the situation discovered, and with their detected irrelevance they became unmeaning and uninteresting. For the present, the greatest contribution which any one experimental school can make to education is precisely the idea of experiment itself, the ideal of the experimental method as the spirit in which a social problem is to be approached.

Fortunately for the promise of the new undertaking, the experimental school of the General Education Board is not a pioneer. There are already a good many experimental schools, and there are a great many more schools not experimental in the main which are experimenting in this or that topic or method. The rigid hold of non-experimental notions —and it is the nature of non-experimental notions to be rigidly dogmatic in spite of their intellectual vagueness—has already been loosened. The soil has been stirred, and seeds are quickening. Experimental work already done makes it possible to find teachers who are themselves capable of assuming the experimental attitude—the most difficult single condition to realize. The proposal comes at the right moment—a moment which makes the enterprise a type, not merely another school. To concentrate the mind of the public upon the need of the open and inquiring attitude, to lead it to realize that education should not be confined to making a choice among already formulated conflicting alternatives, but offers a field for genuine discoveries, to help it see that progress is completely dependent upon a method for controlling discoveries, is itself the achievement. To familiarize the public with the possibility of such a method in education is an event more sensational than that heralded by even the blackest and largest headlines which announced a Rockefeller School.

# 13

## LEARNING TO EARN *

L EARNING to Earn" has a pleasant jingling sound. The "Earn" part of it is attractive also. It is, however, objectionable to some persons to see earning brought into close connection with learning. Since words frequently hide facts from us, we inquire at the beginning what the practice has been in this respect in the past. Contrary to the general opinion, popular education has always been rather largely vocational. The objection to it is not that it is vocational or industrial, but that it serves a poor, one may say an evil, ideal of industry and is therefore socially inefficient. So-called cultural education has always been reserved for a small limited class as a luxury. Even at that it has been very largely an education for vocations, especially for those vocations which happened to be esteemed as indicating social superiority or which were useful to the ruling powers of the given period. Our higher education, the education of the universities, began definitely as vocational education. The universities furnished training for the priesthood, for medicine and the law. This training also covered what was needed by the clerks, secretaries, scribes, etc., who have always had a large part of the administering of governmental affairs in their hands. Some portions of this original professional training ceased to be vocationally useful and then became the staple of a cultural and disciplinary education. For it will be found true as a general principle, that whenever any study which was originally utilitarian in purpose becomes useless because of a change in conditions, it is retained as a necessary edu-

* Address at the annual meeting of the Public Education Association, Hotel Biltmore, February 20, 1917. From *School and Society*, March 24, 1917.

cational ornament (as useless buttons are retained on the sleeves of men's coats) or else because it is so useless that it must be fine for mental discipline. Even today it will be found that a considerable part of what is regarded in collegiate education as purely cultural is really a preparation for some learned pursuit or for the profession of teaching the same subjects in the future, or a preparation for the profession of being a gentleman at large. Those who object most bitterly to any form of vocational training will often be found to be those whose own monopoly of present vocational training is threatened. What concerns us more directly, however, is the fact that elementary education, the education of the masses, has been not only "Learning for Earning," but a badly conceived learning, an education where the ability of the learner to add to the earnings of others rather than to his own earnings has been the main factor in selecting materials of study and fixing methods. You are doubtless weary hearing the statistics of our school morbidity and mortality rehearsed: the fact that of the school population only one in nine goes through the eighth grade, one in sixteen enters the high school, and only one in a thousand goes to college. We don't, however, ask often enough what these figures mean. If we did ask, we should see that they prove that our present scheme of elementary education is in the first place a scheme of vocational education, and in the second place a poor one.

Reading, writing, figuring, with a little geography and a smattering of other things, are what the great mass of those who leave our schools leave with. A few get something more. These things, when nothing else is added on to them, are pretty nearly pure economic tools. They came into the schools when the better-to-do classes discovered that under the conditions an elementary ability to read, write and figure was practically indispensable for salesmen and shop workers. He who is poorly acquainted with the history of the efforts to improve elementary education in our large cities does not know that the chief protest against progress is likely to come from successful business men. They have clamored for the three R's as the essential and exclusive material of primary education—knowing well enough that their own children would be able to get the things they protest against. Thus they have attacked as fads and frills every enrichment of the curriculum which did not lend itself to narrow economic ends. Let us stick to business, to the essentials, has been their plea, and by business they meant enough of the routine skill in letters and figures to make those leaving the elementary school at about the fifth or sixth grade useful in *their* business, irrespective of whether pupils left school with an equipment for advance and with the ambition to try to secure better social and economic conditions for their children than they had themselves enjoyed. Nothing in the history of education is more touching than to hear some successful leaders denounce as undemocratic the attempts to give all the children at public expense the fuller education which their own children enjoy as a matter of course.

Of late years, the situation has changed somewhat. The more intelligent employers have awakened to the fact that the mere rudiments of the three R's are not a good industrial training, while others of the community have awakened to the fact that it is a dangerously inadequate industrial education from the standpoint of the community. Hence there has arisen a demand for vocational and industrial education as if this were an entirely new thing; while, in fact, it is a demand that the present industrial education be so modified as to be efficient under the conditions of present machine industry, rapid transportation and a competitive market.

I have made these bald statements because they indicate to my mind the real issue at the present time concerning industrial education in public education. It isn't whether it shall be introduced in order to supplant or supplement a liberal and generous education already supposed to exist— that is pure romance. The issue is what sort of an industrial education there shall be and whose interests shall be primarily considered in its development.

To understand the *educational* issue is to see what difference is made in the schools themselves according as we take the *improving* of economic conditions to be the purpose of vocational training, or take its purpose to be supplying a better grade of labor for the present scheme, or helping on the United States in a competitive struggle for world commerce. I know that those who have the latter ends chiefly in view always make much of the increased happiness of the industrial worker himself as a product to result from better industrial education. But after all, there is a great difference between the happiness which means merely contentment with a station and the happiness which comes from the struggle of a well-equipped person to better his station. Which sort of happiness is to be our aim? I know, also, that stress is laid upon ability which is to proceed from a better industrial education to increase earnings. Well and good. But, does this mean simply that laborers are so to have their skill to add to the profits of employers increased, by avoiding waste, getting more out of their machines and materials, that they will have some share in it as an incidental by-product, or does it mean that increase in the industrial intelligence and power of the worker for his own personal advancement is to be the main factor?

I have said that the way these questions are answered makes all the difference in the world as to the educational scheme itself. Let me now point out some of the particular educational differences which will be made according as one or other idea of industry in education prevails. In the first place, as to administration, those who wish, whether they wish it knowingly or unknowingly, an education which will enable employees to fit better into the existing economic scheme will strive for a dual or divided system of administration. That is to say, they will attempt to have a separate system of funds, of supervisory authorities, and, as far as possible, of schools to carry on industrial education. If they don't go so far as this, they will at least constantly harp on the difference between a liberal or cultural and a money-earning education, and will endeavor to narrow the latter down to those forms of industrial skill which will enable the future workers to fall docilely into the subordinate ranks of the industrial army.

In the second place, the conception that the primary object of an industrial education is merely to prepare more skilled workers for the present system, instead of developing human beings who are equipped to reconstruct that scheme, will strive to identify it with trade education—that is, with training for certain specific callings. It assumes that the needs of industrial education are met if girls are trained to be skilled in millinery, cooking and garment-making, and boys to be plumbers, electric wirers, etc. In short, it will proceed on a basis not far removed from that of the so-called prevocational work on the Ettinger plan in this city.

In the third place, the curriculum on this narrow trade plan will neglect as useless for its ends the topics in history and civics which make future workers aware of their rightful claims as citizens in a democracy, alert to the fact that the present economic struggle is but the present-day phase taken by the age-long battle for human liberties. So far as it takes in civic and social studies at all, it will emphasize those things which emphasize duties to the established order and a blind patriotism which accounts it a great privilege to defend things in which the workers themselves have little or no share. The studies which fit the individual for the reasonable enjoyment of leisure time, which develop good taste in reading and appreciation of the arts, will be passed over as good for those who belong by wealth to the leisure class, but quite useless in the training of skilled employees.

In the fourth place, so far as the method and spirit of its work is concerned, it will emphasize all that is most routine and automatic in our present system. Drill to secure skill in the performance of tasks under the direction of others will be its chief reliance. It will insist that the limits of time and the pressure for immediate results are so great that there is no room for understanding the scientific facts and principles or the social bearings of what is done. Such an enlarged education would develop personal intelligence and thereby develop also an intellectual ambition and initiative which might be fatal to contentment in routine subordinate clerical and shop jobs.

Finally, so far as such a training concerns itself with what is called vocational guidance, it will conceive guidance as a method of placement—a method of finding jobs. It will measure its achievements by the number of children taking out working papers for whom it succeeds in finding places, instead of by the number whom it succeeds in keeping in school till they become equipped to seek and find their own congenial occupations.

The other idea of industrial education aims at preparing every individual to render service of a useful sort to the community, while at the same time it equips him to secure by his own initiative whatever place his natural capacities fit him for. It will proceed in an opposite way in every respect. Instead of trying to split schools into two kinds, one of a trade type for children whom it is assumed are to be employees and one of a liberal type for the children of the well-to-do, it will aim at such a reorganization of existing schools as will give all pupils a genuine respect for useful work, an ability to render service, and a contempt for social parasites whether they are called tramps or leaders of "society." Instead of assuming that the problem is to add vocational training to an existing cultural elementary education, it will recognize frankly that the traditional elementary education is largely vocational, but that the vocations which it has in mind are too exclusively clerical, and too much of a kind which implies merely ability to take positions in which to carry out the plans of others. It will indeed make much of developing motor and manual skill, but not of a routine or automatic type. It will rather utilize active and manual pursuits as the means of developing constructive, inventive and creative power of mind. It will select the materials and the technique of the trades not for the sake of producing skilled workers for hire in definite trades, but for the sake of securing industrial intelligence—a knowledge of the conditions and processes of present manufacturing, transportation and commerce so that the individual may be able to make his own choices and his own adjustments, and be master, so far as in him lies, of his own economic fate. It will be recognized that, for this purpose, a broad acquaintance with science and skill in the laboratory control of materials and processes is more important than skill in trade operations. It will remember that the future employee is a consumer as well as a producer, that the whole tendency of society, so far as it is intelligent and wholesome, is to an increase of the hours of leisure, and that an education which does nothing to enable individuals to consume wisely and to utilize leisure wisely is a fraud on democracy. So far as method is concerned, such a conception of industrial education will prize freedom more than docility; initiative more than automatic skill; insight and understanding more than capacity to recite lessons or to execute tasks under the direction of others.

The theme is an endless one. All that can be done here is to point out that the real issue is not the question whether an industrial education is to be added on to a more or less mythical cultural elementary education, but what sort of an industrial education we are to have. The movement for vocational educations conceals within itself two mighty and opposing forces, one which would utilize the public schools primarily to turn out more efficient laborers in the present economic regime, with certain incidental advantages to themselves, the other which would utilize all the resources of public education to equip individuals to control their own future economic careers, and thus help on such a reorganization of industry as will change it from a feudalistic to a democratic order.

## 14

## PUBLIC EDUCATION ON TRIAL *

SOCIAL situations are never simple, and in wartime nothing is simple, save emotion. The educational conditions leading up to the dismissal of three teachers in a New York high school afford no exception to this statement. Guidance through the maze may be had, however, by reviewing the matter as a culmination of the established and traditional relationship of official superiors and inferiors in the school system, and as evidence of a sharp clash between two opposed social and educational philosophies. But since these causes have been exasperated by war conditions and war psychology, it is first necessary to say something about the "loyalty" aspect of the matter.

Almost up to the time of the meeting at which the men were dismissed, a reader of at least the editorial columns of the newspapers would have derived the impression that the teachers were accused of disloyalty of some degree or other. But by the time of the final meeting the prosecution had settled on another formula. The men were not charged with overt disloyalty; they were charged with a lack of that active or aggressive loyalty which the state has a right to demand, in wartime particularly, from its paid servants. Now lack, absence, is a negative thing; it is notoriously difficult to prove except when the thing at issue is definite and tangible. Opinions even among experts differ as to the precise constitution of loyal patriotism; no burden of standardization has ever settled upon the exact tests by which its absence is to be determined.

The observer who bears in mind the negative character of

* From *The New Republic*, December 20, 1917.

the charge will have the key to many of the otherwise in-
explicable phenomena of the testimony (I say testimony
rather than evidence advisedly) and the trial. Ordinarily a
person is innocent till proved guilty. The charge of absence
of something, that something not being clearly defined, shifts
the burden. Anybody may then safely be considered guilty
until he can present convincing evidence that he is in possession of the required article—which is, perhaps, one reason
why negative charges have not been encouraged in the
legal procedure of more enlightened countries. Moreover,
charges of lack or absence encourage suspicion. With the
multiplication of accusations and loyalty pledges in the
schools—pledges which naturally such pro-Germans as there
are sign with the greatest regularity and cheerfulness—the
situation was approaching the point exemplified in the old
tale: "There is nobody in the congregation orthodox but you
and me—and I am not quite sure about you." There follows
another lack than that of active and aggressive loyalty,
namely, a lack of intellectual scrupulousness in making and
weighing charges. The lack of active loyalty is assumed to
be so widespread that sacrificial offering, even if somewhat
vicarious, will be welcome to the God of Hosts. It is absurd
to be too particular about positive evidence to prove the
lack of a thing. There are suspicious circumstances; to pun-
ish this man will at least arouse others to a less passive
patriotism.

One who reads the volume of testimony with these things
in mind will have little difficulty in understanding either its
concentration upon views rather than acts, views which
might be entertained on various hypothetical occasions
rather than any views ever actually uttered, or its desire to
entrap individuals into obnoxious statements. Such an atmosphere breeds suspicion, accusation and violent action,
the phenomena of Inquisition, whether of Torquemada,
Salem, the Committee of Public Safety of the French Revolution, Lenin, or New York school authorities.

All this, however, concerns the spirit and atmosphere, the

local color, of the school episode rather than its substance, or structure. These are to be sought, as has already been said, in the only too well-established methods of school administration with respect to teachers. Quite independently of this episode, one of the least sensational of our school superintendents, Mr. Arthur Perry, has written a pamphlet regarding the problem confronting the new Board of Education. In it he frankly states that there is a general feeling that the building of the Board of Education is a circumlocution office; that there is practically no citywide esprit de corps among the teachers; that because of this lack the "tremendous amount of enthusiasm and intelligence in the more than twenty thousand members is going pitiably to waste"; that the devotion of teachers to pupils—which is general— is due to dictates of individual conscience, rather than to leadership, and that the feeling is widespread among teachers that instead of looking to their immediate employers, the Board of Education, for support and aid, they must rather protect themselves *against* their employers by using the pressure of legislation or of public opinion to secure "even ordinary consideration."

This is a temperate, and even tempered, statement. It indicates the background upon which a particular difficulty has been projected. If there has been a lack of "active" loyalty in support of the war, the charge affects not three alone nor yet thirty nor three hundred. But what it reflects is not lack of individual loyalty, but just this absence of leadership on the part of nominal leaders, an undermined esprit de corps, a widespread skepticism and even cynicism, the immediate responsibility for which does not lie at the door of the teaching staff. Not merely the accused teachers but the teaching force has been left without inspiration, and the guidance of any constructive policy, and hence exposed to every sort of irresponsible interference and amateur pressure.

It is matter of common knowledge that the strain in the relations between superior and inferior and the general unrest in the teaching staff have been on the steady increase during the latter years of the Mitchel administration. To the teachers that administration presented its most brutal face. All of the better informed of friends of the now defunct Gary system in New York have been aware for some time that its success was fundamentally compromised if not doomed by the autocratic way in which it was formulated and imposed from above. Under Mr. Churchill, the cultivation of more co-operative relations with the teaching staff had begun; after the fusion administration broke with him, the situation became largely that described by Carlyle as anarchy plus the constable's club.

New York memories are proverbially short. But if anyone will turn back to the newspapers of the pre-election days he will find them full of school riots and school strikes, for which the fusion campaign managers with the ineptitude which characterized their almost every act were holding, by name, Mr. Churchill, Mr. Somers and other members of the Board of Education, responsible. Pupils of De Witt Clinton High School were active in a strike against the imposition of the longer (seven-hour) school day. The merits or demerits of this lengthened school day are of little account for present purposes in comparison with the fact that it presented one more autocratic decree and imposition from above. The teachers immediately affected were not even consulted as to its probable effects or the best way of administering it so as to mitigate the hardships it would work upon the many pupils who spent part of their time in earning money to continue at school. Provoked by these riots and strikes, and presumably as a Tammany man not particularly pleased at having them unjustly charged to Tammany, Mr. Whalen, the chairman of the High School Committee of the Board of Education, said that he would close the schools rather than allow teachers and pupils to "run them."

This utterance seems to have furnished the proverbial straw. Members of the school council, most of whom are among the dismissed and transferred teachers, prepared resolutions condemning Mr. Whalen's attitude as autocratic and called a meeting of the teachers of the school which passed the resolutions almost unanimously. The Inquisition followed. There is no evidence that Mr. Whalen himself instigated it. The variety and number of the coincidences with respect to the teachers called and not called, the questions asked, etc., amount to a mathematical demonstration of the connection between the two things. It was no accident that the inquiry began in and concerns teachers in the De Witt Clinton High School. Moreover this action on the part of teachers in that school did not stand alone. Before this episode the school had been famous—or if any one will—infamous—as a center of unrest, of independence, and of protest against autocratic administration. If an example was needed, here was the place to begin. If specific charges of insubordination had been brought, the hearing might have cleared the air. Underlying causes of friction would have been brought out and the public been placed in a position to determine the balance of rights and wrongs. But it was more tactful to leave the indictment vague and to establish a subtle association between lack of loyalty to official superiors and to the nation.

The direct clash of educational philosophies as to methods of teaching and discipline in dealing with pupils presents the same conflict from another angle. The situation between teachers and pupils corresponds, point for point as the mathematicians say, to that between teachers and their employers. Hence the phrases "teaching instinctive obedience" and "respect for authority as such" (with true metaphysical emphasis upon the "as such") are permanent contributions of the trial to pedagogical literature. Teachers who do not instill in pupils blind "doglike" fealty to every kind of authority are not likely themselves to yield it. Teachers who regard the possibility of utilizing their own thoughtful experience as an important factor in conducting the schools will respect the intelligence of their pupils. This defines the fundamental issue. Is automatic routine habit or the development of habits of reflective consideration to be the dominant aim of teaching and discipline? Never has it been revealed more clearly that the latter is "dangerous" and the former "safe"—dangerous to whom and safe for whom being carefully concealed save as the subtle association with disloyalty may be insinuated. In spite, then, of the temporary prestige which war psychology may give to automatic habit over against thoughtfulness as an educational end, progressives might, were it not for danger of injustice to individuals, well be grateful to the reactionaries for having the issue so unambiguously set forth. The fact that this conflict of ideals and principles is the source of a multitude of other clashes and discrepancies is usually overlaid with irrelevant matter and ornamentally concealed with eulogistic phraseology. The trial has brought it out in a bald, naked, uncompromised form. The record stands. Like most reactionary triumphs after the issue is once revealed, the record will become a milestone in the history of the gradual victory of a progressive over a reactionary social and educational philosophy.

# 15

# EDUCATION AND SOCIAL DIRECTION *

IT IS not surprising that many persons in the United States who are accustomed to think of themselves as belonging to the "upper" and therefore rightfully ruling class, and who are impressed by the endurance and resistance of Germany in the war, should look with envious admiration upon the Prussian system of authoritarian education. To suppose however that they desire a direct importation of the German system of autocratic power and willing submissiveness in order to secure the discipline and massive order of Germany, is to make a blunder. They see America retaining its familiar traditions; for the most part they would be sincerely shocked at a suggestion of surrender of democratic habits. What they see in their fancy is an America essentially devoted to democratic ideals and rising to the service of these ideals with a thoroughness, a unanimity, an efficiency and ordered discipline which they imagine would be secured by a judicious adoption of German methods. Since they do not perceive the interdependence of ends and means, or of purposes and methods, their error is intellectual rather than perversely immoral. They are stupid rather than deliberately disloyal.

It is one of the many merits of Veblen's most enlightening book on Imperial Germany that he makes clear the high human cost of the envied German habit. Under modern conditions social automatism is not automatically self-sustaining. It represents a delicate and complicated piece of machinery which can be kept in proper working order only by immense pains. The obedient mind is not a thing which can be achieved by the segregated means of school discipline alone.

* From *The Dial*, April 11, 1918.

All the resources of all social institutions have to be centered upon it without let-up. "It can be maintained only by unremitting habituation, discipline sagaciously and relentlessly directed to this end." Successful warfare, the effects of warlike preparation, and indoctrination with warlike arrogance are more necessary than the technique of the classroom. Only "bureaucratic surveillance and unremitting interference in the private life" of subjects can, in the face of the disintegrating tendencies of contemporary industry and trade, develop that "passionate aspiration for subservience" which is a marked feature of the Prussian diathesis. If we look these facts in the face, we shall quickly see the romanticism of any proposal to secure the German type of disciplined efficiency and of patient and persistent "industry" by borrowing a few features of the personal relation of teacher and pupil and installing them in the school. Only an occasional pedagogical Dogberry can rise to the level of a New York school administrator who would secure permanent good loyal citizenship by "teaching [sic] instinctive obedience" in the schools.

Taken in this crude form, the desire to Prussianize the disciplinary methods of American schools is too incoherent and spasmodic to constitute a serious danger. A serious danger there is, however, and it lies in the confused thinking which such efforts stimulate and strengthen. The danger lies not in any likelihood of success. Save here and there for a brief period, the attempts run hopelessly counter to the trend of countless social forces. The danger is that the vague desire and confused thought embodied in them will cover up the real problems involved in securing an effectively loyal democratic citizenship, and distract attention from the constructive measures required to develop the kind of social unity and social control required in a democracy. For the whole tendency of current lamentations over the failure of American education to secure social integration and effective cohesion, is to put emphasis upon the futile and irritating relations of personal authority and personal subjection, or else upon the regulative power of blind engrained habits, whose currency presupposes an authoritative deus ex machina behind the scenes to supply the ends for which the habits are to work. And anybody who hasn't put his soul to sleep with the apologetics of soporific "idealism" knows that at the present time the power which would fix the ends to which the masses would be habituated is the economic class which has a selfish interest in the exercise of control. To cater to this class by much talk of the importance of discipline, obedience, habituation, and by depreciation of initiative and creative thought as socially dangerous, may be a quick path to favor. But it represents an ignobility of spirit which is peculiarly out of place in an educator, who above all others is called upon to keep his supreme interest sensitively human.

Unfortunately there is much in the tradition of what is regarded as scientific sociology which lends itself, unwittingly, to such base uses. Sociological science inherited a basic error from the older political science, and has too often devoted itself to a pompous dressing-out of solutions of a problem resting upon a "fact" which isn't a fact. It has taken as its chief problem how individuals who are (supposedly) non-social become socialized, how social control becomes effective among individuals who are naturally hostile to it. The basic supposition is, of course, mythological. Docility, desire for direction, love for protective control are stronger original traits of human nature than is insubordination or originality. The scales are always weighted in favor of habituation and against reflective thought. Routine is so easy as to be "natural," and initiative is so difficult as to require the severe discipline of art. But the sociological antithesis of the individual and the social has invaded educational thought and is employed by the pedagogue to defend unintelligent convention, unexamined tradition, and to feed the irritable vanity of that petty tyrant, the educational administrator, who learns by study of the new sociological pedagogy that the exercise of his personal authority is in reality an exemplar of the great problem of sociology —the "social control" of the unregenerate, unsocialized individual.

This thoughtless sociology does something, however, even more harmful than the rationalization of mere personal authority. It serves to justify the laziness, the intellectual inertia, of the educational routineer. The latter finds it easier, say, to rely upon books than to make himself a well-informed man at first hand. He is solemnly told that textbooks socialize the pupil, for they embody the intellectual heritage of the race. He then puts to one side the onerous task of achieving any personal originality in the subjects he teaches, lest he might fire his students with "individualism" having socially disastrous consequences. An uneasy intellectual conscience tells a teacher that in his methods he is following the lines of least resistance furnished by school customs which he has unreflectively picked up. But he is consoled by being told that thinking merely develops individualism, that custom is the great social balance wheel. And far be it from him to undermine the sanctities of institutionalized habit by a little adventure in personal reflection. He has a sense that his ways of dealing with pupils are external and perfunctory. He feels that if he took pains to acquaint himself with the scientific methods of gaining insight into human nature and applied himself with sympathy to understanding it in its immense diversity, he might be able to work from the inside to release potentialities instead of from the outside to impose conventionalities. But then the solemn guardian of "social control" comes along and warns him of the "social" value of respect for authority as such, and the dangers of "catering" to individuality. A scientific excuse for natural laziness and ignorance can go a long way.

The worst of all this, I repeat, is that it leaves problems which are pressing untouched and ignores the urgent need for the particular kind of social direction fitted to a democratic society—the direction which comes from heightened emotional appreciation of common interests and from an understanding of social responsibilities, an understanding to be secured only by experimental and personal participation in the conduct of common affairs. At this point, the antithesis between individual and social ceases to be merely silly. It becomes dangerous. For the unsolved problem of democracy is the construction of an education which will develop that kind of individuality which is intelligently alive to the common life and sensitively loyal to its common maintenance. It is not an antithesis of social control and individual development which our education requires. We want that type of education which will discover and form the kind of individual who is the intelligent carrier of a social democracy —social indeed, but still a democracy.

# 16

# EDUCATION AS RELIGION *

A FRIEND has been accustomed for many years to urge that there exists only one sure measure for the real progress of education. The test, he has said, is the possibility of bringing suit at law to compel payment of damages by educators to educatees for malpractice. There being no such possibility at present, there is no science or profession of education in existence. However, we are approximating the time when it will be possible to trace specific physical injuries, spinal curvatures, bad eyesight and the like, to specific school procedures so that before long actions may lie for physical damages incurred in consequence of incompetency. After responsibility is socially recognized and enforced for unscientific treatment of the body, intellectual injuries resulting from bad instruction will be actionable. The man who finds when he grows up that he had had habits of mind-wandering foisted upon him or who has lost scientific curiosity or ability to observe accurately will be able to bring suit against the community which subjected him to such injuries through its educational agencies. Then at the final and culminating stage society itself will have legal remedies against schools and teachers who send out into life citizens lacking the capacity and desire to be good citizens.

These remarks seem to be an effective if whimsical way of conveying the fact that at present our educational procedure is still accidental, and that all our pretensions in education will remain mere pretensions until we can analyze the products of home and school rearing, so as to assign with definiteness responsibility for the various conditions and

* From *The New Republic*, September 13, 1922.

forces which have brought about the various elements in the human product. Our backwardness is seen in the general nature of the causes which we assign. They are so vague as to be meaningless; words by which we disguise our absence of insight. Thus we talk about heredity and environment in a grandiose way when we try to explain this or that result. When we become more specific, as in biography, we can hardly do more than to point to the effects of some chance contact, some inspiration derived from meeting some person or the arousing force exercised by some event. Or we fall back on native genius and native depravity, innate "smartness" and stupidity and various other practical synonyms for God and the devil—good and bad forces which control us and which we cannot modify.

Now it may be that things will always remain in this condition. Perhaps it is utopian to expect anything different. But at least we may frankly recognize the situation and its implications. We may clear up our minds. And at present they seem to be badly muddled. We are trying too often to combine two contradictory beliefs. We make a religion out of education, we profess unbounded faith in its possibilities, we point with pride to its advance, we term instruction an art and school management a profession. Faith in education signifies nothing less than belief in the possibility of deliberate direction of the formation of human disposition and intelligence. It signifies a belief that it is possible to know definitely just what specific conditions and forces operate to bring about just such and such specific results in character, intellectual attitude and capacity. But on the other hand, we assume in practice that no one is specifically responsible when bad outcomes show themselves. We assume in fact that education, as a matter of forming character and intelligence, is and must remain an accident. We thus find ourselves in an insincere position. There is supposed to be a profession which has an art based upon scientific knowledge. But when results are undesirable we shrug our shoulders and place the responsibility upon some intrinsic defect or some outer chance which has unaccountably entered in and deflected our correct procedure to a bad outcome. This course suggests the story of the physician who admitted that his patient died, but insisted that nevertheless he died scientifically cured.

It seems almost impossible to measure the extent to which these contradictory ideas are combined in the popular mind. Faith in the possibilities of education is enormous. But the notion that we cannot really direct the processes which lead in actual living human beings to good and bad products is equally widespread. The popular conception of "free will" is a case in point. What is it but a name for the sum-total of forces which resist and pervert our efforts at educational direction? It is a rationalization of our own inabilities to deal with the development of human beings; a shifting of our responsibilities to some unknown mysterious power whose force is greater than ours. The prevalence of the disposition to put blame on others and on circumstances when things go badly is but another evidence of our practical acknowledgement that there is no knowledge upon which to base control. It is the operator, incompetent because of ignorance, who swears at his machine; the intelligent mechanic locates the source of trouble and deals specifically with it. An honest facing of the duplicity of the situation will at least put an end to our Pickwickian idealization of education in combination with our practical denial of the possibility of education in the concrete.

It is possible to be either a pessimist or an optimist about the attainment of real education. One may hold that the art of directing the formation and development of human desires and beliefs is impossible. The past affords some basis for the statement that such controlled guidance is feasible in just the degree in which its fruits are objectionable; that is, that deliberate direction of human development always ends in hardening human nature and narrowing its scope. The one who holds that the complexity and diversity of human beings is such as to render education in any fundamental sense impossible and the one who holds that human nature is so delicate and flexibly tenuous as to render attempts at education dangerous cannot be decisively controverted. But one can also be hopeful about the future without subjecting himself to conclusive refutation. One can point out that the development of science has only just got to the point where we are beginning to have the materials and methods for creating an intelligent art of guiding the formation of intelligence and affections. It may be argued that the failures of the past are necessary consequences of lack of the kind of knowledge that is now coming into our possession. Only the future can decide whether the school of despair or of hope is in the right. But at least the right to hope remains with us. If we have any ground to be religious about anything, we may take education religiously.

For those who choose to exercise the hope and who also wish to be honest about the accidental state of what is called education, the first step is to recognize the enormous gap which divides our talking and writing about education from our practice of it in the concrete. In the former, education is always something generic. It has a general aim which is stated in terms of dignity. The end is indeed diversely named by different schools of thought. By some it is called character, by others culture, by others a disciplined mind, by others good citizenship or capacity for social service or vocational usefulness. The representatives of these schools, the devotees of these ideals, quarrel actively with one another. A considerable part of educational "discussion" is a record of these quarrels. Adherents of different doctrines quarrel as if there were something really at stake as broad and as deep as are the words they employ. They deceive themselves and the innocent bystander, the public, into supposing that there will be some difference in educational practice corresponding to the fervor and import of the outcry for culture or good citizenship, according as one side or another wins the verbal dispute.

"Deceive" is a strong term. But in educational practice

the ends aimed at are not generic and human; they are immediate and technical or specialized, namely the acquiring of some form of skill and item of knowledge. The controlling end is to acquire mastery of fractions or of a Latin declension or ability to bound the state of Tennessee or give an acceptable account of Magna Charta or manage tools so as to make a mortise and tenon joint. The assumption, of course, is that by pursuit of these various specific aims the general end of culture or discipline or good citizenship or whatever is furthered. And here is where the element of deception comes in. Until we have a definite knowledge of just how results in terms of human disposition and quality are achieved, till we can analyze the formation of human disposition into definite factors connected with definite antecedents, our belief in a working connection between this and that study, this and that method, and our desired end is at best a pious aspiration. In consequence, the educator who talks about culture usually means as a matter of fact simply that Latin or Greek should occupy a large place among school studies, while the one who dwells upon the desirability of mental power and discipline usually means in fact that he leans strongly toward grammar and mathematics and formal studies, and the adherent of good citizenship or social service notifies us that he is in favor of the introduction of studies which have recently found their way into the program, civics perhaps or book-keeping or manual training.

I see no ground for criticizing those who regard education religiously. There have been many worse objects of faith and hope than the ideal possibilities of the development of human nature, and more harmful rites and cults than those which constitute a school system. Only if all faith that outruns sight is contemptible can education as an object of religious faith be contemned. This particular form of faith testifies to a generous conception of human nature and to a deep belief in the possibilities of human achievement in spite of all its past failures and errors. Possibly all such faith involves credulity. But this particular credulity is not without its nobility. A faith becomes insincere and credulity injurious only when aspiration and credence are converted into dogmatic assertion; only when the importance of their objects is made the ground of asserting that we already have at hand the adequate means of attaining them, thereby attaining salvation. Worship of education as a symbol of unattained possibilities of realization of humanity is one thing; our obstinate devotion to existing forms—to our existing schools and their studies and methods of instruction and administration or to suggested specific programs of improvement—as if they embodied the object of worship—is quite another thing.

The first act evoked by a genuine faith in education is a conviction of sin and act of repentance as to the institutions and methods which we now call educational. This act must apply not to this and that, here and there, but to the idea which runs through all of it. It is no particular set of educators that is called to repentance. For everywhere there is the same absence of insight into the means by which our professed ends are to be realized, in consequence of which those ends remain nominal and sentimental. However much or little other religions may conflict with science, here we have a religion which can realize itself only through science: only, that is, through ways of understanding human nature in its concrete actuality and of discovering how its various factors are modified by interaction with the variety of conditions under which they operate. Without science this religion is bound to become formal, hypocritical and, in the end, a mass of dogmas called pedagogy and a mass of ritualistic exercises called school administration. Education may be a religion without being a superstition, and it may be a superstition when it is not even a religion but only an occupation of alleged hard-headed practical people.

# 17

# EDUCATION AS ENGINEERING *

M RS. MARY AUSTIN in her illuminating article on "The Need for a New Social Concept" gives an apt expression of the contrast in contemporary behavior between our power in physical engineering and in basic human concerns. We can, as she points out, easily construct a new type of bridge; we cannot create a new type of education. It would be a comparatively simple matter if schools were destroyed to restore them out of a denuded social consciousness; it would be very difficult under like circumstances to recover ability to make a modern bridge. "The reason is that we have been thinking about education long enough to form a pattern in our minds but not long enough of the multitudinous processes involved in the building of steel bridges."

The meaning is clear, and there is nothing to be gained by a meticulous critique of words. But for radical renovation of the school system, a revision, almost a reversal, of wording would seem to be required. Instead of saying that we have thought so long about education—if thinking means anything intellectual—it would be closer to the realities of the situation to say we have only just begun to think about it. The school system represents not thinking but the domination of thought by the inertia of immemorial customs. Modern bridge building, on the other hand, is quite inconceivable apart from the use of materials determined by purely intellectual methods. Our steel cantilever bridges represent precisely the kind of thing that custom unmodified by thought could never achieve no matter how far it was carried. Because bridge building is dependent upon thinking it is easy for thinking

* From *The New Republic*, September 20, 1922.
150

to change the mode; because education depends upon habits which arose before there was scientific method, thinking with great difficulty makes even a little dent.

Consequently if our school system were destroyed, we should not have to recover our "minds"—our intellectual equipment—to restore our schools. It would be enough if we retained our habits. To restore modern bridges we could dispense with formed habits provided we retained our intellectual technique. There is an ambiguity in referring to a "mental pattern" in connection with schools. The pattern is not mental, if we mean a pattern formed *by* mind. There is doubtless a pattern *in* our minds, but that signifies only a sense of a comfortable scheme of action which has been deposited by wont and use. The pattern is so deep-seated and clearly outlined that the ease of its recognition gives rise to a deceptive sense that there is something intellectual in the pattern itself. In engineering the pattern is mental in quite a different way. It summarizes a distinctively intellectual type of behavior.

A sense of this contrast seems essential to adequate reflection on the question of how educational procedure is to become a form of constructive engineering. William James said that anyone grasps the significance of a generalization only in the degree in which he is familiar with the detail covered by it. Now detail means things in concrete existence. We are familiar only with things which specifically enter into our lives and with which we steadily reckon and deal. All concepts, theories, general ideas are thin, meager and ineffectual in the degree in which they are not reflective expressions of acts and events already embodied, achieved, in experience. New conceptions in education will not of themselves carry us far in modifying schools, for until the schools are modified the new conceptions will be themselves pale, remote, vague, formal. They will become thick, substantial, only in the degree in which they are not indispensably required. For they will offer precise and definite modes of thinking only when new meanings and values have become embodied in concrete life-experiences and are thus sustained by them. Till that time arrives the importance of new concepts is mainly negative and critical. They enable us to criticize existing modes of practice; they point out to us the fact that concrete detail of the right sort does *not* exist. Their positive function is to inspire experimental action rather than to give information as to how to execute it.

There was, I take it, no definite art or science of modern bridge building until after bridges of the new sort had been constructed. It was impossible that the new art should precede the new achievement. The formulae for construction, the rules of specific procedure, the specific classification of types of problems and solutions had to wait upon presentation of appropriate concrete material, that is upon successful experimentation. Nevertheless the pioneers had something to go upon and go ahead with, even if they had no specified art of bridge building to rely upon. They had a certain amount of dependable knowledge in mathematics and physics. The difficulty they suffered from was that no one before them had employed this knowledge in building the kind of bridge that new social conditions called for. When they tried to imagine a new type, the minds of all but a few were surely held in bondage by habituation to what was already familiar.

The essential need was thus human rather than scientific. Someone had to have the imagination to get away from the "thought" of the existing easily recognized pattern. This took daring, the courage to think out of line with convention and custom; it took inventiveness in using existing scientific material in a new way, for new consequences. It took intellectual initiative to conduct experiment against almost universal indifference or reprobation; it took intellectual honesty to learn from failure as well as from success in experimentation. The pioneer succeeded in making his bridge—and ultimately making a new art or scientific technique—because he had the courage of a creative mind. Consider the history of any significant invention or discovery, and you will find a period when there was enough knowledge to make a new mode of action or observation possible but no definite information or instruction as to how to make it actual. Every time it was a courageous imagination, a quality which is personal, human, moral, rather than scientific or technical, which built the bridge—in every sense of the word bridge.

There is at present no art of educational engineering. There will not be any such art until considerable progress has been made in creating new modes of education in the home and school. But there does already exist a considerable body of observations and ideas in biology, psychology and the like which serves to criticize and condemn much of our existing practice, and to suggest to a mind not weighed down by fear the possibility of new leads and openings. Given imagination, courage and the desire to experiment and to learn from its results, there is a push toward, a momentum for creative work. Its concrete consequences if subjected to honest or discriminating reflection will afford material for the elaboration of an art, a fairly definite body of suggestions and instructions for the later intelligent conduct of an educative art. But this technique will be largely ex post facto. It is equally fatal to postpone effort till we have the art and to try to deduce the art in advance from the scientific knowledge in biology, psychology and sociology we actually possess. If earlier mathematicians and physicists had attempted to anticipate the result of inventive experimentation in bridge building by deducing from their sciences the rules of the new art, it is certain that they would have arrived only at improved rules for making the old and familiar type of bridge; they would have retarded the day of the new type; they would have concealed from view the necessity of the indispensable human factor—emancipation from routine and timidity. The case is the same with the creation of new types of schools and the ulterior development of an art of education.

There is no question that would-be pioneers in the educational field need an extensive and severe intellectual equipment. Experimentation is something other than blindly trying one's luck or mussing around in the hope that something nice will be the result. Teachers who are to develop a new type of education need a more exacting and comprehensive training in science, philosophy and history than teachers who follow conventionally safe lines. But they do not at present need a translation of this knowledge into a science and art of education. They do not need it because it cannot be had and the pretense of supplying it makes conditions worse rather than better. When, for example, psychology is employed simply to improve the existing teaching of arithmetic or spelling for pre-existing ends, or to measure the technical results of such teaching, let that fact be clearly acknowledged. Let it not be supposed that there is really any advance in the science of education merely because there is a technical improvement in the tools of managing an educational scheme conspicuous for its formation prior to the rise of science. Such "science" only rationalizes old, customary education while improving it in minor details. Given the required intellectual equipment, the further immediate demand is for human qualities of honesty, courage and invention which will enable one to go ahead without the props of custom or the specious pretensions of custom masquerading in the terminology of science.

At present we are still largely in the "rationalizing" stage. Consequently, as was pointed out in the article on "Education as Religion," educational concepts nominally as diverse as culture, discipline, social serviceableness work out in practice to mean only a little more of this or that study. The scope of our rationalizing is seen in the fact that educational theory as taught in our teachers' training schools has been revolutionized in the last generation, largely in a decade. But where is the evidence of any corresponding change in practice? The most optimistic soul, if candid, will admit that we are mostly doing the old things with new names attached. The change makes little difference—except for advertising purposes. We used to lay out a course prescribed by authority for the improvement of the minds of the young.

Now we initiate them into their cultural heritage. The staples used to be taught in certain ways on the ground that the crude and lawless minds of the young needed to be chastened by discipline in things above and beyond them. Now we appeal to "inner motivation." But we teach much the same topics, only in a more gracious, less repellent way. Strange, though, that the opposed needs of external discipline and of inner purpose should be met by so nearly the same subjects and topics!

I am not insinuating that there is personal insincerity in this state of affairs. In part it is due to the fact that docility has been emphasized in education, plus the fact that in the main the most docile among the young are the ones who become teachers when they are adults. Consequently they still listen docilely to the voice of authority. More fundamentally the outcome is due to the fact that a premature attempt is being made to lay down a procedure, definite proper courses of subjects and methods by which teachers may guide themselves, the procedure being nominally derived from our new knowledge in biology, psychology, etc. But as we have seen, this cannot be done; no results so definite as this can be reached until after the change in educational practice is well under way. When the attempt is made in advance to answer specific questions which will arise in the course of employing the new knowledge, to supply in advance definite suggestions as to courses of procedure, it is inevitable that the minds both of "authorities" and of students intending to teach should fall back upon just the old practices which they are nominally striving to get away from. For here alone is there material concrete enough to permit the formulation of definite problems, answers and steps to be undertaken.

In short, at present, both students and teachers of education are excessively concerned with trying to evolve a body of definite, usable, educational directions out of the new body of science. The attempt is only too natural. But it is pathetic. The endeavor to forestall experiment and its failures and achievements, the attempt to tell in advance how successfully to do a new kind of thing ends, at most, in a rectification of old ways and results, plus a complacent assurance that the best methods of modern science are employed and sanction what is done. This sense of being scientifically up-to-date does endless harm. It retards the creation of a new type of education, because it obscures the one thing deeply needful: a new personal attitude in which a teacher shall be an inventive pioneer in use of what is known, and shall learn in the process of experience to formulate and deal with those problems which a premature "science" of education now tries to state and solve in advance of experience.

I do not underestimate the value of the guidance which some time in the future individuals may derive from the results of prior collective experience. I only say that the benefit of such an art cannot be had until a sufficient number of individuals have experimented without its beneficial aid in order to provide its materials. And what they need above all else is the creatively courageous disposition. Fear, routine, sloth, identification of success with ease, and approbation of others are the enemies that now stand in the way of educational advance. Too much of what is called educational science and art only perpetuate a régime of wont and use by pretending to give scientific guidance and guarantees in advance. There is in existence knowledge which gives a compass to those who enter on the uncharted seas, but only a stupid insincerity will claim that a compass is a chart. The call is to the creative adventurous mind. Religious faith in education working through this medium of individual courage with the aid of non-educational science will end in achieving education as a science and an art. But as usual we confuse faith with worship, and term science what is only justification of habit.

# 18

## EDUCATION AS POLITICS *

MATTHEW ARNOLD somewhere quotes with approval the saying of a French writer that the chief advantage of education is the assurance it gives of not being duped. A more positive statement is that the profit of education is the ability it gives to discriminate, to make distinctions that penetrate below the surface. One may not be able to lay hold of the realities beneath the froth and foam, but at least one who is educated does not take the latter to be the realities; one knows that there is a difference between sound and sense, between what is emphatic and what is distinctive, between what is conspicuous and what is important.

Judged by this criterion education is not only backward but it is retrograding. This is the era of bunk and hokum—there is more of it in quantity, its circulation is more rapid and ceaseless, it is swallowed more eagerly and more indiscriminately than ever before. The reasons, of course, for the present reign of bunkum in human affairs are external rather than in any inherent deterioration of intellect and character. Until the last generation or so, the mass of men have been interested for the most part only in local matters, in things and people right about them. For the most part their convictions and thinking had to do with affairs of which they had some direct experience. Their range might be limited, but within it they had shrewdness and employed judgment. They were undoubtedly as gullible about remoter things as people are today. But these remoter things did not come within their scope of action. It makes little difference what notions they

* From *The New Republic*, October 4, 1922.
157

entertained about them; they were hardly more than material for yarns.

The railway, telegraph, telephone and cheap printing press have changed all that. Rapid transportation and communication have compelled men to live as members of an extensive and mainly unseen society. The self-centered locality has been invaded and largely destroyed. Men have to act in view of remote economic and political conditions, and they have to have some notions about the latter upon which to base their actions. Since their notions influence conduct, beliefs are now something more than fancies and entertainments; their correctness is a matter of moment. At the same time, it has become an object for some men to influence the beliefs the masses hold; control has become less a matter of established habits and more a matter of opinions. Control opinion and you control, for the time being at least, the direction of social action. Cheap printing and cheap distribution afford the opportunity to put the control of opinion into effect. Given the new curiosity and the new need of knowing about distant affairs on the one hand and the interest in controlling their exercise on the other, and the era of bunk, of being systematically duped, of undiscriminating sentiment and belief, is ushered in.

Carlyle was no lover of democracy. But in a lucid moment he once declared that when the printing press was invented democracy was inevitable. Cheap printing made it necessary to take the public into partnership in governmental affairs; it extended the number as well as the geographical area included in a particular political society. It converted the theory of government by consent of the governed into a reality. But the conversion did not guarantee the sort of thing to which consent is given; it did not guarantee—as Walter Lippmann has so ably pointed out—that the policies to which consent was given should be in fact what they are in form or that they should correspond with the realities of the situation.

The industrial revolution made necessary the forms of con-

sulting the "voice of the people." But printing and circulation also made it easier to induce the people to speak loudly
on unreal issues, and by very multitude of clamor to
conceal facts and divert attention. It is as idle therefore to
attack democracy at large as it is to eulogize it at large. As a
current form of government it does not spring from personal desire or from opinion: it came about through external
forces that changed the conditions of contact and intercourse
among men. What needs consideration and criticism is the
quality of popular government, not the fact of its existence.
Its quality is inseparably bound up with the quality of the
ideas and information which are circulated and to which belief adheres.

Doubtless the régime of propaganda brought on by the
war has had much to do with forcing upon us recognition of
the dominant role in social control of material put in circulation by the press. The bulk and the careful organization of
propaganda are testimony to two outstanding facts: the new
necessity governments are under of enlisting popular interest and sentiment; and the possibility of exciting and directing that interest by a judiciously selected supply of "news."
But the vogue of propaganda is more significant in calling
attention to the basic fact than it is in constituting that fact.
As against one item in circulation that represents deliberately
invented or consciously colored fact there are a dozen items
that represent prejudice and ignorance due to laziness, inertia of custom and prior mental habits caused by bad education.

Human psychology is such that we attribute to conscious
design and set purpose most of the bad consequences to
which attention is suddenly called. That is one chief reason
why reformers so frequently fail. Real causes of the evils
against which they contend usually lie much deeper than
the conscious intentions and voluntary plans of the individuals against whom they direct their efforts. Consequently
they are dealing with symptoms rather than with forces.
What Mr. Lippmann has so well called stereotypes are more

responsible for confusion and error in the public mind than is consciously invented and distorted news. Those who are most concerned in setting in social movement or circulation the material which blinds and misleads the public, themselves more than half believe the tenor of what is given out; they share the intellectual confusion and ignorance which they propagate. Acting upon the belief that the end justifies the means, it is easy to add the spice, the emphasis, the exaggeration, the suggestions which will convey to the mass what they themselves conceive to be fundamentally true.

Back of the education supplied by print and news is, in short, the earlier and deeper education which influences equally those who give out the news and those who subscribe to what is given out. We are brought back to our original statement. Our schooling does not educate, if by education be meant a trained habit of discriminating inquiry and discriminating belief, the ability to look beneath a floating surface to detect the conditions that fix the contour of the surface, and the forces which create its waves and drifts. We dupe ourselves and others because we have not that inward protection against sensation, excitement, credulity and conventionally stereotyped opinion which is found only in a trained mind.

This fact determines the fundamental criticism to be leveled against current schooling, against what passes as an educational system. It not only does little to make discriminating intelligence a safeguard against surrender to the invasion of bunk, especially in its most dangerous form—social and political bunk—but it does much to favor susceptibility to a welcoming reception of it. There appear to be two chief causes for this ineptitude. One is the persistence, in the body of what is taught, of traditional material which is irrelevant to present conditions—subject-matter of instruction which though valuable in some past period is so remote from the perplexities and issues of present life that its mastery, even if fairly adequate, affords no resource for discriminating insight, no protection against being duped in facing the emergencies of today. From the standpoint of this criterion of education, a large portion of current material of instruction is simply aside from the mark. The specialist in any one of the traditional lines is as likely to fall for social bunk even in its extreme forms of economic and nationalistic propaganda as the unschooled person; in fact his credulity is the more dangerous because he is so much more vociferous in its proclamation and so much more dogmatic in its assertion. Our schools send out men meeting the exigencies of contemporary life clothed in the chain-armor of antiquity, and priding themselves on the awkwardness of their movements as evidences of deep-wrought, time-tested convictions.

The other way in which schooling fosters an undiscriminating gulping mental habit, eager to be duped, is positive. It consists in a systematic, almost deliberate, avoidance of the spirit of criticism in dealing with history, politics and economics. There is an implicit belief that this avoidance is the only way by which to produce good citizens. The more undiscriminatingly the history and institutions of one's own nation are idealized, the greater is the likelihood, so it is assumed, that the school product will be a loyal patriot, a well-equipped good citizen. If the average boy and girl could be walled off from all ideas and information about social affairs save those acquired in school, they would enter upon the responsibilities of social membership in complete ignorance that there are any social problems, any political evils, any industrial defects. They would go forth with a supreme confidence that the way lies open to all, and that the sole cause of failure in business, family life or citizenship lies in some personal deficiency in character. The school is even more indurated from a frank acknowledgment of social ills than the pulpit—which is saying a good deal. And like the pulpit it compensates for its avoidance of discussion of social difficulties by a sentimental dwelling upon personal vices.

The effect is to send students out into actual life in a condition of acquired and artificial innocence. Such perceptions as they may have of the realities of social struggles and problems they have derived incidentally, by the way, and without the safeguards of intelligent acquaintance with facts and impartially conducted discussion. It is no wonder that they are ripe to be gulled, or that their attitude is one which merely perpetuates existing confusion, ignorance, prejudice and credulity. Reaction from this impossibly naïve idealization of institutions as they are produces indifference and cynicism. It is astonishing that the professed conservative molders of public opinion take so little notice of the widespread cynicism of the mass at the present time. They are even more credulous than those whom they appear, superficially, to dupe. This attitude of indifference and opposition is now passive and unorganized. But it exists as a direct result of the disillusionment caused by the contrast between things as they are actually found to be and things as they had been taught in the schools. Some day some more or less accidental event will crystallize the scattered indifference and discontent into an active form, and all the carefully built up bulwarks of social reactions will be washed out. But unfortunately there is little likelihood that the reaction against reaction will be more discriminating than the previous state of things. It too will be blind, credulous, fatalistic, confused.

It seems almost hopeless to name the remedy, for it is only a greater confidence in intelligence, in scientific method. But the "only" marks something infinitely difficult of realization. What will happen if teachers become sufficiently courageous and emancipated to insist that education means the creation of a discriminating mind, a mind that prefers not to dupe itself or to be the dupe of others? Clearly they will have to cultivate the habit of suspended judgment, of skepticism, of desire for evidence, of appeal to observation rather than sentiment, discussion rather than bias, inquiry rather than conventional idealizations. When this happens schools will be the dangerous outposts of a humane civilization. But they will also begin to be supremely interesting places. For it will then have come about that education and politics are one and the same thing because politics will have to be in fact what it now pretends to be, the intelligent management of social affairs.

## 19

## MEDIOCRITY AND INDIVIDUALITY *

INDIVIDUALISM is about the most ambiguous word in
the entire list of labels in ordinary use. It means anything
from egoistically centered conduct to distinction and uniqueness. It is possible to say that excessive individualism is an
outstanding curse of American civilization, and that absence
of individualism is our marked deficiency. When the former
remark is made, economic and legal conditions are in mind;
when the latter, intellectual life is in question. Individuality
is a surer word; it carries with it a connotation of uniqueness
of quality, or at least of distinctiveness. It suggests a freedom
which is not legal, comparative and external but which is
intrinsic and constructive. Our forebears who permitted the
growth of legal and economic arrangements at least supposed, however mistakenly, that the institutions they favored
would develop personal and moral individuality. It was
reserved for our own day to combine under the name of individualism, laudation of selfish energy in industrial accomplishment with insistence upon uniformity and conformity in
mind.

Now that we have reached the point of reverence for mediocrity, for submergence of individuality in mass ideals and
creeds, it is perhaps not surprising that after boasting for a
long time that we had no classes we now boast that we have
discovered a scientific way of dividing our population into
definite classes. Just as Aristotle rationalized slavery by showing how natural it was for those superior by nature to constitute the ends for others who were only tools, so we, while
marveling perhaps at the callousness of the Greek philoso-

* From *The New Republic,* December 6, 1922.

pher, rationalize the inequities of our social order by appealing to innate and unalterable psychological strata in the population.

Thus Mr. George B. Cutten in his inaugural address as president of Colgate University recently informed us that it is now "discovered" that "only fifteen per cent of the people have sufficient intelligence to get through college." From this "discovery" he draws the conclusion that as we have never had a real democracy, so "the low level of the intelligence of the people will not permit of our having one." He not only makes the undeniable statement that we are ruled by an aristocracy in industry, commerce, professions and government, but he terms this aristocracy an *intellectual* aristocracy! The adjective seems incredible. But President Cutten thinks there is the same scientific warrant for assuming that conspicuous success under present conditions is a sign of innate intellectual superiority as for saying that twenty-five per cent of the population are mentally subnormal and that only fifteen per cent are capable of higher education.

Mr. Cutten begins his presidential career with a startling view of the social stratification which is to be the ultimate outcome of an educational classification based on intellectual classifications by means of mental testing. We are to arrive at a caste system like that of India, "but on a just and rational basis." For "when the tests for vocational guidance are completed and developed, each boy and girl in school will be assigned to the vocation for which he is fitted." There will be no difficulty about filling the ranks of unskilled labor and mechanical operators, for Mr. Cutten implicitly believes the yarn that the army tests have shown that the "average mentality" of the population is slightly over thirteen years. Considering only the energy and unspoiled curiosity of the average thirteen-year-old in comparison with the dulled observation and blunted vigor of the average adult, one might hope that this statement were true. It would be most encouraging. But it is more to the point to remark that, as Mr.

Lippmann has so clearly shown, the statement interpreted as Mr. Cutten means it, is like saying that perhaps sixty-five per cent of the population rank below the lowest fifty per cent; it takes absolutely what is only a comparative statement, thereby rendering it literally senseless. What makes this performance more than a mere individual mistake is that it affords striking evidence of the habit of ignoring specific individualities, of thinking in terms of fixed classes, intellectual and social.

But why has it been so generally assumed among our cultivated leaders that a purely classificatory formula gives information about individual intelligence in its individuality? To say that Johnnie Jones who was born in 1913 has in 1922 a mental age of eight or of ten years only means that he belongs, on the basis of his performance of certain exercises, to a class of persons at least over a million in number, who were born in 1912 or 1914 respectively. Why then is it so frequently supposed that the individual mentality of John Jones has been definitely determined? To say that one belongs in a class which is a million or so large, with respect to which one is accelerated or retarded by a year in comparison with another class of a million, does not, after all, throw much light on the intrinsic capacities of a given individual.

The assumption seems to indicate one thing. We are irretrievably accustomed to thinking in standardized averages. Our economic and political environment leads us to think in terms of classes, aggregates and submerged membership in them. In spite of all our talk about individuality and individualism we have no habit of thinking in terms of distinctive, much less uniquely individualized, qualities. The inference to be drawn from the popular reception of mental testings concerns the acquired habits of intellectual spokesmen, rather than the inherent intellectuality of the populace. This fact is indeed significant for the prospects of democracy. But the reason it is ominous for democracy is radically different from that often assigned. For it reflects not upon the innate mentality of the mass but upon the acquired intelligence of men in high positions. It shows how their education, that given by their surroundings as well as by their schools, has fixed in them the disposition to judge by classification instead of by discrimination, and by classifications which represent the average of massed numbers, mediocrities instead of individualities.

We may be thought to ignore the interest which many testers have shown in pupils of superior abilities. For some of the testers tell us that one of the chief beneficial consequences of testing is that it enables us to pick out the superior tenth, to rescue the saving remnant from the ruck in which they are now submerged. But the seeming exception proves the rule. The idea of classification still fatally pursues and dominates. "Superior" is still a classificatory word. The size of the class is reduced, say from a million to a hundred thousand. But what kind of superiority marks a particular individual is still unrevealed to us.

The practical educational use to which testers propose that the results of testing should be put strengthens the proposition that even cultivated minds are dominated by the concept of quantitative classes—so much so that the quality of individuality escapes them. For many of them are now telling us that the chief use of the results of the tests is to secure a more accurate ranking or grading of pupils. Instead of mixing up together a lot of pupils of different abilities we can divide them into a superior, a middle and an inferior section, so that each can go its own gait without being kept back or unduly forced by others. An individual is not conceived as an individual with his own distinctive perplexities, methods and rates of operation. The classificatory submergence of individuals in averaged aggregates is perpetuated: it is standardized and rendered more efficient. It may turn out that the net result will be to postpone the day of a reform of education which will get us away from inferior, mean and superior mediocrities so as to deal with individualized mind and character. The movement is on a par with the movements to make instruction more efficient while retaining that notion of teaching which emphasizes the receptively docile mind instead of an inquiring and pioneering purpose.

These remarks are in no sense a hostile criticism of the scientific procedure of mental testing. They are an attempt to suggest its proper goal and to indicate the stage which has now been reached in moving toward that goal. The goal is a method of discrimination, of analysis of human beings, of diagnosis of persons, which is intrinsic and absolute, not comparative and common. Before this goal can be reached it is necessary that certain average statistical norms should be determined. But their function is scientific, not practical either for schooling or for the conduct of democracy. They are of value in working out a system of tests to be used ultimately in analysis of an individual. You cannot be sure, for example, that you have a good test for mechanical ingenuity in a particular person until you have seen how large numbers react to different exercises. The pity is that a scheme for testing tests which are ultimately to be employed in diagnosing individuality has been treated as if it already provided means of testing individuals.

Life insurance is impossible, for example, without extensive statistical investigations, establishing quantitative mean norms. Individuals are graded as to their degree of insurable risk on the basis of these norms. But no one supposes that the result determines the fate of any particular person. If to be accepted as a good risk were a guarantee of long life, clearly no one after being accepted would insure himself. And similarly to a sensible person rejection is not a fatalistic sign of sure death. It is a warning to have a thorough individual examination made, and to undertake individualized remedial measures on the basis of this individual diagnosis. An I.Q. as at present determined is at most an indication of certain risks and probabilities. Its practical value lies in the stimulus it gives to more intimate and intensive inquiry into individualized abilities and disabilities.

As a matter of fact, President Cutten's educational outlook in the concrete is much more intelligent and humane than is indicated by his credulous use of the army tests. He saves himself by losing his logic. He says that education is conservative as compared with theology and philosophy; he declares that if we are teaching the wrong subjects, the better the teaching the more disastrous the results; his conviction that we are largely teaching the wrong subjects is perhaps indicated by his statement that our curricula have not changed much in the last millennium. He points out that the whole system is strong on its receptive side and weak on the creative side; and that the consequence is the comparative scarcity of creative artists and thinkers among us. Students who merely pass in college and who are conspicuous for breaches of discipline become later in life leaders and executives.

Is it possible to admit these facts and not also admit that as a practical measure we should devote ourselves to changes in education which are within our control rather than worry about innate differences which are not within our control? If there prevailed from the elementary school up the kind of inquiring and creative education which President Cutten desires for the college, perhaps democracy, in spite of native inequalities and inferiorities, would not be in such a parlous condition. Until we have tried the educational experiment, we simply do not know and shall not know what individual capacities and limits really are. For it is not just the quantity of our education which is confessedly at fault; it is its quality, its spirit, method and aim.

A change from a receptive education to a creative one, to one which as President Cutten well says would result in "ability to meet a unique situation," obviously implies studying and treating individuals in their distinctive and unique qualites. It involves getting away from that class and averaged education to which the current interpretation of the results of mental testing the more rigidly commits us. One appeals with unusual pleasure from President Cutten dealing with a subject matter of a science in which he is a somewhat credulous non-expert to the field of education in which he is a wise expert. From an *ad hominem* point of view, the difference of attitude in the two fields indicates how much what is termed intelligence is an acquired matter, due to opportunity and experience.

No matter how much innate qualities may set limits, they are not active forces. Experience, that is to say education, is still the mother of wisdom. And we shall never have any light upon what are the limits to intelligence set by innate qualities till we have immensely modified our scheme of getting and giving experience, of education. Barring complete imbecility, it is safe to say that the most limited number of the populace has potentialities which do not now reveal themselves and which will not reveal themselves till we convert education by and for mediocrity into an education by and for individuality.

# 20

# INDIVIDUALITY, EQUALITY AND SUPERIORITY *

IN "Mediocrity and Individuality" I pointed out that the
current reception of the results of mental testing proves
the extent to which we are given to judging and treating individuals not as individuals but as creatures of a class, a quantitative class which covers up truly individualized traits. Our
mechanical, industrialized civilization is concerned with
averages, with per cents. The mental habit which reflects
this social scene subordinates education and social arrangements to stratifications based on averaged gross inferiorities
and superiorities. We accept standards of judging individuals which are based on the qualities of mind and character
which win under existing social conditions conspicuous success. The "inferior" is the one who isn't calculated to "get
on" in a society such as now exists. "Equals" are those who
belong to a class formed by like chances of attaining recognition, position and wealth in present society.

This intellectual acceptance of standards for valuing individuals of a society which every candid mind admits to be
lopsided and disordered gives occasion for a re-examination
of the fundamental ideas of superiority and equality. What
do these words means? Professors have one measure of superior ability; captains of industry another. One class es-
teems aptitude for learning academic subjects; the other
class appraises in terms of power in execution. Suppose that
investigators and artists were so socially dominant that they
were effectively articulate. Should we not then employ quite
other standards of measurement? At present superior races

* From *The New Republic*, December 13, 1922.

are superior on the basis of their own conspicuous achievements. Inferior races are inferior because their successes lie in different directions, though possibly more artistic and civilized than our own.

Superiority and inferiority are meaningless words taken by themselves. They refer to some specific outcome. No one should use the words until he has asked himself and is ready to tell others: Superior and inferior in *what?* Is a student inferior for purposes of reciting lessons, of fitting into a school administration, of influencing companions, of "student activities" or what? Is an adult superior in money-making, in music, in chicanery and intrigue, in being a wise parent or good neighbor, as a homemaker, a chauffeur or a librarian, a congenial companion, a confidence man, an investigator of higher mathematics, an expert accountant, a tractable worker or a revolutionist, in writing acceptable movie scenarios or in research in the laboratory?

There are as many modes of superiority and inferiority as there are consequences to be attained and works to be accomplished. And until society becomes static new modes of activity are continually developing, each of which permits and exacts its own specific inferiorities and superiorities. There is doubtless some degree of correlation between traits which promote superiority in more than one direction. But the idea of abstract, universal superiority and inferiority is an absurdity. The current loose use of these conceptions suggests overcompensation on the part of those who assume that they belong to a superior class. It appears like an attempt to escape from the limitations and incapacities which we all know, subconsciously at least, that we possess.

When classifications are rigid, the quantitative, the more or less, phase of superiority is inevitably conspicuous. Castes are ranks or grades of superiority; within each caste the hierarchical order of higher and lower is repeated. The endeavor to discover abstract degrees of mental superiority which fit for "leadership" in the abstract is evidence of the hold upon us still exercised by feudal arrangements. Our new feudalism of the industrial life which ranks from the great financier through the captain of industry down to the unskilled laborer revives and re-enforces the feudal disposition to ignore individual capacity displayed in free or individualized pursuits. Sometimes in theory we conceive of every form of useful activity as on a level with every other as long as it really marks the performance of needed service. In these moments we also recognize in idea at least that there are an infinite number of forms of significant action. But these ideas are usually restricted to religiously accented moments. When it comes to "practical" matters, the very person who in his religious moods asserts the uniqueness of individuality and of opportunity for service falls back upon a restricted number of conventionally formulated and esteemed occupations and is content to grade persons in a quantitative comparative scale.

It was once supposed, at least by some, that the purpose of education, along with equipping students with some indispensable tools, was to discover and release individualized capacities so that they might make their own way with whatever of social change is involved in their operation. But now we welcome a procedure which under the title of science sinks the individual in a numerical class; judges him with reference to capacity to fit into a limited number of vocations ranked according to present business standards; assigns him to a predestined niche and thereby does whatever education can do to perpetuate the present order. The motto concerning genuinely individual distinctions is that of the tank corps. "Treat 'em rough"—except as they give promise of success in this or that established social classification. Otherwise, the person might grow up to be a conscientious objector or a social innovator, or be inclined to demand social recognition for activity in free scientific inquiry or in art or some other luxurious and ornamental calling.

The irony of the situation is that this course is usually taken in the name of aristocracy, even of intellectual aristocracy, and as part of an attack upon the tendencies of democracy to ignore individuality. It may be that the word democracy has become so intimately associated with a particular political order, that of general suffrage and elective officials, which does not work very satisfactorily, that it is impossible to recover its basic moral and ideal meaning. But the meaning remains whatever name is given it. It denotes faith in individuality, in uniquely distinctive qualities in each normal human being; faith in corresponding unique modes of activity that create new ends, with willing acceptance of the modifications of the established order entailed by the release of individualized capacities.

Democracy in this sense denotes, one may say, aristocracy carried to its limit. It is a claim that every human being as an individual may be the best for some particular purpose and hence be the most fitted to rule, to lead, in that specific respect. The habit of fixed and numerically limited classifications is the enemy alike of true aristocracy and true democracy. It is because our professed aristocrats surrender so gladly to the habit of quantitative or comparative classifications that it is easy to detect snobbery of greater or less refinement beneath their professed desire for a regime of distinction. For only the individual is ultimately distinctive; the rest is a matter of common qualities differing merely in degree. Even in the crudest pioneer democracy there was something more distinctive, more aristocratic, than in that smoothed-off communal worship of qualities belonging to certain classes which is characteristic of present-day critics of democracy.

The most ardent of the early advocates of equality never fell into the stupidity of alleging that all persons are qualitatively alike. Rousseau was one of the first to insist upon natural differences, psychological and physical. It was his profound conviction of the intensity and scope of these differences which made him so insistent upon political, legal and, within certain limits, economic equality. Otherwise some form of native superior energy would result in the enslavement of the masses, adding artificial enfeeblement to their natural deficiencies, while corrupting those of superior ability by giving them an artificial mastery over others and a cruel, contemptuous disregard for their welfare.

In our own earlier history, John Adams is perhaps the chief proponent of the unavoidable necessity of recognizing the aristocratic principle in politics because of inequality of natural endowments. But Adams was a realist. He did not assume that superiority of gifts meant intellectual superiority or that aristocracy in practice means the rule of the mentally and morally superior. He saw that the native superiorities which were bound in any political system to find outlet and to warp institutions to their ends are of indefinitely many kinds—power, power to command and influence the action of others, being their only common divisor. In his own realistic words: "Any aristocrat is any man who can command two votes, one besides his own." And this superior influence may be due, he points out, to virtue, talent or intrigue and debauchery; to loquacity or taciturnity, to frankness or reserve, to goodfellowship or fraud, violence and treachery, to deism or atheism. Powerful is as powerful does. Adams never fell into that mealy-mouthed sentimentalism of contemporary defenders of aristocracy who assume that native superiorities are all in the direction of talent and virtue, and inferiorities all in the opposite direction.

Thomas Jefferson is associated with the democratic school. But he writes to John Adams: "I agree with you that there is a natural aristocracy among men. . . . The natural aristocracy of virtue and talents is the most precious gift of nature. . . . That government is best which provides the most effectively for selection of these natural aristocrats into the offices of government." And he proceeds to state that the difference between Adams and himself concern the means which are best calculated to secure this result. Adams thought that some express and definite institution was necessary; Jefferson thought that such explicit recognition would encourage the "tinsel" aristocracy of wealth and birth at the expense of natural aristocracy; for the wealthy will manage to protect themselves anyway and need no artificial protection against the feebleness of the poor. Both agreed that equality is moral, a matter of justice socially secured, not of physical or psychological endowment.

No intelligent defender of democratic equality has ever believed anything else. Today he is not as sure as men were a century ago that any legal and political system can of itself prevent the untoward working of native differences of power. He sees very clearly that a régime of economic anarchy like the present overstimulates many of the least desirable forms of superior native power, and that the result overrides the legal and political bulwarks of moral equity. In consequence he sees that moral equality cannot be conceived on the basis of legal, political and economic arrangements. For all of these are bound to be classificatory; to be concerned with uniformities and statistical averages. Moral equality means incommensurability, the inapplicability of common and quantitative standards. It means intrinsic qualities which require unique opportunities and differential manifestation; superiority in finding a specific work to do, not in power for attaining ends common to a class of competitors, which is bound to result in putting a premium on mastery over others. Our best, almost our only, models of this kind of activity are found in art and science. There are indeed minor poets and painters and musicians. But the real standard of art is not comparative, but qualitative. Art is not greater and less, it is good or bad, sincere or spurious. Not many intellectual workers are called to be Aristotles or Newtons or Pasteurs or Einsteins. But every honest piece of inquiry is distinctive, individualized; it has its own incommensurable quality and performs its own unique service.

Upon reflection, however, it is apparent that there is something academic in confining the models of moral equality to art and intellectual pursuits. Direct personal relationships, the affections and services of human companionship are its most widespread and available manifestations. The snobbery of the snobbish, who call themselves aristocrats, is nowhere as evident as in their neglect of the superior gifts and attainments of the humble of the earth in these respects. No contact of this human sort is replaceable; with reference to it all are equal because all are incommensurable, infinite. Democracy will not be democracy until education makes it its chief concern to release distinctive aptitudes in art, thought and companionship. At present the intellectual obstacle in the way is the habit of classification and quantitative comparisons. Our pseudo-aristocrats with their flourishing of abstract and uniform superiority and inferiority are now the main defendants of a concept of classes which means only the mass divided into smaller portions. The democrat with his faith in moral equality is the representative of aristocracy made universal. His equality is that of distinction made universal.

# 21

## CULTURE AND PROFESSIONALISM IN EDUCATION *

IN education as in sport the amateur has always had a higher ranking than the professional, even when the latter had greater skill and won more successes. There may be some snobbery mingled with this state of affairs, but in the main it is due to the idea that the amateur cares for the thing itself and pursues it, whether golf or learning, from love of the activity, while with the professional the activity, whether science or a game, is subservient to pecuniary rewards and other external consequences. It is not surprising accordingly that large numbers of persons are deeply concerned about present tendencies in education, especially in the higher schools, for they seem to see everywhere an irresisted movement to professionalize teaching and learning. The amateur of learning hardly seems to be holding his own as well as the amateur in sport.

It is not hard to make out a case. Disinterested love of inquiry and idealistic devotion to the things of the mind in science and art are not flourishing in our high schools, colleges and universities as are the studies that prepare for what is called practical life. The campus of almost every large educational institution in the country presents to the observer professional schools of business or commerce, of teaching and of journalism added to the traditional schools of law, theology and medicine, while the branches of technical study in engineering and agriculture have been indefinitely multiplied. Many colleges have a large part of their

* Address given at the opening exercises of Columbia University on September 26, 1923. From *School and Society*, October 13, 1923.

undergraduate work so arranged as to overlap work in the professional schools so that they are in effect professional preparatory schools. Hence there is lively solicitude as to whether our higher schools are going to surrender to the practical and industrial spirit of the age, until that discriminating love of thought and its products that we call culture shall have been buried under modes of training that prepare students for their future vocations.

I, for one, should not wish to deny that there are deplorable features in the present situation and dangers for the future. I think, however, that a consideration of its causes is more helpful than lamentation and scolding. In the main, these causes seem to be twofold. In the past, liberal studies and culture were the almost exclusive possession of a leisure class, which however was not an idle class. For the leisure class was in general control of political affairs and through the responsibilities and contacts of social management secured a wide horizon and a serious and dignified outlook on life. Moreover the social status of the members of this leisure class was hereditary, so that there was opportunity for the development of a continuous and cumulative tradition of taste and interest. The masses of the people were occupied as they always have been with getting their daily living. They had no part in the direction of society; they were not consulted in political affairs, domestic or foreign. Their interests were confined to their own parish and dooryard, and they naturally had no share in any education except the most elementary practical and vocational apprenticeship.

At the present time there is no social class predestined to play the major role in politics and in social management. Actual control has passed largely into the hands of practical businessmen, but this class is not a closed class but is ever changing its personnel with the ups and downs of economic fortune. The masses have been politically emancipated and in theory at least share in the control of society and the state. They have free time and material resources as their forefathers had not; they have access to cheap and varied reading matter. In consequence of this great social revolution, the leisure class, with which the whole tradition of culture and education in the past was bound up, tends to disappear or to become a merely idle class. Its representatives in our higher schools do not go in for professionalism but neither do they go in for culture; they are devoted to luxury and sport. And in comparison with the nominal concern of this class for the traditional liberal studies, and their actual lack of any intellectual interests, the assiduity and seriousness of students with professional aims stands out in a refreshing way. Large numbers who had neither opportunity, money nor motive for getting a higher education in the past now have the chance, the means and good hope of improving their careers by getting an education. The tradition behind them being by force of necessity that of industrial endeavor and achievement, it is natural that the same standards should persist for a generation or two at least. It is thus not practical or vocational education which is new; that has always been the only education received by the great mass of mankind. What is new is the opportunity to get this education somewhere else than in the home or shop and in some other manner than by indenture and by imitation of associates.

The rapid growth of professional tendencies and aims in higher education appears then to be the effect of the social and economic changes of the last century and a half. No such political and industrial dislocation could possibly occur without a great educational change. The decline of the traditional leisure class has given a shock to the studies and intellectual interests associated with it. The economic and political elevation of the masses has intensified the studies and interests which have been in the past the pre-occupation of the masses while it has also afforded facilities for realizing their practical ambitions.

Even if it could be proved that the present movement toward professionalism in education were historically inevitable, it would not follow that it is wholly desirable or admirable. But the placing of the movement in its historic setting shows that if there has been loss on one side there has been gain on the other. Large numbers of students may not be getting the most ideal education, but at all events they are getting some scientific training and intellectual outlook, while their ancestors only a few generations ago were not getting any higher schooling at all, and not much lower instruction. It is even possible that it is only in ratio that professional have gained so much upon liberal studies and that in absolute amount the latter have not appreciably lost.

But the chief value of the historic interpretation is, it seems to me, the ground it gives for believing, with some reasonable confidence, that present tendencies are transitory since they are the expression of a very rapid and recent social transition. It is natural, as was said, that newcomers to an intellectual and liberal tradition should bring with them their own old tradition. Since by necessity and through no fault of their own their background is mainly that of getting a secure livelihood and obtaining success in a career, why should not this aim be projected by them into education when they get a chance at it? Meantime there is some contact with intellectual pursuits and aims, some degree of reshaping of thought and purpose; and it may well be that a new and much more widely and solidly established tradition of culture is in process of development. The great universities of the Middle Ages in Europe were groups of professional schools, and yet it can not be doubted that they were largely the authors of the free artistic and intellectual movement that we call the Renaissance.

After all, the friends of liberal and so-called cultural studies are somewhat to blame for the existing state of affairs which they deplore. They have often made a cult out of culture, and treated it as a sacred and highly protected industry. Our ultimate faith must be in the intrinsic appeal which things of the mind make to the human mind when the mind is brought in contact with them. An imagination sensitive to things of intellectual value and a power of discriminating choice among the values that surroundings offer are the chief marks of the cultivated mind. Even if, at first, these traits are only secondary accompaniments of pursuit of knowledge and mental discipline for the sake of professional ends, yet if they are as worthy and delightful as we friends of culture think they are, even incidental acquaintance with them ought to breed a more whole-hearted interest and devotion, that is, from the training of the professional there ought to emerge the person who has all the interests of the amateur combined with the seriousness and trained skill of the professional.

I do not believe however that we should sit idly by and wait passively for this hope of a future transformation of professional tendencies to be realized. There are things that can be done to facilitate and hasten the process. I hesitate to call culture a by-product because the word might seem to insinuate that it is unimportant. But culture is not a specific and direct aim. As moralists have said that happiness is best attained by not aiming directly at it but by devotion to things that bring happiness in their train, so it is with culture. It is a fruit and reward of other activities. There is nothing in the subject-matter or method of professional studies that prevents them having this fruitage. It is a question after all of the spirit in which they are carried on. A school of law, medicine, engineering or theology that teaches only enough science to be a directly practical tool and teaches it only as a subordinate tool or device and not for the sake of insight into its principles will not be favorable to culture. But that is the fault of the spirit of the teaching and learning, not of the subjects taught or of the fact that useful application is ultimately to be made of the things learned. In other words, the more the scientific spirit of inquiry and love of thinking is introduced into professional teaching, the surer is broad and liberal intellectual interest and taste to be the product.

Again while professional studies have to be conducted with ultimate application in practice in view, this application may be to personal success, pecuniary and competitive, or it may be more widely social. There is a great difference in the attitude, for example, of the engineer who looks upon his special training as a means to the material success of himself or his employer, and the one who also sees in it a means of solving some of the most acute social problems of the present. In the degree in which the broad human factor enters in, culture is a consequence.

I think our friends in the professional schools will not take offense if we say that many of us who are engaged in non-professional fields of inquiry and teaching often feel some misgivings at present tendencies, and wonder whether because of these tendencies consideration of philosophy and history, and the natural and social sciences is going to suffer. Fundamentally we are coworkers. The more theoretical studies do not attain their highest development until they find some application in human life, contributing indirectly at least to human freedom and wellbeing, while the more practical studies can not reach their highest practicality save as they are animated by a disinterested spirit of inquiry. At present the current sets your way rather than ours, and time it did, you may think, in view of so much of the past of educational history. But in our common interest, we may ask that we join together to foster in any and every department of the university, interest in inquiry and liberal discussion and love of scientific thinking, that is of free and disinterested thinking. When all teaching whether labeled primarily liberal or professional has this love as its goal, we shall develop in our schools what may be called the amateur professional: the man and woman who unites the seriousness, unity of purpose and skill of the professional with the breadth and freedom of thought and desire characteristic of the amateur.

# 22

# THE PROSPECTS OF THE LIBERAL COLLEGE *

AMERICAN colleges call themselves colleges of Liberal Arts. The historic reason for this use of the word is familiar. In its literal signification liberal means free and it means generous. Aristotle fixed the terminology over two thousand years ago in its application to education.

To write, however, upon the liberal college in America and its prospects in narrow adherence to this point of view would be irrelevant, if not a cowardly evasion of burning issues. The old distinction between the vocational and the liberal, the professional and cultural has lost somewhat of its force as the distinction between the slave, the bond-serf and the free citizen has disappeared. Service is no longer a term of enslavement and reproach. Today the word liberal is applied to an educational institution to denote opposition to the reactionary and the ultraconservative, not to denote just preoccupation with intellectual and ideal matters. The word has taken on economic and political significance in connection with the human struggle for economic independence and political emancipation.

Such a quotation as follows perhaps indicates the issue that many persons associate with the problem of the liberal college: "Liberals know only too well that predatory wealth is determined to destroy every vestige of academic freedom in America." The question of the place and prospects of liberal institutions of higher learning in America is bound up in the public mind with economic and political affairs that are in the focus of heated and partisan strife. A wide space

* From *The Independent*, April 26, 1924.

divides these matters from the traditional academic definition of a liberal institution.

Yet, at the risk of being suspected of Laodicean indifference to burning issues, I am bound to say that I believe that
the base-line of discussion of current actual tendencies in
American education should be the ancient definition—interpreted out of abstract generalities so as to apply to present
conditions. Hospitality of mind, generous imagination,
trained capacity of discrimination, freedom from class, sectarian and partisan prejudice and passion, faith without
fanaticism:—these things are still rare, difficult to attain and
sorely needed. Indeed, in one respect the task of the liberal
college in creating these attitudes is harder today than ever
before.

The multiplication of the printed word has well-nigh
robbed words of meaning and deprived ideas of reality.
There never was a time when narrow class interests so self-
consciously arrayed themselves as public interests, and were
as virtuously indignant in reproving all ends and beliefs except their own; never a time when all causes clothed themselves so distractingly with idealistic phrases and emotions.
Modern education in its universal range is the child of
the printing press, but if it is to nurture the liberal
mind it must protect itself and us from other offspring of its
progenitor. Mankind was ever subject to passion, dogma,
self-interest, partisanship and propaganda. But these causes
have lost whatever frank, stout downrightness they once
possessed. They have acquired a muddled insincerity. These
things are now suspect when they offer themselves for what
they are, and hence seek all kinds of disguise. They find
entrance into the mind invested with a protective sheen of
loyalty, sanity and security, progress, or whatever ideals are
in fashion. To discriminate, to see things for what they are, to
maintain consistent poise for any length of time, is to go
against the current of show, of deteriorated standards, of
flashy novelties that sweep us away.

Therefore the problem of the liberal college is urgent, and

the consequences of success and failure in achieving it are momentous. It is bound up with sustaining in existence an intelligence both emancipated and generous, both critical and sympathetic. Its foes are many and powerful.

In almost all controversies both sides already possess fixed convictions upon whose solid and unshakeable nature they pride themselves. They have settled in advance just what studies and methods are liberal and what illiberal; they are not content to nurture the liberal mind and then trust it to do its own perceiving and form its own beliefs. It is held to be certain in advance just what beliefs a truly liberal mind will hold. It is therefore established that the way to create the liberal mind is to instill these beliefs. Quarrel concerns just what set of studies, what "curriculum," methods and beliefs are characteristic of the liberal mind, and are to be employed and inculcated. Now such direct effort to gain specific ends is itself proof of the operation of the illiberal mind.

One side confuses truly liberal education with what is so traditional that it may be safely called classic. Studies and methods that at some time in the past were associated with the culture of a gentleman are liberal studies, and all else is professional, technical, utilitarian. Freedom of mind is the result of discipline; and the studies that provide discipline and cultivate the liberal mind are the classical languages, mathematics and a suitably selected modicum of what is safest, most "fundamental" in modern literature, science and history. Immature and inexperienced minds exposed to strictly modern issues and problems without previous grounding in cherished fundamental subjects contract wild intellectual Bolshevisms which they mistake for liberty; a solemn reminder of the difference between liberty and license is in order.

Liberty, yes, but liberty under law. What law is does not need to be ascertained by a mind that has been freed; it is inscribed in the obvious constitution of things. And if liberty in consequence gets so far under law that it cannot lift its head and look about, the safer for all concerned, including the sacred interests of a truly liberal education. Now even supposing the adherents of this school were correct in their specific educational prescriptions, their spirit and method demonstrate nevertheless the failure of the education they recommend to produce the liberal mind. For their assurance of just what a liberal mind is and contains, just what will it do and believe, is the root of intellectual and moral illiberalism.

Unfortunately, however, the claims and assertions of the professedly liberal school in education are not always unlike those of their opponents. Perhaps the number of those is not large who honestly believe in a conspiracy of interlocking directorates, representing the deliberate purpose of "predatory wealth" to eliminate from colleges every trace of intellectual freedom. But the readiness with which every difficulty in collegiate personnel and administration which reaches the newspapers is adjudged to be a conflict between established economic interests and progressive ideas, suggests that many estimate liberal temper on the basis of preoccupation with contemporary social issues, and teaching "advanced" views about them. Thus the tenets of political and economic liberal faith are made the criterion of a liberal education and mind. And here also it may be stated that even if these views are sound, the mark of a liberal mind is not that they are held, but is the *way* in which they are reached and accepted.

These remarks indicate that obstacles to the development of the liberal college are not found primarily within the college. They lie rather in the temper of the American public. In spite of complaints about the academic isolation of higher education, the modern college is not a secluded monastery. The phrase "within college walls" is highly metaphorical today. The connection of the college with life is exhibited in every newspaper during the season of sports and at every alumni banquet, even though it is not flaunted on the printed pages that describe the offerings of the curriculum. Union of academic life with the life of the community is now so pervasive that it is as inept to impute the weaknesses of the former to some single particular cause, like deliberate economic pressure, as it is to ascribe to it superior virtues. Our college life shares in the defects and excellencies of our general life. Until this fact is clearly the point of departure in our discussions I do not think we shall arrive anywhere. In the degree in which our colleges are not liberal, it is because the spirit of the American communal scene is dense, given to both cocksureness and conformity, prone to sudden and short-time excitements, shifty, in love with immediate and showy success, addicted to a savage-like alternation between adoration of fetishes and whipping them.

I do not mean to imply that the hand of finance is not laid upon our colleges or that the weight of this hand is not depressing. It would be impossible for money, business and material success to occupy the place they do occupy in our national activities and scale of values, and education remain unaffected. But if we are to indulge in blame we should put the blame where it belongs, at the source. I am perfectly willing to concede that predatory wealth would be capable of carrying on a campaign to destroy intellectual freedom. But I also know that it does not need to do so, and that it is not so stupid as to undertake what is unnecessary. This remark is not so cynical as it may sound; it does not imply that there is no need, because there is no intellectual freedom to be suppressed. It signifies that enemies of a liberal temper of mind are so varied, so deeply engrained in affairs, and affect so many other matters than economic and political thinking, that undeniable occasional efforts of financial interests to discourage free investigation and criticism are after all but emphatic expressions of a common intellectual temper to whose existence they owe their efficacy.

It is difficult to write in this vein and not appear to be an apologist for the colleges, or perhaps even an apologist for predatory wealth. I trust that the discerning mind will realize, however, that a statement that college activities in administration, inquiry and teaching suffer and suffer deeply from the low esteem in which thinking is held by the community, and the high esteem in which belief as distinct from thought is held, is not exactly a defense. Nor is the statement that economic interests concerned for the perpetuation of their present power and influence derive their potency for evil interference in academic concerns from the same causes exactly an apologia. Such statements are an attempt to locate the source of the trouble, not an attempt to palliate. The utmost that will be said in apologetic mitigation respecting the colleges is that an academic experience of some forty years has convinced the present writer that, upon the whole, freedom of thinking and devotion to standards of intelligent thought are upon a distinctively higher level among the members of the teaching profession in colleges and universities than they are, group for group, in the general community; and that the larger institutions, popular belief to the contrary notwithstanding, are freer from the influence of interests and beliefs hostile to the independent life of reason, than are the smaller ones.

To make this assertion is not to claim a great deal. It would be shameful indeed if it were not true that the specially selected representatives of impartial thinking and communication of knowledge, maintained a wider and deeper allegiance to their professed cause than others. The criticism that they are not sufficiently the leaders of the community in behalf of their nominal cause is justified. This defect cannot be remedied by exhortation to greater independence and courage. It can be altered only by changing the causes which create subservience and timidity.

# 23

## THE LIBERAL COLLEGE AND ITS ENEMIES [*]

AMONG the extrinsic causes that make for subservience, timidity and illiberality in the American college I should place first the peculiar conditions under which higher education originated in the United States. For they were such as to create a closer bond between the colleges and the level of contemporary public opinion and sentiment than exists in the Old World. It is futile to institute comparisons, whether invidious or favorable, between American universities and those of Great Britain and the Continent. The latter have behind them a tradition reaching back hundreds of years: they have, for good and for evil, an independent status, dignity and momentum that our parvenu institutions do not and cannot have. Nor is the difference limited to the difference made by length of life and the cumulative tradition this long life has developed. European institutions were products of general social aristocratic conditions, and of a special intellectual élite. Until almost our own day, when the world is being progressively "Americanized," it would have been meaningless to talk about a general social responsibility in connection with English and Continental universities. Such social responsibility as they possessed was to Church and State, both of them also separate and seclusive, aristocratic, nstitutions. Even those who, like the present writer, believe that in the long run the more intimate connection of education and the common life will prove the better of the two systems are compelled to note that remoteness from common affairs has a protective value for a certain

[*] From *The Independent*, May 24, 1924.

kind of free intellectual life and has rendered possible the growth of independent standards of intellectual excellence. It was not without historic reason that Voltaire feared the "canaille" even more than he feared authorities of Church and State. The latter could annoy; the former might destroy. A more widespread social, or as we say "democratic," responsibility, of higher education means of necessity greater susceptibility to influences proceeding from the ordinary tone and level of beliefs. If leadership is to exist it must be by boring from within; it cannot be an aloof and detached leadership. Newspapers report that a canvass of one of our university faculties as to the six English words appraised as having greatest significance, concluded by nominating "loyalty" to pre-eminent position. Although the institution in question has a record of theological connection, God, freedom, immortality and the soul gave way to loyalty. If newspaper reports are to be trusted, it was not even deemed important to state to *what* objects loyalty should be given. That it should not be judged necessary in a university to specify loyalty to thought, inquiry and discriminating judgment says more than volumes of amplification could say. While I cannot join those who deplore the currency in education of the ideal of "service," it must be admitted that there is a deplorable absence of any statement as to *what* the colleges should serve, and just how it should serve. As long as these matters are left vague, or dressed up in conventional decorative garb, service is near to subservience, and loyalty to blind conformity.

Another cause of present limitations is found in the dependence of rapidly expanding institutions upon the good will of the public for financial support, and the popular conviction, accepted too tamely by scholars, that scholarship, like virtue, is its own reward. There may be some advantages in the fact that the pecuniary rewards of teaching and investigating are far below those which the same degree of ability and industry may procure in other callings. But a precarious economic status is not favorable to independence of thought and expression. A family to support is still a hostage given to fortune. Martyrdom was never fashionable, and its present vogue is well-nigh *nil*. Meantime, while the flow of funds into higher institutions of learning is immense, college administrators are subject to the influence of the American fetishes of size and expansion; and, speaking with some exaggeration, these latter interests always take precedence of that of rendering more secure free inquiry and teaching.

In a country which began with no provision for higher education, in which population is rapidly expanding and where wealth is growing and so diffused that the children of those who were themselves forbidden a college education are in a position to gratify ambition to "go to college," expansion is necessary. It is not necessary to allege conspiracy when it is discovered that members of college boards of trustees are largely men of wealth and that men of wealth are quite likely to be directors of corporations. It would be matter of surprise were it otherwise, where education is in process of constant expansion which requires constant increase and profitable investment of funds. The fact that boards of trustees do not confine their functions to the care of funds, leaving the cure of souls to the instructing body, is an historic accident, which none the less makes for a lowered standard of intellectual productivity—which it must always be remembered is synonymous with intellectual freedom.

The resulting limitations upon liberality of mind are less flagrant, crude, and direct than popular opinion supposes. The work is done indirectly, subtly. An institution that has a well-deserved reputation for jealous protection of academic freedom may in fact have its activities hedged in from inconvenient participation in troublesome social questions by a tradition of what is good form. Another institution, in which greater freedom is exercised, may be in the public eye as a conspicuous sinner against academic freedom simply because of a conjunction of locality and enterprising newspapers with greater independence from canons of good form on the part of its faculty.

In general, interference comes from supervising, officious faculty members who take aside a young man who shows signs of entering upon ice labeled "dangerous," and who warn him in the kindliest manner against anything which might damage his prospects. Contrary, again, to popular belief, infringements of this nature occur almost universally with younger men, not well known, whose career is still at stake, and they do not find their way into public print. Individually, they are slight and almost intangible; cumulatively their restrictive effect is considerable. A less selfish-appearing appeal is made on the ground of possible danger to the interests of the institution as a whole. Where the ideal of "loyalty" is as highly developed as it is in our society, this appeal, in spite of or because of its vagueness, has a deadening effect. If it is permissible to cite, without undue egotism, personal experience, I may say that the only case of either direct or indirect interference which I ever met, was when a university president with heartfelt personal interest told me that he should be sorry to have to report that I had prevented the university from securing an added endowment. And to avoid misapprehension, it should be said that the matter was administrative, and had no connection with any controverted religious, economic or social question.

Among the intrinsic causes which restrict intellectual liberality is the undue importance given to administrative activities, which then encroach upon the time and energy which should go to study and teaching. It is hard to say how much of this condition is an inevitable accompaniment of a period of expansion and of transition, and how much is due to our American worship of keeping busy, of organization and those modes of mechanical distraction which are unaccountably termed efficiency. But as long as chief prestige attaches in the American mind to outward signs of conspicuous activity rather than to scientific and artistic achievement, intellectual life will pay the price. Genuine intellectual activity occurs in the closet rather than on the house-top. But academic closets are pretty highly specialized and departmentalized affairs. Specialism is the vogue of the day in scholarship. While some degree of specialism is indispensable, in excess it contributes to decline of liberality of mind.

Paradoxically enough, a high degree of intellectual freedom in a narrow and technical line is in effect a restriction of intellectual freedom. A scholar deprived of a generous liberty in matters that touch religion, morals and social faiths, compensates for the loss by finding freedom within his library and laboratory, where as the *nouveau riche* said of his "study," in the illustration in *Punch,* what he does "is nothing to nobody." The point is delicate and not easy to grasp and state. But one may be reasonably sure that a cause for the aloofness of philosophy, and of the failure of the enormous achievements of modern science to make any serious impression upon general habits of thought and belief is that an unconscious protective reaction has led them into technical vocabularies and, except where discoveries have some obviously desirable practical application, into remote channels of effort. Till men are encouraged to theorize freely upon "practical" matters, there will endure a hateful division of theory and practice.

The other intrinsic cause of limitation to be mentioned is the uncertain state of the sciences or inquiries that deal with social matters. This condition is consequent upon their being so extremely new. History indeed is old, but it is undergoing transformation as a science and an art, a change which affects not merely special methods but the more important matter of perspective, of judgment of what is important and what unimportant. Many kinds of history, all kinds that are primarily antiquarian, are wholly "safe." An economic interpretation is both new and hazardous. Political economy, political science—it deals with realities and not with sacerdotal forms and rites,—social morals, social psychology, sociology, anthropology as the theory of human cultures, are newly forming disciplines. The old human dread and irritation in the presence of the new and unexplored still persists much more than most of us admit. In addition, these disciplines because they are still forming have of necessity much that is inchoate, tentative, unsettled. This estate lends them to ready contrast with the eternal truths of the time-tested creeds of the conservative. Youth needs, it is readily arguable, to be protected from their crudities and untested speculations until it shall have attained maturity—which means in effect till it shall have become so inculcated with the traditional folk-ways that it will be immune to the disturbing influence of a new idea. Add to this fact the other fact that investigators and teachers in these subjects, being human, may substitute dogmas for hypotheses, mistake propaganda for teaching, novelty for depth, and the very subjects that most need free inquiry and that may most readily excite intellectual interest in young people, become subject to a kind of perversion, influential in the measure of its vague intangibility.

To name causes for a state of affairs is not to excuse it. Things are justified or condemned by their consequences, not by their antecedents. To discover causes is to indicate the points at which endeavor is to be directed if the situation is to be changed. But the enormous task of liberating the American public mind and of securing for the American college its rightful place in assisting this liberation is only hampered by the prevalence of a scapegoat-and-devil complex. The present situation as to liberality of mind is not desirable either within or without the college and university. But it is no evidence of a liberal spirit to seek a simple and single force or two upon which may be unloaded the blame. The problem is interesting as well as difficult just because it is so complex, because it lays hold upon so many factors in our customs and habits. Since this article has dwelt by intent upon the unfavorable phases of the present situation, it is the more incumbent to add that in the opinion of the writer the situation has steadily improved and not grown worse in the last twenty-five years. Something of the acuteness of the problem at present is a sign of the development of a spirit which subjects to criticism things which in their kind were not long ago taken unconsciously for granted.

The greatest assurance of the prospects of further improvement of the status of the liberal college lies in the integrity of intelligence itself. Thinking makes way slowly, but as fast as it makes way, it gains momentum and accelerates its movement. The hope for the liberal mind and the liberal college is not in the spread of liberal beliefs, but the hope for the spread of liberal ideas is in the development of the liberal mind. The meaning of this perhaps obscure saying is illustrated in the undoubted growth of liberal if not radical opinion in all departments of the social disciplines in university teaching in the last twenty-five years. With a few exceptions, the teachers had no antecedent bias in that direction. They have not been moved by sympathy with practical agitators and propagandists. They have wished rather to exercise their minds fully upon the topics that presented themselves, and to follow up whatever significant clews they could find by which to understand social phenomena; they have gone whither the clews led. This frame of mind is what is meant by intellectual integrity. Intellectual standards have something self-protective and self-moving about them. And in spite of narrow specialization, conceit, and the other enemies within and without, intrinsic interest in thinking and inquiry, in their power to attract, hold and direct the mind of teacher and student, is, in the long run, the object of our liberal faith and hope.

In specific matters, the free mind is always being defeated, and its progress always being arrested. Yet history reveals that it moves on, and that its enemies of a few centuries ago are now obscure and shadowy figures, objects of contempt even by its foes of today. If the fight of today were between conservative reactionaries on one side and those of liberal faith on the other, I should be skeptical about the chances of the latter and of the liberal college. But the fight is not really at that point. It is between the reactionary and the method and spirit of scientific method, the interest in the full play of the human mind. Faith in the continuous triumphing of the latter is not due to a "Messianic complex." The faith is grounded in the history of the last few centuries, when there have been overcome enemies much more deeply entrenched in custom, in ecclesiastic, economic and political institutions than are the present foes of the liberal mind. It is confirmed by the fact that whatever is gained by intelligence at once is consolidated for further use. It alone persists. It alone corresponds with the actual movement of things, and thus opens the road for further activity. Vested prejudices, class interests are deeply rooted, but not as deeply rooted in the nature of things as the joy of discovery and of communication.

If the growth of the free mind to fullness of stature and social recognition was to have been prevented, it should have been strangled at birth. It is now too late. Hostile influences may and will deflect and retard its progress. Individuals will be annoyed and suffer harm. But the spirit of thought and inquiry will never be beaten by weapons of flesh and blood. If reactionaries knew the force against which they were fighting they would desist. As it is, I fancy that their attack adds subtlety, vigor and grace to the free movements of the human spirit. Our deliberations close, then, as they began, with the conviction that the hope and dependence of the liberal college lie in the growth of the free mind and the perfecting of standards of thought and inquiry. These things, rather than the spread of liberal opinions in politics and economics, are its ground and guarantee. If progress is slow it is because we are constantly putting effects before the cause and thereby defeating ourselves.

# THE DIRECTION OF EDUCATION *

**D**OUBTLESS many have been embarrassed in meeting questions put by European visitors concerning the school system of the United States. Foreign students who carry in their minds the systems with which they are familiar and who naturally employ this knowledge as a standard of judgment are perplexed when confronted with American educational institutions. They inquire into our system and they find from their standpoint no system at all but what strikes them as chaos. In one part of the country they find townships almost a law to themselves, and learn that even fractions of civil units called districts enjoy an almost complete educational autonomy. In other regions, they learn that counties are the units of organization; and that while in a few states the state itself exercises considerable regulative and supervisory authority, this authority manifests great diversity in actual operation. While all states lay down certain regulations as to minimum requirements for the length of the school year, certification of teachers, character of school buildings and subjects to be taught, there is often little attention paid to any close supervision that sees to it that these regulations are locally enforced. Actual control is mainly exercised by custom. And of a national system, as they understand it, the visitor finds not more than a trace. Instead of a minister in the national cabinet clothed with the powers every European state takes for granted, he finds hardly more than a clerical bureau gathering and distrib-

---

* Address delivered on the occasion of the installation of Dean William Fletcher Russell, Teachers College, Columbia University, April 10, 1928. From *School and Society*, April 28, 1928.

uting information, but without administrative authority.

I have referred to these familiar facts to place before you the background of the development of American education and to suggest the way in which that development has been attained. For there has been a growth; there is a record of accomplishment. No one is wholly satisfied, least of all such an audience as is here represented. But nevertheless things have happened educationally in spite of the lack of official leadership and regulation. Where has direction of the movement come from? There is of course but one alternative to official or state direction: voluntary and personal leadership, internal ferment and contagion. What has been done has been largely done by inspiration and stimulation issuing from individuals and from educational centers not clothed with authority to impose on the schools their ideas and ideals. Education has been mainly promoted by the processes of education rather than by state administration. Ideas have been communicated by word of mouth, by periodicals, by books and by observation of the efforts and results of other teachers. New ideas and practices in the field of administration, methods of instruction or subjects of study have spread rather than been enacted and instituted. The spreading has taken place by the same sort of contact, radiation, infiltration and contagion that changes social habits and beliefs in other fields that do not fall within any governmental regulation.

I am not here to make a comparison of the respective merits of the two systems, or, if you please, of system and lack of system, much less to glorify the method which we have for the most part unconsciously adopted because it corresponds to the conditions of our social life. I have introduced the contrast only by way of calling attention to the intellectual and moral responsibilities that are necessarily involved in our accepted procedure. Exemption of political government and officials from responsibilities that are elsewhere incumbent upon them places corresponding responsibilities upon individuals and institutions. With all our drifting, there must be leadership somewhere, or absence of governmental system will signify lack of all unified and co-operative educational movement. But leadership that is not official can only be intellectual and moral leadership. It is not merely leadership *in* education but it is leadership *by* education rather than by law and governmental authority. Indeed, it is a kind of leadership that gives a new meaning to the word. It is a process of guidance. It takes effect through inspiration, stimulation, communication of ideas, discovery and report of facts, rather than by decree. It is compelled to trust for the most part to the power of facts and ideas and to the willingness of the community at large to receive and act upon them.

Numbers make an institution big but not great; what has made Teachers College great has been its firm grasp upon an idea, the perception of the public need for educational guidance, and its devotion to the fulfillment of this need.

To enumerate the various fields in which Teachers College has pointed the way to educational advance and directed practical movements to their realization would be like calling the roll of its departments. For when an educational need has shown itself, this institution has answered "Here." A random mention of a few movements to which Teachers College has lent its powerful support and some of which it may be said to have originated will suffice to indicate the quality and scope of the intellectual and moral service it has rendered in lending direction to American education. There come to mind the development of measurements and tests; the project method; school surveys and study of administration; the transformation of kindergarten theory and practice; the nursery school and the scientific study of pre-school children; domestic science and art and the placing of education of nurses on a more dignified and self-respecting, because more intellectually responsible, plane; contributions to industrial training and vocational guidance; to rural schools; Americanization through education, religious education; to international phases of education.

The things mentioned are not spoken of by way of mere congratulation, but as indications of the way in which an educational institution can give voluntary and unofficial direction to an otherwise confused and dispersive scene.

Although no one a generation ago could have possibly predicted the development of the last thirty years, it is not too much to say that the work is only in its initial stage. Certain things have been demonstrated. It has been proved that education is a proper field for scientific research; that it ranks with any subject as a proper and richly rewarding topic for university study; it has been redeemed from the academic contempt that so long was felt toward pedagogy; especially has its fruitfulness been demonstrated as a means of correlating a vast variety of specialized topics and interests, scientific and social, so as to bring them into vital unity in a human and humane perspective. The training of teachers is no longer a mere matter of equipping students having a somewhat inadequate prior intellectual preparation with the means by which to deal with the immediate problems of the schoolroom. The simple discovery that education is first of all a problem for study, for investigation and research, and a problem so complex and diversified as to demand prolonged and thorough training, marks in itself almost a revolutionary departure from the older attitude.

Indeed, I should be willing to say that this discovery is that which gives Teachers College its distinction. Important as are all the special contributions that have been alluded to, the recognition of the necessity of regarding education in all its phases as an intellectual problem, a philosophical and scientific problem, is the most important. For the attitude contained in this recognition has been the inspiration of these movements and the source of their directive value.

The idea that activities like medicine and agriculture are proper fields for scientific exploration and that they can prosper only when conducted upon the basis of the conclusions of patient and prolonged inquiry has pretty well made its way into popular consciousness. I do not think a similar statement can be made as yet regarding education. The air is full of glittering generalities and of sentimental appreciation of its supreme importance, but not of steady and definite realization of its significance as an intellectually grounded art. This fact is natural. Education is the most complex, intricate and subtle of all human enterprises. Its intellectual emancipation and elevation was compelled to wait until other inquiries and sciences, physical, mathematical even, as well as social and psychological, had developed to the point where they could make their contributions. In consequence, the art of education will be the last of the arts to come into its own scientifically.

The pioneering stage of this great idea is not past. This fact is an inspiration, for this stage in any subject is that of greatest ardor and utmost devotion.

# 25

# GENERAL PRINCIPLES OF EDUCATIONAL ARTICULATION *

THERE are two ways of approaching the problem of elimination of waste in the educative processes of the schools. One is the administrative. This takes the existing system as a going concern, and inquires into the breaks and overlappings that make for maladjustment and inefficient expenditure of time and energy on the part of both pupil and teacher—useless and therefore harmful mental motions, harmful and not merely useless because they set up bad habits. The other may be called personal, psychological or moral. By these adjectives is meant that the method starts from the side of personal growth of individual needs and capacities, and asks what school organization is best calculated to secure continuity and efficiency of development. It sets out from the side of pupils and asks how the successive stages of the school system should be arranged so that there shall be a minimum ˙f blocks, arrests, sudden switches and gaps, futile repet˙ᴬons and duplications, as the children and youth pass from one state to another, from kindergarten to elementary, from this to high school, from the latter to college, etc.

This statement of two modes of approach does not imply that there is a necessary opposition between the two. They should be complementary. What is common to both is that each looks at the educational system as a whole and views each part with respect to what it does in making education really a whole, and not merely a juxtaposition of mechan-

* Address before the general session, Department of Superintendence, Cleveland, February 26, 1929. From *School and Society,* March 30, 1929.

ically separated parts. Each avenue of approach is equally concerned to eliminate isolations and render the function of each part effective with respect to the others. There is no more necessary opposition between the two than there is when engineers in tunneling a mountain bore from opposite ends. Before they start work, the tunnel must be considered as a single thing and the work done from either end must be thought out and undertaken with reference to examination of the entire project. But a preliminary intellectual survey of the whole is necessary to make the two modes of approach meet at a center.

When the consideration of the problem is undertaken from either side without regard to the considerations which necessarily exist at the other side, there are dangers and evils that can not be avoided. Thus an approach from the exclusively personal side will overlook certain administrative necessities that seem to be inherent in the situation. An important consideration here is pointed out in the general introductory report of the commission. The area of the region drawn upon and the different numbers of children and youth who go to school in the elementary and higher grades must be considered. Younger children as a rule must be in buildings nearer their own homes, and because of their greater number there must be a certain amount of physical segregation from older pupils. Moreover, for the older pupils there must be a greater variety of courses, differentiation of teachers and amount of equipment. These facts demand a large number of pupils in the high school and this in turn demands that they be drawn from a wide area. Hence consideration from the personal development side must take into account administrative necessities.

Consideration of the latter must, however, be checked at every point by taking into account the conditions that make for effective mental and moral growth of individuals as individuals. Undue attention to the administrative side tends toward "rationalization" of the divisions that happen at a given time to be institutionalized. Reasons are found which justify their continued existence as more or less independent units. Then the problem of articulation becomes an external one, that of smooth transitions from one to another and getting rid of the more obvious sources of friction. This is a gain as far as it goes, but it does not go far enough to touch the basic matter of securing adequate and complete personal growth. In consequence of this external approach, there will be a tendency to assume that mental and moral growth is marked by "epochs" which correspond, at least roughly, to the isolated units of the school system. The fact that interests and capacities change with age is undeniable; that the boy and girl of sixteen differ markedly from those of twelve, and those of the latter age from those of eight and the latter, in turn, from those of five and six is too evident to escape notice. But the underlying problem is whether the changes occur gradually and almost insensibly or by sharply marked off leaps which correspond to the conventional institutional school divisions. This is a question which must be investigated and the answer found by independent study of the facts of development in individuals. The need of this independent inquiry as a check and test is the more acute because the divisions that exist among school units react upon personal development. Hence it is in consequence easy to assume that changes in personal growth are inherent, when in fact they may be the relatively artificial products of the existing school divisions and in so far abnormal and undesirable.

For this reason the study of the best methods of articulation can not be complete without a comparative study of schools in which division into units is minimized; that is, so-called unified schools in which children of different ages, from primary to high school, are found together and wherein there is no administrative break between junior and senior years in the high schools. Only by such a comparative study can the elements, if any, that are artificial and conventional in the schools where units are emphasized be detected. This statement does not contradict what was said earlier about the problems of area of distribution and the need of increased variety of courses and equipment in higher grades. For, in the first place, cities vary greatly in population and there may be median range of size to which the unified school is well adapted. In the second place, the results of comparative inquiry would throw light upon the methods of organization to be adopted in the schools of towns of such a large size that the unified system can not be literally adopted. For there is a question of limits, and educators can work in either of two directions, toward opposite poles —either to that of independent units, or to the maximum possible of relative unification of the assembling of pupils— without carrying either principle to its logical extreme. This consideration seems to me to be fundamental in the whole problem of articulation. Mere convenience of administration should not be permitted to override it.

It is recognized that *adequate* treatment of the fundamental problem here—the mutually complementary character of the administrative and the moral psychological development of individuals—must wait upon command of greater knowledge of the actual process of normal growth than anybody now possesses. Nevertheless, reference to the latter is important, for it indicates, in the first place, the necessity of continued study of personal growth as an inherent factor in the problem of articulation from the administrative side. And in the second place, it serves as a warning, a caveat. It cautions us against a too ready assumption that the present institutional division into separate units has necessary inherent value on account of corresponding "epochs" of personal development. It warns us against attaching too great value, decisive value, to matters of administrative habit and inertia. A complete examination of the question of articulation can be attained only when the experiences of classroom teachers in immediate contact with pupils are procured and utilized, as well as the experiences of administrators. This statement does not signify that principals and superintendents in their reports do not take advantage of the experiences gained in actual classroom work, much less that there is any antagonism between the point of view of classroom teachers and of administrators. It is, however, a reminder that specialized experience always creates a one-sided emphasis, in habits of thought as well as of outward action, and always needs to be checked. There is much evidence in the various reports of the extent to which conference and exchange of reports and information already obtain as necessary methods of avoiding unduly sharp breaks in subject-matter and methods and harmful repetitions. What I am pleading for is a more direct obtaining of data on the whole subject of continuity of personal development from classroom teachers, and a *direct* inclusion of such reports in the gathering and interpretation of material along with those of superintendents and supervisors and principals. The findings of experimental and progressive schools must also be included, not as models, but as providing data regarding processes of personal development under different conditions.

Conceding that we have not *adequate* knowledge of the course of mental development in individuals, I propose now to consider the bearing of what is available in this respect upon the general problem of articulation. I begin with a statement which is so general that it can hardly arouse dissent. The ideal is that the achievements at any one period of growth be the tools, the agencies and instrumentalities, of further growth. The statement is not one that refers simply to the transition from one unit to another. It is of constant application. That is, whatever the pupils gain at any period, whether in skill or knowledge, should be promptly funded into something actively employed in gaining new skill and knowledge. A new level of intellectual achievement should mark off each successive month and week of school life, and not be thought of as occurring only in the transition from one unit to another. The bearing of this principle upon the specific problems of articulation which the various reports of the commission bring out may be postponed until another basic principle has been stated.

The idea of ripening, maturing, is evidently fundamental in the question of individual growth. Now what needs to be especially borne in mind with reference to maturing is that it is plural, that is, various powers and interests mature at very different rates. Maturing is a continuous process; the mature fruit may appear, as with fruits on a tree, only at some later stage, even if we assume, which it is probably wrong to do, that there is any such completely matured fruit in the case of a person as in that of a plant. But the normal maturing as a process goes on all the time; if it does not there is something the matter with conditions. Arrest of growth and incapacities to cope with subject-matter and inabilities to respond to methods employed at a later period are all of them always signs of something wrong. They need to be studied as symptoms and be diagnosed with a view to constructive remedies.

Since maturing is a continuous process and also a plural one, it is not a uniform four-abreast thing. One has only to observe a baby to note how one ability ripens before another, the ability to fixate objects with the eye, to grasp, to sit up, to creep, to walk, to talk, etc., and how each operation as it matures is utilized as a factor in bringing about some maturing of another ability and adaptation. No parent ever makes the mistake of overlooking this plural nature of maturing. When we come to schooling, however, I wonder if there is not too much of a tendency to assume an equal, uniform, four-abreast maturing, and if that does not underlie the conception of "epochs" of growth which correspond to various units of the school system. If the assumption is not made in a positive form, it is made in a negative way, that is, by overlooking the specific needs and capacities that are ripening, or that may ripen, during each year and month of school life. It is this neglect which is responsible for the idea that each stage is merely preparation for some later stage, particularly that the aim of the early years of the elementary school is chiefly the purpose of gaining social tools to be independently employed and enjoyed later on.

I am always surprised and disturbed when I find persons who insist that the high school must not be dominated by the idea of college preparation ready to assume as a matter of course that the first two or three primary years must have as their main purpose the securing of "social tools" for later use, instead of being devoted to gaining those experiences which are appropriate to the powers that are ripening at the time. I must express my profound dissent from the position that sets up a dualism between the actual experience of children in the early years and the requirements imposed and dictated by the needs of later school years.

At this point, the two principles laid down cease to be innocuous generalities. The way to get possession and command of a tool for later use is by having the experiences proper to the immediate time—experiences which awaken new needs and opportunities and which, just because they are achievements, matured developments, form the natural agencies or tools for later activities. Any theory which sets out by denying that this is possible so misstates the problem of articulation that its "solution" is bound to be defective. Unless powers as they ripen are put to immediate use in acquiring new knowledge and skill, tools are not shaped for later use. The real problem is not one of early maturing for a fruitage to come in a later unit. It is, from the side of earlier years, the problem of discovering those particular needs, interests and capacities which are ripening, not attempting a premature introduction and forcing of others; and then of finding that use and application of them which passes insensibly into the ripening of other more complex tendencies. From the side of later years, it is the same problem, with the added factor of adjusting subject-matter and methods so that the powers already relatively ripened shall be used in developing new powers that are showing themselves. Only in this way can the maximum of continuous growth be secured and an internal rather than mechanical articulation be secured.

The point and force of the two principles laid down is

found in their concrete application. I propose, accordingly, to consider some phases of isolation and waste, of non-articulation, in their light.

In the first place, they suggest that reasonable integration within the school can not be secured by limiting the problem to what goes on in the school. The fundamental problem of articulation takes us outside the school to articulation of its activities with the out-of-school experience of the pupils. It is for this reason, of course, that the problem of curriculum is so fundamental; to articulate successive phases of subject-matter with one another there must be an articulation of the curriculum with the broadening range of experiences had at home, in the neighborhood and community. This principle applies at the beginning and all the way through. I remember hearing an intelligent parent complain that kindergarten teachers seemed to assume that children came to them blanks, and treated them as if everything had to begin afresh, thereby boring children with things they could already do and were familiar with, and failing to utilize the capital they had already acquired. This complaint was made over thirty years ago; doubtless cause for it no longer exists. But it is typical of what is meant by the present point. Except for highly specialized matters, the ripening of powers does not go on exclusively nor mainly in school. This fact gives great significance to matters contained in the various reports which at first sight are remote from the question of school articulation: matters of health, nutrition, regularity of attendance, home life, reading and occupations out of school, economic status of parents and children, as well as the general changing demands of a rapidly changing civilization. But it extends to the whole matter of utilizing in school the experiences gained in school.

More specific points are involved in the application of the two principles. One of these is the principle of alternate concentration and remission of work in special lines. While great improvements have taken place, there is still an undue tendency to a uniform four-abreast treatment of the subjects that make up the school program. Certain studies tend to appear in every month and in every year of a school program. There is need for flexible experimentation in periods of intensive concentration upon such things as reading and number work in the elementary grades, followed by periods of relaxation in which achievements gained are capitalized in concentration upon other studies. The same principle applies to history, geography, nature study and science. Each might be made for a time the relative center with subordination of other factors. The effect would be to disclose better than does the uniform method special aptitudes and weaknesses, and would, I think, greatly minimize the breaks that now come with change of pupils to a new year and new unit.

Other difficulties in the present situation arise, I believe, from the isolation that comes from the confining of teachers to single years. The pupils are the only ones who come into direct contact with the whole process. Artificial breaks, sudden introduction of new demands and new methods of discipline, teaching of new kinds of subjects, duplications and need of review of subjects already supposedly mastered are the result. They are in large measure due, I think, to the isolation of the teacher resulting from too exclusive confinement to a single year. Articulation is secured only as, at each stage of the school system, pupils' activities are directed in reference to a continuing wholeness of growth. One year is too short a span in which to survey the process of growth. Much has been done, as appears from the reports in exchange of records and data, and in joint committees to form the curriculum; unified supervision helps. But these things do not cover the whole situation. There are administrative difficulties attending transfers of teachers from one grade to another, or in having a teacher give instruction during the same year in more than one grade. But I do not believe that, without a greater use of these methods, teachers can get that real appreciation of continuity of school movement which will enable them to secure articulation from within.

One aspect of this matter involves the question of having younger children in contact with more than one teacher. I recognize the objections dealing with departmentalization in the elementary grades. But these objections have to be offset not only against the point already made regarding the need of intimate acquaintance on the part of the teacher with children at different stages of development, but against the evils of the conditioning of a child to the habits and methods of a single person, and against the fact, frequently noted, of the friction that arises when the pupils enter a unit in which departmental teaching does exist. It does not follow, because departmental teaching can easily be overdone in the early grades, that children may not profitably get used to more than one teacher even in the first grade. It is a concrete question of proportioning. Nor does it follow that in high schools teaching should be rigidly departmentalized. We need a little more "give" at both ends. Still less does it follow that departmentalized teaching in high schools should be confined to a teacher having many sections of algebra or geometry or physiography in only one year of the school. Genuine correlation or integration and genuine continuity of articulation may depend upon a teacher having more than one topic and in teaching a subject through more than one year. As Ella Flagg Young used to remind teachers many years ago, what often passes for departmentalization is in reality only a subdivision of labor such as obtains in a factory where each worker is confined to making a part of a shoe, which part is then passed on to the next worker.

Another point frequently mentioned is connected with the last two. Attention is called to the difficulties arising from the fact that teachers in training often specialize on some one phase or unit, to the neglect of knowledge of the system as a whole. It would seem to follow that all teachers in training should have at least one thorough course to familiarize them with the system in its entirety, with special reference to the place, in the whole, of that part of the system for which they are specially preparing. If this were a regular procedure, it is possible that the reluctance of teachers to change from one grade or one unit to another might give way to desire for a broader experience. In connection with the training of teachers there are so many problems relevant to the issue of articulation that it is possible to select only one.

Graduate schools of universities are in a large measure training schools for teachers in colleges and in an increasing degree in high schools. Through instruction given to those in colleges who go out to teach in high schools there is, in any case, a reaction into high-school teaching. These conditions account in large measure for the gaps and maladjustments frequently referred to in articulation of senior high schools with the junior, and in general of high schools with upper elementary grades. I allude, of course, to the distinction often drawn between greater attention to development of pupils on one side and to subject-matter as such on the other. I must content myself with calling attention to the problem; no survey of the causes of bad articulation is complete that does not take into account the influence, direct and indirect, of the training of future teachers in graduate schools of universities. It is a phase of the old question of the isolation of normal schools from colleges with the greater emphasis of one upon method and of the other upon subject-matter. Although the problem is not as acute as it used to be, since there has been reapproachment from both sides, it is still a factor not to be neglected.

Time permits only of these few selected illustrations of some of the meanings contained in the two general principles when they are applied. I conclude by recurring to the original statement of the problem: that of co-ordinating the administrative approach with the psychological-moral approach through personal development. It makes a great difference how we take up the problem of articulation. If we accept too readily any existing distribution of units as even rela-

tively fixed, I am skeptical of any solutions being found
which do more than eliminate some of the more striking
cases of external friction. It is a natural trait of the human
mind to "rationalize" what exists—that is, to find adventitious
reasons that justify what is found. We should, it seems to
me, view the problem of articulation as one of *differentiation.*
The metaphor of organic growth is helpful if not pressed
too literally. The problem of co-ordinated physiological
growth is not one of co-ordinating bones, muscles, lungs and
stomach, etc., together: not until mal-co-ordinations have
been established does the latter problem arise. There is gradual differentiation of different organs and functions, each
co-operating with the others.

Analogy fails with educational process of growth because
the former takes place so largely intrinsically, requiring from
without only provision of normal conditions. In education
there is no such inherent internal development; direction
by means of provision of suitable environment, of both
things and personal associations, is relatively more important. But the problem of such external guidance may still
be conceived as one of bringing about differentiation in a
consecutive way. The meaning of this general statement can
be only briefly illustrated. For this purpose I select once
more a portion of the introduction of the commission which
in its implications appears to diverge from the principle.
I refer to the contrast which is set forth between the earlier
years and later with reference to docility of a passive type
and personal independence and individualistic initiation in
the latter, and the conclusions about legitimate separation
of units drawn from the alleged fact. The statements seem
to overlook several facts, such as that well known to parents,
the fact called "contrary suggestion" in very early years:
the fact that development in the school years comes through
activities, and also the adoption of the method of socialized
activities in the kindergarten. Receptivity and assertive activity are *constant* functions. What differs with different
stages of growth is the range of exercise and the fields in

which they are exercised. Because a child of six or seven can not assume the same active responsibilities that he can when he is eight or nine does not mean that some field for its exercise is not available at the earlier age nor that it is not an indispensable factor in normal development. The problem is to find the particular ripening activities which are operative. To generalize wholesale from the regions in which the capacity does not exist, and infer from them that the willingness of children to accept what is put over on them "dictates" certain subject-matters at that period, is to fail to prepare pupils for greater independence in other fields later, and thus puts a premium upon excessive "individualism" later. The problem is one of constant differentiation of powers of independent action through prior utilization of those which already exist. A normal differentiation will create in pupils a willingness to recognize later on their need of guidance and receptivity in respects in which they are not developed to the point of independence, and thus reduce an abrupt and undesirable "individualism."

The example is taken from a limited field, but it applies throughout. At each stage the pupil, whether in elementary grades, junior high school or college, has a certain region of experience in which he is relatively at home and has certain tendencies which are relatively mature. Attention to these things as the agencies to be connected with in securing new powers of independent and responsible action in wider fields of experience gives the key to a continuous process of differentiation which will place the problem of articulation in its proper light.

# 26

## HOW MUCH FREEDOM IN NEW SCHOOLS? *

I T IS not easy to take stock of the achievements of progressive schools in the last decade: these schools are too diverse both in aims and in mode of conduct. In one respect,
this is as it should be: it indicates that there is no cut-and-
dried program to follow, that schools are free to grow along
the lines of special needs and conditions and so to express
the variant ideas of innovating leaders. But there is more
than is suggested by these considerations in the existing
diversity. It testifies also to the fact that the underlying motivation is so largely a reaction against the traditional school
that the watchwords of the progressive movement are capable of being translated into inconsistent practices.

The negative aspect of progressive education results from
the conditions of its origin. Progressive schools are usually
initiated by parents who are dissatisfied with existing schools
and find teachers who agree with them. Often they express
discontent with traditional education or locally available
schools without embodying any well-thought-out policies and
aims. They are symptoms of reaction against formalism and
mass regimentation; they are manifestations of a desire for
an education at once freer and richer. In extreme cases they
represent enthusiasm much more than understanding.

Their common creed is the belief in freedom, in esthetic
enjoyment and artistic expression, in opportunity for individual development, and in learning through activity rather
than by passive absorption. Such aims give progressive
schools a certain community of spirit and atmosphere. But
they do not determine any common procedure in discipline

° From *The New Republic*, July 9, 1930.

or instruction; they do not fix the subject matter to be taught; they do not decide whether the emphasis shall be upon science, history, the fine arts, different modes of industrial art, or social issues and questions. Hence the diversity of the progressive schools, and hence the great difficulty in appraising them. Adverse criticisms may be readily and often effectively answered on the ground that they do not apply to specific schools.

Strong and weak points go together; every human institution has the defects of its qualities. Colonel Francis W. Parker, more nearly than any other one person, was the father of the progressive educational movement, a fact all the more significant because he spent most of his educational life in public rather than private schools—first at Quincy, Massachusetts, and then at the Cook County Normal School in Englewood, Chicago. I do not know whether he used the phrase which has since come into vogue, "child-centered schools." One of his most frequent statements was that teachers had been teaching *subjects* when they should be teaching *children*. He engaged in aggressive warfare against the burden of ready-made, desiccated subject matter formulated and arranged from the adult point of view—in other words, against the stock in trade of the conventional curriculum. He pleaded for subject matter nearer to the experience and life of the pupils. He strove to throw off the yoke of fixed and uniform disciplinary measures. He introduced many things, innovations in his day, which are now almost commonplaces in the public schools which lay any claim to being modern —for example, the school assemblies conducted by the pupils themselves.

Even such an inadequate statement as the foregoing brings out an antithesis which has persisted to a considerable extent in the later movement of progressive education: that between the human and personal element represented by the pupils, the children, youth, and, on the other hand, the impersonal and objective factor—the subject matter of studies, the body of knowledge and organized and skilled accomplishment. In saying that the antithesis thus set up has resulted, upon the whole, in a lack of balance, I do not mean in any way to hold the work and influence of Colonel Parker responsible. I mean that the same reaction against dead, formal and external studies which affected his early reforms has continued to operate with his successors, and to produce a one-sided emphasis—that upon pupils at the expense of subject matter.

That there was need for the reaction, indeed for a revolt, seems to me unquestionable. The evils of the traditional, conventional school room, its almost complete isolation from actual life, and the deadly depression of mind which the weight of formal material caused, all cried out for reform. But rebellion against formal studies and lessons can be effectively completed only through the development of a new subject matter, as well organized as was the old—indeed, better organized in any vital sense of the word organization —but having an intimate and developing relation to the experience of those in school. The relative failure to accomplish this result indicates the one-sidedness of the idea of the "child-centered" school.

I do not mean, of course, that education does not center in the pupil. It obviously takes its start with him and terminates in him. But the child is not something isolated; he does not live inside himself, but in a world of nature and man. His experience is not complete in his impulses and emotions; these must reach out into a world of objects and persons. And until an experience has become relatively mature, the impulses do not even know what they are reaching out toward and for; they are blind and inchoate. To fail to assure them guidance and direction is not merely to permit them to operate in a blind and spasmodic fashion, but it promotes the formation of *habits* of immature, undeveloped and egoistic activity. Guidance and direction mean that the impulses and desires take effect through material that is impersonal and objective. And this subject matter can be provided in a way which will obtain ordered and consecutive development of experience only by means of the thoughtful selection and organization of material by those having the broadest experience—those who treat impulses and inchoate desires and plans as potentialities of growth through inter-action and not as finalities.

To be truly self-centered is not to be centered in one's feelings and desires. Such a center means dissipation, and the ultimate destruction of any center whatever. Nor does it mean to be egoistically bent on the fulfillment of personal wishes and ambitions. It means rather to have a rich field of social and natural relations, which are at first external to the self, but now incorporated into personal experience so that they give it weight, balance and order. In some progressive schools the fear of adult imposition has become a veritable phobia. When the fear is analyzed, it means simply a pref-erence for an immature and undeveloped experience over a ripened and thoughtful one; it erects into a standard some-thing which by its nature provides no steady measure or tested criterion. An adult cannot attain an integrated per-sonality except by incorporating into himself the realities of the life-situations in which he finds himself. This operation is certainly even more necessary for the young; what is called "subject matter" represents simply the selected and organized material that is relevant to such incorporation at any given time. The neglect of it means arrest of growth at an im-mature level and ultimate disintegration of selfhood.

It is, of course, difficult to use words that are not open to misapprehension. There may be those who think that I am making a plea for return to some kind of adult imposition, or at least to readymade and rather rigidly predetermined topics and sequences of study. But in fact many of the cur-rent interpretations of the child-centered school, of pupil initiative and pupil-purposing and planning, suffer from ex-actly the same fallacy as the adult-imposition method of the traditional school—only in an inverted form. That is, they are still obsessed by the personal factor; they conceive of no alternative to adult dictation save child dictation. What is wanted is to get away from every mode of personal dictation and merely personal control. When the emphasis falls upon having experiences that are educationally worth while, the center of gravity shifts from the personal factor, and is found within the developing experience in which pupils and teachers alike participate. The teacher, because of greater maturity and wider knowledge, is the natural leader in the shared activity, and is naturally accepted as such. The fundamental thing is to find the types of experience that are worth having, not merely for the moment, but because of what they lead to—the questions they raise, the problems they create, the demands for new information they suggest, the activities they invoke, the larger and expanding fields into which they continuously open.

In criticizing the progressive schools, as I have indicated already, it is difficult to make sweeping generalizations. But some of these schools indulge pupils in unrestrained freedom of action and speech, of manners and lack of manners. Schools farthest to the left (and there are many parents who share the fallacy) carry the thing they call freedom nearly to the point of anarchy. This license, however—this outer freedom in action—is but an included part of the larger question just touched upon. When there is genuine control and direction of experiences that are intrinsically worth while by objective subject matter, excessive liberty of outward action will also be naturally regulated. Ultimately it is the absence of intellectual control through significant subject matter which stimulates the deplorable egotism, cockiness, impertinence and disregard for the rights of others apparently considered by some persons to be the inevitable accompaniment, if not the essence, of freedom.

The fact that even the most extreme of the progressive schools do obtain for their pupils a degree of mental independence and power which stands them in good stead when they go to schools where formal methods prevail, is evidence of what might be done if the emphasis were put upon the rational freedom which is the fruit of objective knowledge and understanding. And thus we are brought to the nub of the matter. To conduct a progressive school is much more difficult than to conduct a formal one. Standards, materials, methods are already at hand for the latter; the teacher needs only to follow and conform. Upon the whole, it is not surprising that, in history, science, the arts and other school "studies," there is still a lack of subject matter which has been organized upon the basis of connection with the pupils' own growth in insight and power. The time-span of progressive schools has been too short to permit very much to be accomplished. What may rightfully be demanded, however, is that the progressive schools recognize their responsibility for accomplishing this task, so as not to be content with casual improvisation and living intellectually from hand to mouth.

Again one needs to guard against misunderstanding. There is no single body of subject matter which can be worked out, even in the course of years, which will be applicable all over the country. I am not arguing for any such outcome; I know of nothing that would so completely kill progressive schools and turn them into another kind of formal schools, differentiated only by having another set of conventions. Even in the same school, what will work with one group of children will not "take" with another group of the same age. Full recognition of the fact that subject matter must be always changing with locality, with the situation and with the particular type of children is, however, quite consistent with equal recognition of the fact that it is possible to work out varied bodies of consecutive subject matter upon which teachers may draw, each in his own way, in conducting his own work. The older type of education could draw upon a body of information, of subject matter and skills, which was arranged from the adult standpoint. Progressive education must have a much larger, more expansive and adaptable body of materials and activities, developed through constant study of the conditions and methods favorable to the secutive development of power and understandir weakness of existing progressive education is due to the meager knowledge which anyone has regarding the conditions and laws of continuity which govern the development of mental power. To this extent its defects are inevitable and are not to be complained of. But if progressive schools become complacent with existing accomplishments, unaware of the slight foundation of knowledge upon which they rest, and careless regarding the amount of study of the laws of growth that remains to be done, a reaction against them is sure to take place.

Such reference as has been made to the subject matter of a worth-while and continuously developing experience is too general to be of value in actual guidance. The discovery of such subject matter, which induces growth of skill, understanding and rational freedom, is the main question to be worked upon co-operatively. The question may be raised, however, of whether the tendency of progressive schools has not been to put emphasis upon things that make schooling more immediately enjoyable to pupils rather than upon things that will give them the understanding and capacity that are relevant to contemporary social life. No one can justly decry the value of any education which supplies additions to the resources of the inner life of pupils. But surely the problem of progressive education demands that this result be not effected in such a way as to ignore or obscure preparation for the social realities—including the evils—of industrial and political civilization.

Upon the whole, progressive schools have been most successful in furthering "creativeness" in the arts—in music, drawing and picture making, dramatics and literary composition, including poetry. This achievement is well worth while; it ought to assist in producing a generation esthetically more sensitive and alive than the older one. But it is not enough. Taken by itself it will do something to further the private appreciations of, say, the upper section of a middle class. But it will not serve to meet even the esthetic needs and defaultings of contemporary industrial society in its prevailing external expressions. Again, while much has been achieved in teaching science as an addition to private resources in intellectual enjoyment, I do not find that as much has been done in bringing out the relation of science to industrial society, and its potentialities for a planned control of future developments.

Such criticisms as these are not met by introducing exercises and discussions based on what are called "current events." What is needed is something which may indeed connect intellectually in time with what currently happens, but which takes the mind back of the happenings to the understanding of basic causes. Without insight into operative conditions, there can be no education that contains the promise of improved social direction.

This fact brings us back again to the enormous difficulty involved in a truly progressive development of progressive education. This development cannot be secured by the study of children alone. It requires a searching study of society and its moving forces. That the traditional schools have almost wholly evaded consideration of the social potentialities of education is no reason why progressive schools should continue the evasion, even though it be sugared over with esthetic refinements. The time ought to come when no one will be judged to be an educated man or woman who does not have insight into the basic forces of industrial and urban civilization. Only schools which take the lead in bringing about this kind of education can claim to be progressive in any socially significant sense.

27

# THE DUTIES AND RESPONSIBILITIES OF THE TEACHING PROFESSION *

AMONG those who accept the principle of general objectives, there seems to be at the present time a general consensus as to the nature of these objectives. On the psychological or individual side, the aim is to secure a progressive development of capacities, having due regard to individual differences, and including a physical basis of vigorous health, refined esthetic taste and power to make a worthwhile use of leisure, ability to think independently and critically, together with command of the tools and processes that give access to the accumulated products of past cultures. On the social side, this personal development is to be such as will give desire and power to share in co-operative democratic living, including political citizenship, vocational efficiency and effective social goodwill. Disagreement seems to concern the relative emphasis to be given the different elements among these aims and the best means for attaining them, rather than the objectives themselves.

On the other hand, there is a marked tendency in other groups to discard all general objectives and to seek instead for specific aims. In this case, the latter are usually sought for in analysis of existing social occupations and institutions (present adult life in general). Their unstated general objective appears to be that education should prepare, by means of blueprints of society and the individual, students to fit efficiently into present life.

I. Under these circumstances, the first need is that the

* Used as a basis for discussion at the meeting of the National Council of Education, June 28, 1930. From *School and Society*, August 9, 1930.

teaching profession as a body should consider the nature of the social function of the school. The question of general *versus* specific objectives goes back to the question of whether the schools should aim to fit individuals for the existing social order, or whether they have a responsibility for social planning. The latter objective clearly involves preparation of students to take part in changing society, and requires consideration of the defects and evils which need to be changed.

The first thesis or proposition is, accordingly, that apart from and prior to consideration of changes in actual school programs, curricula and methods, the teaching body, as a body, should arrive through discussion within itself at conclusions concerning the direction which the work of the school should take with respect to social conditions. Does this involve responsibility for planning and leadership or only for producing conformity?

II. As far as the conclusion points in the former direction, the question arises as to the handicaps and obstacles from which the American public school suffers in performing this function. (A) It is stated that social sentiment, especially that of influential interests, will not permit the discussion of controversial questions in the schools and is even opposed to the introduction of objective and impartial subject-matter relating to them. (B) It is also stated that teachers as a class are not equipped to take part intelligently in the discussion of such questions or to lead in consideration of them. My second proposition, accordingly, is that there should be a clearer idea obtained, through discussion within the teaching body, of the existing handicaps to the realization by the school of its social function. This would include the state of the teaching body, and the question of how far it may be better prepared for social participation and leadership, including both teachers in service and the changes which would be required in training schools. The discussion should involve attention to the problems of adult education and of how far there is at present a lack of harmony between the processes of child education and those of adult education, since the ideal of continuity of education implies that there should be consonance and not conflict.

III. There is the problem of how objectives should be determined and formulated. There is the tendency, illustrated perhaps by the present paper, to begin at the top and pass the formulations arrived at down through a series of intervening ranks until they are handed over to the classroom teacher. This procedure conflicts with the principle of democratic co-operation. It suggests the proposition that there is need that classroom teachers, who have immediate contact with pupils, should share to a much greater extent than they do at present in the determination of educational objectives as well as of processes and material.

These three main propositions may be rendered more concrete and definite by raising questions which are involved in them.

1. How far should the educational process be autonomous and how can it be made such in fact? Is it the duty of the schools to give indoctrination in the economic and political, including nationalistic, principles that are current in contemporary society? Should criticism of the existing social order be permitted? If so, in what ways? Can pupils really be educated to take an effective part in social life if all controverted questions are excluded?

2. To what extent is it true that in spite of formulation of objectives by leaders, the educational system as a whole is goalless, so much so that there is no common and contagious enthusiasm in the teaching body, a condition due to lack of consciousness of its social possibilities? Do students go forth from the school without adequate consciousness of the problems and issues they will have to face? As far as it is true, can this state of affairs be remedied without a realization of responsibility for social planning on the part of the teaching body and administrators?

3. Can a vital professional spirit among teachers be developed unless there is (a) greater autonomy in education

and (b) a greater degree of realization of the responsibility that devolves upon educators for the social knowledge and interest which will enable them to take part in social leadership?

4. It has been stated from high quarters that the individuality and freedom of the classroom teacher are lessening; that "the teacher is becoming more and more of a cog in a vast impersonal machine." How far is this statement correct? What are its causes and remedies? Is the work of administrators too far removed from that of teachers? What is the tendency of the present administration of standardized tests? Does it tend to fix the attention of classroom teachers upon uniformity of results and consequently produce mechanization of instruction? Does it foster a grading and division of pupils with respect to mastery of standardized and predetermined subject matter at the expense of individual development? What tests and what method of their administration would tend to greater release of creative work on the part of teachers? How much of present administrative procedures is based upon distrust of the intellectual capacities of classroom teachers? Can these capacities be increased without giving these teachers a greater degree of freedom?

5. Can the power of independent and critical thinking, said to be an objective, be attained when the field of thought is restricted by exclusion of whatever relates to controverted social questions? Can "transfer" of thinking habits be expected when thinking is restricted to technical questions such as arise when this social material is excluded?

6. What are the concrete handicaps to development of desire and ability for democratic social co-operation?—for this is also stated to be a cardinal objective. Can such questions as the relation of capital and labor, the history and aims of labor organization, causes and extent of unemployment, methods of taxation, the relation of government to redistribution of national income, co-operative *vs.* competitive society, etc., be considered in the schoolroom? Similar questions

arise in connection with family relations, prohibition, war and peace.

7. The principle is generally accepted that learning goes on most readily and efficiently when it grows out of actual experience and is connected with it. How far does this principle imply, logically and practically, that the structure of economic and political activities, which affect out-of-school experience, should receive systematic attention in school?

8. How far is the working purpose of present school work to prepare the individual for personal success? How far are competitive incentives relied upon? How far are these factors compatible with the professed objective of democratic co-operation?

9. How far can and should the schools deal with such questions as arise from racial color and class contact and prejudice? Should questions relating to Negroes, North American Indians, the new immigrant population, receive definite consideration? What should be the attitude of the schools to differences of cultural tradition and outlook in the schools? Should they aim to foster or to eliminate them? What can and should the schools do to promote greater friendliness and mutual understanding among the various groups in our population?

10. The same questions come up regarding our international relations. Does the teaching of patriotism tend toward antagonism toward other peoples? How far should the teaching of American history be designed to promote "Americanism" at the expense of historical facts? Should definite questions of international relations, such as our relation to the Caribbean region, the use of force in intervention in financial and economic questions, our relation to the World Court, etc., be introduced?

These questions are suggested as means of making the three principles laid down more concrete in their meaning. They are tied together by certain convictions. First, the formulation of objectives, whether general or specific, tends to become formal, empty and even verbal, unless the latter are translated over into terms of actual school work. Secondly, the isolation of the school from life is the chief cause for both inefficiency and lack of vitality in the work of instruction and for failure to develop a more active professional spirit. Third, the closer connection of school with life can not be achieved without serious and continued attention by the teaching body to the obstacles and handicaps that lie in the way of forming such a connection. Fourth, it is necessary to enlist the entire educational corps, including the classroom teacher, in consideration of the social responsibilities of the school, especially with reference to the larger issues and problems of our time.

Underlying these convictions is a faith that the public will respond positively to the assumption by teachers of recognition of their social function; that much of the present adverse reaction of the public to free consideration of social questions is due to the failure of the teaching profession to claim actively and in an organized way its own autonomy.

# 28

## MONASTERY, BARGAIN COUNTER OR
## LABORATORY IN EDUCATION? *

SOME years ago when I was in the Adirondacks, I climbed Mt. Marcy, the highest peak of those mountains. There, near the top, is a marshy space with a little brook trickling down, apparently insignificant. A few rods away, after a slight rise of land, there is a second little brook, likewise apparently insignificant. I was told that the first one I speak of is the headwaters of the Hudson River; that the waters a short way off, separated by a watershed only a few feet higher than this swampy land, finally empty into the St. Lawrence. These little streams, that are hardly to be called streams but rather rivulets, at their source are only a few yards apart, but traversing very different lands and seeing very different scenes they finally reach the Atlantic Ocean hundreds of miles away from each other. This metaphor for purposes of comparison is trite, yet it seems to me that in its way it is representative of what happens historically. Great movements are not often great in their beginnings. Taken in themselves their inception is as seemingly insignificant and trivial as the little trickles of water near the top of that mountain. It is only when after long periods of time we look back to see what has come out of these little beginnings, that they appear important; just as it is when we see the Hudson River after it has become a majestic stream that the small rivulet at the top of Mt. Marcy gains importance.

You remember Emerson spoke about men who build

* An address at the Barnwell Foundation, February 4, 1932. From *The Barnwell Bulletin*, February, 1932.

better than they know. It seems to me that all great historic movements may be said to build either much better or much worse than those who started them knew or intended. This is true in the history of the founding of our own country. You will recall that most of the leaders in the Revolution, George Washington himself included, hoped that there would not be a complete break with Great Britain. They had certain objects which they wanted to gain, but they did not contemplate a really new political world. They felt rather that they were protesting against abuses of the liberties which belonged to British subjects, and just as their English forefathers had protested against the tyranny of the Stuarts, so they, in protesting against the despotism of the Georges in their own day, were walking in the footsteps of their ancestors.

Certainly those who started the educational system in America had no idea and no intention of founding a new educational system. Indeed, they looked backward rather than forward. Some of them looked back to Holland, others to England; and their highest ambition was to imitate or, if possible, to reproduce those schools in which they themselves had been trained. They were in a new country, the greater part still a wilderness, and naturally their highest ambition was to come as near as possible to recreating on American soil the kind of school which they themselves had known when they were children. This attempt to continue the educational system of the Old World persisted for a long time. Upon the whole it continued in this country until—we can only speak roughly—until, say, some time after the Civil War. Up to that time our education in the main was still a perpetuator; an effort to maintain the higher culture of our European source.

That type of education had certain quite definite features. In the earlier period of the elementary school the instruction was essentially an education in the three R's, reading, 'riting and 'rithmetic, with a little history of our own country and geography of the world, but more especially the geography of our country, superadded. There was a tendency to divide the subjects and methods of instruction. The mass of pupils who had received a training in the rudiments of learning did not go on with their education in higher schools. When they left the elementary school, their education was continued mainly through serving apprenticeships in trades and callings of various kinds, entered into either by formal indenture or in an informal way. In the service of a master and from the contact arising from this relation, the apprentice acquired skill in a trade. A small number of pupils, however, continued with higher education. For them the backbone of advanced education was the ancient languages, Greek and Latin, for those going into the learned professions of law and medicine, with the addition of Hebrew for those entering the ministry. Some history was also added, but classic history, the history of Greece and Rome with the literatures of those ancient countries. In those days there was no English literature in the higher courses, and there were no modern languages. The education, as you see, for the most part was in the symbols of knowledge and in the written and printed expression, especially in the languages and literatures of antiquity. It almost seems as if it was supposed that the material was better and more precious, the further away from the present it was both in space and in time.

This type of education I have taken the liberty of calling that of the monastery. This is a metaphor which is not to be taken too literally. But it was an education intended for the few rather than for the mass of the people. It was derived from the European tradition in which it was expected that only a few would continue beyond the mere rudiments of learning into what would be really an education. And the material of it, as I have just said, was largely the symbol of learning. Mathematics was the symbol of numbers, and the written and printed word that of grammar and literature, and so on. There was an aloofness from ordinary every-day living, which perhaps does not make the term "monastery education" entirely inappropriate.

Now this type of education, derived essentially from European sources though modified in some details, (since after all there was the ocean between it and its source) persisted longer than we might have expected. There were probably two main causes for the long persistence of this older education on the new soil, which in the meantime had developed a new political and to a considerable extent a new social system. One cause was that in the first decades of our Republic the practical education of the great majority of people was still obtained out of school. In the main we were still a rural and agrarian people. We were still in an age in which industry was chiefly carried on in the home and in the neighborhood by means of handicraft. If there was machinery, it was comparatively simple. There were local shops in the villages, country communities and towns to which everyone had comparatively easy access. I remember the village in which stood my grandfather's house, where in my childhood I went to spend the summer vacation. There in the village was the old-fashioned sawmill, the old-fashioned gristmill, the old-fashioned tannery; and in my grandfather's house there were still the candles and the soap which had been made in the home itself. At certain times the cobbler would come around to spend a few days in the neighborhood, making and repairing the shoes of the people. Through the very conditions of living, everybody had a pretty direct contact with nature and with the simpler forms of industry. As there were no great accumulations of wealth, the great majority of young people got a very genuine education through a kind of informal apprenticeship. They took part in the home-made duties of the household and farm and activities of the neighborhood. They saw with their eyes, and followed with their imaginations, the very real activities about them. The amount of genuine education, and of training in good habits that were obtained in this way under our earlier pioneer conditions, is not easy to overestimate. There was a real education through real contact with actual materials and important social occupations.

On the other hand, knowledge in the form of the written and printed word then had what economists call a "scarcity value." Books, newspapers, periodicals, in a word reading matter of all kinds, were much rarer and more expensive than they are today. Libraries were comparatively few. Learning, or rather the mastery of the tools of learning, the ability to read and to write and to figure, had a high value, because the school was the one place where these tools of learning could be mastered. We all have heard the story of Abraham Lincoln and other backwoodsmen and of their devotion to learning, of the great difficulties they had to contend with, of their going barefooted for miles to school, of their sitting up at night to master by candle light the rudiments of learning. For in those days, the monastery education was the only avenue to the larger world of the culture of the past. And that is why, I think, this older type of education, that seems to us today rather barren and meager, persisted so long and relatively was so effective in achieving important results.

Gradually, with the change of those social conditions, there was brought about a very great change, a change so great as to be called a revolution, in our whole educational system. I think of the old gristmill of my boyhood days in contrast with the great flour manufactories of today as symbolical. Then we could go into the mill, we could see the grain, we could watch it being ground in those great stone hoppers; we could see it passing through the pipes, and we could follow it with our eyes until it was turned into bran, flour and the rest of it. Today if we go into one of these big flour mills, we would not even see the grain going into the hopper! We may follow the whole process and see practically nothing, not even the finished flour as it is automatically put into barrels. The youth of today have no access to the basic realities of living, social, material, economic, at all to the extent to which the youth of a few generations ago had. This is what I mean by the illustration of the mills, if we take it symbolically. That fact has made it necessary for the schools to branch out in their instruction and to take up many things which used to be taken care of in the life of the boys and girls, of the young men and young women, out of school. In addition the situation is reversed in reference to language and books. Printed matter is almost a drug; it is cheap, accessible, voluminous. It would require considerable ingenuity for one growing up in the city to escape it. Machines take over the work of calculation and penmanship. On the other hand, however, opportunities have vanished for the learning and for the practical discipline which used to be had in open fields under the skies, and in shops where a few persons worked in close contact with one another, using their own judgment and receiving recognition for their personal achievements. They are now fenced-in roads where there used to be open fields inviting the inventive to take short cuts to their goals. The roads, moreover, are crowded and there is much standing in line; individual pace is regulated by the movement of the mass.

There are two outstanding facts which have changed the course of our inherited education in schools. To maintain the idea of democratic equality, schooling was made universal and compulsory. In the last thirty years we have done something to make this ideal a fact. The number of boys and girls who go to high school and college is five or six times greater, in proportion to the population, than it was even thirty or forty years ago. And then the change in the character of life, the change from the agrarian to the industrial, compelled a shift of emphasis in the material of instruction. At first there was merely the attempt to give to the many the education which had in the old country been intended for the few. But as time went on, the very fact that it was the many who were to be schooled compelled a vast change; a change, which has been called a revolution, in things taught, in the ends for which they were taught, and in the methods by which they were taught.

The nature of this revolutionary change was determined largely by the economic factor of life. The great change which goes by the name of the industrial revolution, that is to say, the substitution of mechanical power for the muscular power of animals and man, began, of course, in England, not in the United States. But the relatively sparse population in our country together with the abundance of natural resources, including unused and unappropriated land, the great distances which had to be knit together in transportation and communication, stimulated and almost compelled in this country the rapid and unhindered growth of the new methods of production and distribution. Moreover there was another factor of great importance. In England and in Europe generally, the new industry not only developed more slowly, but also in and against a background of traditions and institutions which were long centuries old. The latter did more than check its rapid growth; they formed the banks within which the economic and industrial movement was confined. In the United States there were no such counterbalancing forces. The industrial conquest of a continent became almost by sheer force of circumstances the dominant occupation of the American people. Physical mastery tended to absorb, almost to monopolize, the energies which in Europe were expended in a variety of channels. It was impossible, humanly speaking, that this engrossing interest should not leave its deep impress upon education in the schools and in the interplay of forces outside of the school which shape disposition and form habits.

Moreover, the development of the arts and industries was more and more dependent upon techniques which ultimately rest upon scientific knowledge; chemistry and physics were making discoveries which displaced the routine, rule-of-thumb methods which earlier generations had acquired through imitation and apprenticeship. Many lines of activity which were not themselves of a high order from the intellectual point of view felt the infection. They had to seem to adopt a scientific technique whether they actually rose above the level of empirical routines or not. Science obtained such a high prestige value that every conceivable human activity now has its corresponding "science"—writing advertisements, doing laundry work, keeping accounts, cooking meals, stenography and typewriting, and so on through the whole inventory.

While many, perhaps most people, regard the broadening of education to meet the needs of the greater number, and especially the inclusion of a larger amount of the vocational element, as an enrichment of education, there are others who hold a contrary view. And this brings me to the second catchword in the caption of my remarks. The persons in the hostile group say that our education has deteriorated through catering to the needs of larger numbers; that what we now have is a bargain-counter education; that the older kind of education relied upon the wisdom and the culture of the past to determine what was good for young people, inexperienced and unwise, to study; that the present theory and practice of education is rather to spread everything out on the educational counter, to provide some study and some course for every taste, so that the buyer, not the person who provides the education but the immature person who is to get the education, determines what kind it will be. Hence they say that the school is now a store where the storekeeper spreads out all kinds of goods in the hope that, by so doing, some one thing which catches the eye will appeal to the taste of one person, while some other thing will gratify the wants of another. And so they say that our education has become a scattered education; that it has been diluted and attenuated; that the elements of the earlier education, which made for discipline and culture, have been more and more eliminated; that the principle on which the schools are now conducted is simply that of giving young people what they want or what they think they want. They claim that education in meeting these demands has become utilitarian, "practical" rather than cultural, that its aim is simply to help an individual make his way industrially, so that he can earn money more easily, or get a better job than he could if he did not have this training. Accordingly, our universities and colleges, and also our high schools, and to some extent even our elementary schools, have been under attack on the grounds that this broadening out instead of being an enrichment is a thinning, while dilution and attenuation have made a course of study congested. The training which the youth now gets lacks depth—it is something merely on the surface.

While I do not wholly agree with these criticisms, I have nevertheless ventured to take the title "bargain-counter education" as a characterization of certain phases of the present education. It is hardly possible to discuss how far these criticisms are really justified. The reason is that different people have such very different standards. If one person thinks that closer connection with life is an advance in education, and another thinks that it is a term of condemnation since the essence of culture is that it shall not be too closely related to the practical needs of everyday life, there is clearly no point of contact between them. They will judge what is going on very differently because they have different standards. Thus if Mr. and Mrs. Smith think it is a fine thing for education to become more vocational, since it then takes into account the fact that the majority of people have got to make their living; while on the other hand their neighbors, Mr. and Mrs. Jones, believe that this kind of education is a step backward, obviously they will appraise the present system quite differently. But this is too large a question to go into here. Some of these criticisms, I may say, seem to be justified. In several respects our present education is spread out too thin, is too scattered; it lacks definiteness of aim. Very often the courses which are called practical are not really practical except in their label. Some of these courses try to teach things which can only be learned in the actual business or calling itself, while they do not take sufficient account of the rapid changes that are going on, since the teachers are out of contact with industry and teach the way things were done five or ten years ago rather than the way they are done now in the actual callings of life. And they are still less in contact with the way things are going to be done five years from now. In consequence, even the so-called practical courses in the long run are often not very practical.

We may make all these admissions about certain tendencies in our present system of education, and may yet say that we have accomplished one very important thing: we have at least broken down the obstacles and barriers which in the traditional education, the so-called cultural education, stood between the mass of the people and the possibility of their receiving anything worthy of the name of education. We have at least taken the first step in making education universally accessible, so that there is more reality than there used to be in the ideal of equality of opportunity for all. We have also at least broken down the wall that used to exist between what was called culture and vocation; for in fact the older type, that which I have called the "education of the monastery," (or which I might have called that of the pulpit, if I had another social class as a type), assumed that the people who were to acquire culture were people of leisure. Only those who had a substantial economic background which rendered it unnecessary for them to engage in any calling or business received education. On the other hand it was assumed that people who went into the active callings of life, especially those which in any way involved the use of the body and the hands, were people who were, of necessity, shut out from any high culture, being condemned to a life of contact.with physical, material things, so that in their callings there was no avenue to things of value intellectually and artistically. This bargain-counter education, therefore, even taking it at its lowest level, had got rid of this dividing line, this complete separation between vocation and culture; or, in other terms, between theoretical things and practical things; between action and doing on the one hand, and knowledge and understanding on the other.

The bargain-counter education has then at least prepared the way for another type of education, to which, also somewhat metaphorically, I have given the name of the "laboratory." For as the very word laboratory suggests, there is action, there is work, there is labor involved in it. The term is of course usually confined to the scientific laboratory, that of physics, chemistry or biology. But the idea inherent in the word extends further than this restriction. The first great characteristic of a laboratory is that in it there is carried on an activity, an activity which involves contact with technical equipment, as tools, instruments and other apparatus, and machinery which require the use of the hands and the body. There is dealing with real materials and not merely, as in the old, traditional education, with the symbols of learning.

There is no reason why the idea of the laboratory should not be extended to include also the workshop. There is no reason why the kitchens, if you please, where the girls learn cooking, or the rooms where they have contact with textiles, and the manual training shops where boys learn something of the arts while using their hands, eyes and bodies, should not embody the principle of learning through action by dealing with realities. There is no reason why there should not be extended to them the kind of learning which goes on in the physics laboratory or in the chemical laboratory. There is no reason why the workshop, whether in the upper grammar school or in the high school or in the college, should be confined merely to imparting manual skill and to giving an external ability to carry on a particular trade or calling. Through active contact with a wide range of materials, an opportunity is offered for an introduction into all the resources of science. Indeed, I often think that probably for the majority of young people the shops would make a better avenue of initiation into the elements of scientific knowledge than do our laboratories. For the concepts of physics and chemistry when approached directly, as in the study of the molecule, the atom or the electron, are technical, difficult and abstract, often quite as abstract and certainly as far removed from sense-perception as anything found in the older type of education. Through the medium of such things as the automobile, the airplane and the radio, there is a direct avenue to the principles of physics, chemistry, the structure of materials, which is on the line of least resistance, and yet which is capable of giving young people a personal and intelligent grasp of scientific principles. Such knowledge then comes to them in terms and through means which are associated with their daily experience; it means something to them in terms of their life instead of in abstruse and remote technical symbols.

Through the work when conducted as a laboratory, that is, as a means of learning and discovery, there is also the opportunity of arousing the curiosity of pupils and of equipping them with the methods for finding out things. The laboratory education also offers a means of access to an understanding of society. For after all, our society is largely what it is today because of the scientifically controlled occupations which are carried on in it. It may not be advisable to subordinate or limit our education to the making of farmers, engineers and merchants, but since the very large majority of the young people who come to our schools go into these various callings, it does seem desirable that they who are to be farmers shall be intelligent farmers, capable of intellectual invention, having initiative and mental control of their materials; and similarly, that the persons who are to enter the other callings shall have an education which will equip them to be flexible and independent in their judgments and original in their outlook. This is the education I would call the laboratory type. Beginning with activity, it would through that activity bring the student into actual contact with real things, and would then use this contact with objects for intellectual training and for arousing a thirst to understand, and not merely to fit pupils into some narrow groove of later trade and business life.

There is one other characteristic of what I call the laboratory education. The older traditional education was based on the thought that the teacher or the textbook knew in advance what the young ought to learn. The teacher or the textbook told the student what was so. The student's effort was largely confined to passive absorption and reproduction—a process which we might call a pipeline education; the teacher and the textbook, pouring the information into the student, who was supposed to be a reservoir which received the knowledge and which on suitable occasions (chiefly those of the examination period), gave out what it had received. This method of education might also be called a phonographic education. For the mind of the student was regarded as a phonographic disc upon which certain impressions were made by the teacher, so that when the disc was put on the machine and the movement started (which, again, would be during the examination period), it might reveal what had been inscribed upon it. The laboratory education, however, to which the bargain-counter type is at least a transitional stage, puts much more responsibility upon students themselves. The method of the laboratory is an experimental one. It is a method of discovery through search, through inquiry, through testing, through observation and reflection—all processes requiring *activity* of mind rather than merely powers of absorption and reproduction.

To go back now to my original metaphor. At first at the original watershed were the elementary district schools, started by parents in localities who wanted their children to have some of the opportunities which the Old World afforded, but which could not be had in the New World unless the parents themselves started the school. Then there were the universities, intended very largely as you will remember to train the clergy. Our ancestors were for the most part a pious folk who wanted pastors, and educated pastors to conduct the services in the churches. Within the past one hundred and fifty years, but more especially and with increasing acceleration during the last thirty or forty years, the streams originating in the traditions and conditions of past times have been growing into a broad current. This current is often meandering, dividing up, getting thin and superficial. But still it has potentially the energy to create a new and significant kind of education; an education which will be universal not merely in the fact that everybody will have the chance of going to school, but universal in the sense that it will be adapted to all varieties of individual needs and abilities. Society, instead of having simply the benefit of the training of a limited class, then will be able, through the development of every individual composing it, to get the benefit of the vast resources of all its members, resources which in the past have been latent because so few people have had the opportunity of realizing their full capacities. Public education will then also be public not merely in the sense that it is conducted by the State at public expense through taxation, but in the sense that it really trains all individuals for some kind of social service. After all, it is through vocations of one sort or another that society is ultimately served, and not by those individuals who, however cultivated they may be, regard their culture as so personal and private a matter that it is not put into vital and organic connection with the work of the world. When these capacities and potentialities are fully brought out by our education, we shall have in this country a genuinely new type of education. This new education will also give the promise and potentiality of a new type of culture, one in which old barriers will be broken down, and in which learning and the pursuit of knowledge will be regarded as public trusts exercised for the benefit of society.

But as yet our education has not found itself; the stream has not reached port and the ocean. It has left behind traditional education; it can never return to its source. It has to meet the problems of today, and of the future, not of the past. The stream just now has gathered up a good deal of debris from the shores which it has flooded; it tends to divide and lose itself in a number of streams. It is still dammed at spots by barriers erected in past generations. But it has within itself the power of creating a free experimental intelligence that will do the necessary work of this complex and distracted world in which we and every other modern people have to live.

# 29

# POLITICAL INTERFERENCE IN HIGHER EDUCATION AND RESEARCH *

IT IS not easy to define political interference in higher education. It may cover anything from meddling with a particular appointment, so as to do a favor to a friend, to a deliberate attempt to control the personnel and educational policies of an institution in the interest of a party or a faction. It is not easy to draw the line between interference for economic and other social reasons and political interference. The alleged reason for dismissal of Professor Miller at Ohio State University was a supposed indiscreet remark made in India, tending to cast discredit on Great Britain. This certainly was not a case of domestic politics. Since the British Government made no diplomatic representations it was hardly a case of foreign politics. What was it? Or if, as was indicated by some evidence, domestic prejudice about race and color entered in, under what heading does that come?

The activities of the "Power Trust" in subsidizing a certain number of college instructors by a variety of means were primarily economic in nature; they did not proceed from any political office, but their intention was admittedly to discourage consideration of public ownership of utilities and to secure a public opinion favorable to legislation in behalf of private ownership and management. Economic in origin, it was political in effect.

---

* Presented as a part of the symposium program under the Committee of One Hundred on Scientific Research at the New Orleans meeting of the American Association for the Advancement of Science, 1932. From *School and Society*, February 20, 1932.

Under a somewhat similar heading would come the organized efforts of persons connected with the War Department to prevent speakers suspected of pacifism from getting a hearing by students, and similar efforts by persons influential in the community to prevent socialists or others holding radical economic views from being heard. For while these latter moves do not concern regular classroom instruction, they do affect students' access to ideas and information having a bearing upon legislation and political administration.

If I mention these cases which seem to lie upon periphery, it is for two reasons. One is that direct interference from state officers, from those clothed with evident political authority, and having an evident political aim in view, is universally reprehended, and is for the most part confined to those parts of the country which are admittedly backward. On the other hand, the cases of mixed origin and motive are much more common; they are found in states which pride themselves upon their educational and cultural advancement, and in institutions of high academic status. Because they operate indirectly, employing relatively subtle means, they are much more dangerous in the long run than direct attacks upon educational integrity undertaken for obvious political reasons. They are, moreover, often condoned by university instructors and by the educated public who would be indignant at interference proceeding from a governor of a state or some political board responsible to the governor.

In political matters, even of the narrower sort, indirect interference is much commoner, more insidious and more injurious than the overt cases which attract public attention. The Board of Regents of one state university adopted the following bylaw: "If any professor or teacher of the university shall become a candidate for any public office or for a nomination thereto, or be a delegate to any political convention, or openly seek a nomination thereto, he should be taken and considered as having resigned his position." Inquiry has not disclosed that any other state has a similar regulation on the books. But pressure accomplishes the same result in other cases. A professor of one of the largest and most populous states in the union is on record to the following effect:

> There is not an institution of higher learning in the state supported by the taxes of the people where any member of the faculty from the president to the humblest instructor would be permitted to engage in any kind of political activity, at least of such a character that it would be pronounced or conspicuous.... If a professor has political convictions that he wishes to express in an effective manner there is only one course open to him, and that is to give up his job.... Institutions of learning under the auspices of religious groups have their shortcomings and disadvantages, but in this state their presidents and faculty members take a much more active part in public affairs, especially where the question of politics may be involved, than is the case in state institutions.*

That cases of direct political interference are more readily and effectively dealt with than the covert and indirect cases is seen in the instance of the educational institutions of the state of Mississippi. During June and July, 1930, wholesale dismissals and demotions were made at the four chief state-supported educational institutions. This action, instigated from political sources, stirred up an immediate reaction of the public. Various professional bodies of educators took action. The Southern Association of Colleges and Secondary Schools suspended the four state institutions from membership as a manifestation of "disapproval of political interference with state-owned schools"—a courageous action which was much resented locally, but which, coming from the neighboring states, had great influence. The American Society of Civil Engineers took similar action as far as engineering schools were concerned. The Association of American Medical Colleges placed the School of Medicine of Mississippi on probation for one year. Such organizations as the American Chemical Society, the Association of American

---

* Bulletin of the American Association of University Professors, for 1931, pp. 572-3.

Universities, the Association of University Professors, passed resolutions of condemnation.

The case of Mississippi is especially cited because it demonstrates so clearly that obvious overt political interference will call out widespread protests which are pretty sure in the end to be effective. Professor Bates, chairman of the committee on academic freedom of the Association of University Professors, states in the report for 1923, that cases of "open and clear interference with freedom of speech will be few. The more baffling cases are those in which a steady and powerful, but almost invisible and impalpable pressure of an academic hierarchy suppresses, discourages and seriously interferes with the usefulness and development of the independent and original thinker."

We might add to the list of cases in which the political activities of teachers are curtailed, the cases of suppression of liberal clubs among students and of extreme censorship of college publications when their utterances seemed to have a radical tinge, economic or political. Such instances do not directly affect instruction in the classroom. Many persons, including some university teachers who strongly resent interference with their freedom of research in their own special lines, are not sensitive to interference with activity outside the classroom. Permission of such outside activity involves, as does all free action in any line, some risk. But its denial, whether by direct action, as in the case of the bylaw cited above, or by indirect pressure, sterilizes thinking on the part of a class to whom, by reason of their especial education, a democratic community might be supposed to look for guidance; it lowers the whole tone of political opinion and action; it reacts unfavorably in classroom instruction by producing a type of teachers who have the habit of suppressing their real views and who finally cease, in consequence, to have any significant convictions.

Teachers and investigators in the more developed and exact branches of science are sometimes so aware of the relative crudity of the state of the social and political subjects that, because of personal economic and political conservatism, they tend to condone restrictions placed on outside activities of teachers in other branches. But they should recall the struggle their own sciences once underwent in order to get a hearing, and be convinced that the social subjects can not attain a more scientific status so long as those who teach them suffer from suppression.

Upon the whole, direct political interferences will, with growth of popular enlightenment in the backward states, tend to become fewer. Local sentiment always resents outside criticism and yet almost always modifies local action because of such criticism when it is fair. At the same time, I do not think the time has come when scientific men through their organizations can afford to be quiescent. If our different professional organizations are alert for infractions upon the integrity of inquiry and teaching of a direct sort, they may profitably extend their activity to take more cognizance than they have done in the past of indirect infractions. Public opinion among educators is tending, as far as I have been able to observe, in the following direction. Let the American Association of University Professors institute a list of accredited colleges and universities. Membership in the association should be confined to those teaching in the accredited institutions. Violation on the part of any institution of the principles of freedom of inquiry and expression should, when proved after investigation, be sufficient cause for removing the institution in question from the accredited list; this would automatically carry with it the dropping from the rolls of the association of members from that institution. All the more special organizations, having scientific and professional aims, should adopt the same course. Both the professors and the scientific associations should have suitable and stringent rules regarding the conditions under which an institution once dropped could be restored to the list.

If the public opinion of the profession could be organized first for its own enlightenment and then for express action along the lines indicated, there would be every prospect, I believe, that cases of infringement of freedom of investigation, speech and writing, including those of political interference, would be reduced to a minimum.

## 30

## EDUCATION AND OUR PRESENT SOCIAL PROBLEMS *

THE present interest in social reconstruction and the present desire of many educators to have the schools assume greater responsibility for achieving it remind me of a somewhat similar stir in the last years of the World War. At that time, too, it was in the air that a great social transformation was imminent and educators were urged to play their part in bringing it about. We all know what happened. There was a hurried and thoughtless "return to normalcy" and in the years following affairs generally were more completely in the grip of reactionaries than ever before in our history.

I do not wish to suggest that the two situations are wholly similar and the present outcome likely to be that of the early twenties. Much less do I wish to join the chorus of those who point to such episodes as proof of the futility of all liberal aspiration for social reform. There are doubtless reasons why the thinking and discussion that attend the present stir will not be as transitory as they were fourteen years ago. But I think the earlier experience conveys a warning and raises a question. At least I shall employ reference to it to state a question which in any case is important. Instead of considering our social problems as such, I shall ask: What is the method by which educators should approach them? Where shall he take his stand in viewing them? Is there any road of approach that will help us ward off the failure which has

* An address delivered before the Department of Supervisors and Directors of Instruction at Minneapolis, Minnesota, March 1, 1933. From *Educational Method*, April, 1933.

accompanied so many idealistic and humane movements in the past?

The question is not raised in a complete vacuum nor even in the upper air. There are, it seems to me, already signs of an approach on the part of educators which is not likely to be productive of enduring results. Of late years we have got in the habit of starting out by listing objectives to be attained. Now this procedure in itself is intelligent and admirable. We want to know what we are after, what we are striving to accomplish. But there is an underlying question: Whence shall we derive our objectives? Do we pluck them out of the air, dig them out of the ground about us, extract them from our inner desires, or what? Much of what we like to think of as American idealism and which we congratulate ourselves upon frames ends out of what appears to be desirable in general, apart from means at hand. I have, for instance, quite lately heard good people ask whether it was quite moral to use the debts which foreign nations owe us as a means of securing drastic reduction of armaments, by making this reduction a condition of abating the debts. And educators may set up social objectives which are inherently fine and noble by starting too remote from present conditions and needs, and hence isolated from the only means by which what they wish can be attained.

A union of idealism of purpose with realistic survey and utilization of existing conditions seems to me the only way in which our objectives can be saved from becoming empty, sentimental, and doomed to defeat. We must frame our social objectives on the basis of knowing the forces and causes which produce the evils from which we suffer, and must frame them on the basis of those forces and conditions in the actual situation which supply means for their realization. I do not know whether charity always begins at home. But I am sure that understanding and the framing of practicable ends and ideals begin as nearly at home as possible. If this principle is applied to education in relation to social problems, it will prevent us as educators from going too far afield at the beginning, and will fix our minds on asking what we can do in terms of the means at hand for doing what we want to do. It is better to do something positive and enduring than to ascend into the high heavens in a balloon that hits the ground with a bump as soon as the gas gives out.

If we adopt this course, we shall begin with the situation in which education now finds itself, with the predicament of the schools affecting students and teachers alike. Ascertaining as best we can the full facts regarding this situation, we shall then try to find out the causes for this state of things, the forces which are responsible for the evils from which the schools are suffering and the even greater evils which are threatened. We shall then move out to the whole social field in which these forces are operating and inquire what counteracting and remedial forces there are with which we may co-operate, and shall frame our ends and objectives on the basis of these surveys.

I cannot pretend to go into the full consideration of the immediate troubles in education in relation to the social and economic forces which have produced them. There are at least two recent authoritative statements: one is· that of the official committee headed by Professor Mort; the other is that of the Citizens Conference in Washington, held in January at the call of President Hoover. The title of that Conference, as nearly official as anything of the sort can be, tells the essential story: The Crisis in Education. Those gathered here know, if the general public does not, the various elements which define the crisis. They know about reduced appropriations at the time when the schools have increased responsibilities put upon them by increasing numbers of pupils and other factors due to the economic collapse; they know about closed schools, reduced school years, enlarged classes; failure to build and equip to keep up with increase in population and obsolescence of old equipment; the closing of kindergartens; elimination of manual training, art work, music, physical training, domestic arts; abolition of special classes for the backward and handicapped; scores of thousands of graduates of normal schools and training colleges added to the unemployed; salaries cut and unpaid; night and continuation schools abandoned. These are samples of forces which are threatening (I speak without exaggeration) to wipe out the gains in security of teachers and in enrichment of instruction which are the great gains of the last forty years. And, of course, we are in the early stage of the movement—not at its close.

In effect and to some degree—how great it is hard to judge —in deliberate intent, the public schools are under attack. The fountain heads of the attack everywhere are large taxpayers and the institutions which represent the wealthier and privileged elements in the community. Those who make the least use of the public schools, who are the least dependent upon them because of superior economic status, who give their children at home by means of private teachers the same things which they denounce as extravagances when supplied in less measure to the children of the masses in schools, these are the ones most active in the attack upon the schools. Under cover of the depression and the cry of economy (interpreted to mean reduction of expense and not removal of sources of waste and disorder), the efficiency and attractiveness of the schools are being threatened. The standards won by hard work over many years are being undermined.

That the causes of the situation do not lie within the schools is too obvious to need exposition. That the causes are in the general state of society itself is equally evident. And any child who can listen and read knows that they lie in the economic institutions and arrangements of present society. On one side is the crisis in education; on the other side are the social problems. There is no doubt about the close connection of the two. The causes of the economic catastrophe are the causes of the educational crisis. Whatever will remove or mitigate the forces which brought about the collapse of industry, the terrible insecurity of millions of our people, the breakdown in government due to decrease of revenues,

will have the same beneficial effect on education. There is no
other way out. We must do what we can at once to protect
the schools from the forces which are imperiling them. In so
doing we shall not be defending merely our personal interests. Of various suggestions regarding "economy" in school
expense passed on "by way of illustration" from the National Chamber of Commerce to local chambers, only two
*directly* affect the income of teachers in service. Others include reduction of the length of school day and year, increase in size of classes, discontinuance of kindergartens and
continuation schools, postponement of capital outlay (thus,
incidentally, keeping up unemployment), simplification of
curricula—an obvious euphemism—taking away one year
from both elementary and high school students, imposition
of fees on high school students, etc.*

I have indicated but not described in any detail the situation which educators find themselves in if they take the
advice to begin the study of their relation to social problems
at home, in what lies closest to them. This method of approach will not merely disclose, as I have already said, the
economic nature of the social problems now pressing upon
the nation and world, but it will, if it is pursued any distance at all, remove from teachers the illusion which many
of them have entertained—that their vocation and vocational
interest are so distinctive, so separated from that of other
wage earners and salaried persons as to justify them in an
attitude of aloofness. The demonstration that the vocation of
education is not and cannot be shut off and shut up within
itself is complete. The educator as a human being, as a
member of the community and as an educator, whether

* The Chamber of Commerce has issued an apologetic statement to the
effect that the suggestions did not originate in their office but in the agenda
of the Citizens Conference and were enclosed in a questionnaire by way of
illustration. The Chamber of Commerce forgot to mention who prepared
the agenda and the fact that these items were deliberately rejected by the
Conference. And it omitted to enclose even by way of illustration the contrary suggestions adopted by the Conference. It is not surprising accordingly that their document made no reference to the spirited opposition of
the American Federation of Labor.

teacher or administrator, must concern himself with economic interests, conditions, needs, possibilities, plans for reconstruction, if he is to be secure and effective in performing his educational function.

Here, then, we are to look for an avenue of approach to social problems which is most likely to produce results that will be enduring and so direct activities that they will not evaporate with a change in the curve of the economic cycle. As the educator travels this road he will see that social problems are not something outside him and his work, but are directly his own concern, and, once more, that they are not so just because they affect his own tenure and wage, but because of education itself. For this very reason he will see that "social problems" signify problems which affect large numbers in common. They are not things like thunderstorms or cyclones, to be looked at outside; they arise from general social causes and have general social effects and hence are to be dealt with socially, that is, by the educator in common with others. There is a curious quirk in human nature which makes us think of social problems as something external although their effects are something personal and private. We as educators need first of all to recognize that the social problems are something of our own; that they, and not simply their consequences, are ours; that we are part of the causes which bring them about in what we have done and have refrained from doing; and that we have a necessary share in finding their solution. Moreover, we have it not just in any outside way called "social" but in the educational interest which is an integral part of society.

In short, a social problem is one which the educator has in common with the farmer, with the factory worker, the small merchant, the white-collar worker. The problem is social because it is common. Put in another way, the causes which produce the suffering of men and women in these groups are the causes which have generated the crisis in education. Hence if we begin to study the social problem from where the educator is, at home so to speak, we shall learn that our interests as teachers are one with those of these other persons. Unless we realize the identity of interest which binds us together, I fear our interest in the social problems will remain on the academic level. Or, at best, it will be more sentimental than practical.

This community of interest is not confined to the fact that teachers, like members of the other groups, require personal security and due reward for their work. Security of useful function, of service necessary to society, is at stake. The educator is aware that he performs an indispensable social function. Present conditions make him alive to the fact that the performance of that function requires protection. But the same is true of every other group. Society could not exist without the farmers, the workers in factories and shops. All the groups alike are victims of anti-social forces. For nothing can be imagined more fundamentally anti-social than the conditions and factors which cripple and paralyze those engaged in performing necessary social forces, which prevent them from doing their work and thus deprive society as a whole of what it needs, while it also demoralizes the workers themselves. Unless the world is a crazy bedlam, unless order and justice are foreign to its constitution, such a state cannot indefinitely continue.

The relation of education to social problems is not, then, external and academic. It resides first of all in the community of interest of educators with all workers who are genuine producers of social necessities. This community of interest has both its negative and positive poles. Educators and others alike need protection against personal unsettlement, insecurity, overhanging disaster. Both must have guaranteed to them the effective ability to perform the services which the whole community requires. I would insist then that the first step for educators to take is the full recognition of this community of interest. Unless the start is made at this point, I fear lest the newly aroused interest of teachers in basic social problems will operate at arm's length and, lacking leverage, will with a return of moderate prosperity grow faint.

The second step which follows naturally upon realization of community of interest is, of course, an alliance in sympathy and in action. The province and function of education are not of course limited to children, though teachers as a whole have had their share in execution of this function limited to children and youth, leaving to the press and other agencies formation of the judgments and sentiments of adults. As long as educators think of their work as something apart from that of other workers and of their interests as separate, this state of affairs is practically sure to persist. The alliance of educators with others who are at a disadvantage because of the chaotic and inequitable economic order of society is, as far as I can see, the only way of changing this state of things so as to enable educators to take part in the normal education of adults.

One reason they cannot do so at present is that they are not prepared to do so, even intellectually. They share in the economic illiteracy which is so common. And much of this ignorance is due in turn to remoteness of teachers from the mass of people upon whom the disordered economic scheme weighs most heavily. Educators themselves can get the education which will enable them to help others only through the effective realization of the community of interest of which I have been speaking. The same identification of sympathy and thought will also break down the moral barriers which now divide teachers from members of other groups and make the latter more or less suspicious of them.

A great deal is now said about the importance of social planning in order to secure the integration and co-ordination which our sick society so badly needs. As I read the report of the Committee on Social Trends, the trend most emphasized is that toward a condition of unbalance due to the independent and unrelated growth of the different parts of the social mechanism. And according to those who report, with scientific moderation, on the trends, the unrelated development of the economic phase, both as a whole in relation to other interests and internally in the relation of its parts to one another, is the thing chiefly responsible for the existing unbalance. To-day the need for planning and co-ordination is, in theory at least, almost a commonplace. But it cannot be realized on paper nor by means of plans on paper however perfect in theoretical principle. The problem is more than one of ad-justing certain impersonal functions, like production and consumption. The human element comes in. The work has got to be done by people. It will not be done as long as people, as human beings, do not understand one another and sympathize with one another. Teachers will not have even a modest share in building a new social order unless they have broken down personal remoteness and indifference as to the things they have in common with farmers, factory workers, the white-collar class generally, and have ceased to think of their interests as being separate or exclusively linked with those of purely professional groups.

The work that has to be done in the further social educa-tion of the teachers themselves in economic matters and in the work they have to do with the young cannot, in short, be properly performed except as teachers, beginning at home with their own activities and function, widen their outlook and sympathy until they come into that practical association with other workers which will create common bonds and exchange of experiences and ideas in a common practical effort. The duty to educate the young for citizen-ship is universally recognized in words. At present much of the work done in this line is barren because the importance of the economic factor in good citizenship does not receive attention. I do not see how it can get proper attention with-out that realization of community of interest and consequent alliance in sympathy and understanding for which I have been pleading.

In conclusion let me say that one of the first steps to be taken practically in effecting a closer connection of educa-tion with actual social responsibilities is for teachers to assert themselves more directly about educational affairs and about the organization and conduct of the schools—assert themselves, I mean, both in the internal conduct of the schools by introducing a greater amount of teacher responsibility in administration, and outside in relation to the public and the community. The present dictation of policies for the schools by bankers and other outside pecuniary groups is more than harmful to the cause of education. It is also a pathetic and tragic commentary on the lack of possession of social power by the teaching profession. Teachers will not do much for the general settlement of social problems (outside of the indirect influence of academic discussion) until they have asserted themselves by taking an active share in the settlement of the educational problems which most directly concern teachers in their own local communities. Beginning at home is again the lesson to be learned.

# 31

# THE ECONOMIC SITUATION: A CHALLENGE TO EDUCATION *

SINCE the present economic collapse is a challenge to every institution in our present civilization, it surely is also a challenge to our schools. This fact is so evident that it is useless to dwell upon it. The important thing is to know how the schools might and should meet this challenge. But, when statesmen falter, industrial chieftains are bewildered, and economists hesitate to express a judgment regarding either causes or remedies, those of us who approach the matter from the educational side may well be at a loss. I am so far from knowing what the schools can actually do to prevent the recurrence of a similar breakdown in the future that I shall have to confine myself to one aspect of the problem. I believe that if we, in common with others, can honestly and courageously face the situation, our combined wisdom, if it holds the problem steadily in view over a long time, can accomplish what overwhelms the mind of any one individual.

In the first place, let me say that the words I have just used, "honest and courageous facing of the elements in the problem," suggest the main thing of which I wish to speak. It takes a good deal of courage for educators to face the situation, and it requires an unusual amount of mental energy to be honest in fact and not merely in intention. One of the functions of education is to equip individuals to see the moral defects of existing social arrangements and to take an active concern in bettering conditions. Our schools have

* A paper read at the general session of the Department of Supervisors and Teachers of Home Economics of the National Education Association in Washington, D. C., February 22, 1932. From *Journal of Home Economics*, June, 1932.

failed notably and lamentably in that regard. We are depressed just now, and trouble makes persons more willing to think and certainly more willing to criticize and to listen to criticism. But foresight and prevention are better than afterthought and cure, socially as well as medically. The atmosphere in our period of seeming economic prosperity tended to suppress serious thought on fundamental social matters and to encourage a complacent emotional acquiescence in and laudation of things as they are, or were.

One illustration will indicate what I mean. I heard a debate the other evening on military preparedness. A speaker, who held that this preparedness tended to provoke war, cited the fact that Holland held Java, perhaps the richest colonial possession in the world, and yet was free from all danger of attack although having no army and navy to speak of. He said that during most of the nineteenth century the United States with negligible military forces was secure, and that only after adoption of an imperialistic policy, which had made us feared and disliked, did the cry for a big army and navy arise. I am not concerned here to consider the justice of these remarks, although to me personally they seem sound. My point concerns the reception they received. General Fries, speaking for military preparedness, said that if the speaker and others like him thought so highly of Holland while he criticized the United States, why didn't they go to Holland to live and leave the country they thought so poorly of. There was great applause from a certain part of the audience, and members of so-called patriotic societies rose to their feet to lead the cheering.

The episode in itself is trivial or even childish. But as an illustration it has tremendous significance. It is typical of an attitude which has too nearly dominated teachers, and increasingly so, ever since the outbreak of the World War at least. It is "unpatriotic" to point out or even to admit that there are any weak spots in our institutions and habits and to suggest that there are matters in which we might learn from other countries. There has been a heavy pall of "hush-hush" imposed upon teachers, and the easy way for them, the way of inertia, has been to become "yes" men and women.

I do not know how it is today, but only a few years ago the names of some of the leaders of thought in this country were on the black books of departments in Washington as dangerous characters, potentially seditious because they had indulged in criticism of our tendencies in industry and were not afraid to put their fingers on sore spots like suppression of free speech. The branch of the War Department which is responsible for military training in colleges in one of its published statements for use in stimulating military spirit in the colleges called Jane Addams, whom most Americans call the best beloved woman in America, the recent recipient of the Nobel prize, the "most dangerous woman in America."

Again, such an instance, taken by itself, seems silly to the point of childishness. Miss Addams has obviously come to no harm. But for the few who by temperament and fortunate circumstances can rise above such attacks there are scores and scores who are induced to keep quiet, to gloss over social ills, and to accustom students to believe that all is for the best in this best of all possible countries. The representatives of large economic interests have been especially sensitive to anything approaching criticism of the existing economic regime and have pretty well succeeded in attaching to critics of it the epithet of "red" or "Bolshevist"; so much so that the publicity agent of the power interests is on public record as advising that all teachers who discuss public ownership favorably should be branded Bolshevists.

Now, when such a spirit prevails through the schools, it is impossible that education should accomplish its social function. For the primary social duty of education is not to perpetuate the existing social order—economic, legal, and political—but to contribute to its betterment. This work is constructive and positive, but it cannot be effected by indiscriminate laudation of the *status quo* any more than a physician can better the health of a patient by carefully averting attention from everything which ails the latter. And the doing of the work depends on the courage and energy of teachers.

The result is that the great majority of the students in our schools go forth unprepared to meet the realities of the world in which they live. They have been filled with highly idealized pictures of the actual state of things, idealizations created in part by omission of any reference to ills and unsolved problems, partly by excessive glorification of whatever good things exist. Then the graduates find themselves in a very different kind of world. The split between their generous beliefs and liberal hopes and what they get into is often tragic; for the sensitive and thoughtful it requires a painful readjustment to find the gap which exists between what they had been taught to believe and things as they are. But even if they succumb without a struggle and accommodate themselves to the *status quo* in the hope of getting ahead individually, they are not qualified to cope with the causes which produce such catastrophes as our present economic breakdown. They are rather positively disqualified. Consequently, we all stand aghast and impotent, while some resort to measures of desperation like pumping oxygen into a sinking patient.

This actual incapacitation, much worse than mere failure to prepare, comes from the fact that the policy of concealment and laudation which is so strongly encouraged by the ruling economic elements gives students the impression that they live in a static world where pretty much everything has been fixed and settled and where all that is necessary is for individuals to take personal advantage of what is provided for them. I remember the experience of those of us who almost fifty years ago went to take graduate work in Johns Hopkins University. The previous schooling of most, if not all of us, had been conducted as if the book of knowledge had already been written full to the last page and that all we as students had to do was to absorb something from its finished pages. But there we found ourselves breathing a new atmosphere. Everywhere was the feeling that what was known was little in comparison with what remains to be found out and that it was possible for us to contribute; that we could and should transform ourselves from mere absorbing sponges of what was already known into active creators of new knowledge.

In this instance, the sudden change was salutary and inspiring. For the readjustment was only intellectual. But the change from the fixed and finished world of an idealized social *status quo* to the moving, dynamic, changing world of actual existence demands a practical readjustment which most persons fail to make because they are not equipped to meet it. In reading lately Merriam's book on *The Making of Citizens,* I was much struck by the testimony of this scholar of politics. He says,

... the state must make its case not once and for all, but continuously for each new generation and each new period.... Plans of civic training that do not reckon with the social background of political power are defective.... The appearances of power are deceiving.... Facing the stern lines of authority with its steel and stone, and looking perhaps into haughty faces equally steely and stony, it is difficult to realize the poverty of power.

He speaks also of the "false front of omnipotence and unassailability."

Dr. Merriam is speaking of political institutions and power. If their fixity is so illusory, what shall we say of the stability of other social forms and arrangements, the everyday and secular affairs of men in industry, business, and finance, affected by almost every new scientific invention and changing with every change in the desires and plans of human beings? Over against this scene of constant change we have our schools, of which it is not too much to say that they engage in eulogistic contemplation of the false front of an unassailable stability.

The point which I am making may seem remote from the question of just what education can do about such things as the present economic depression. But it is my conviction that it cannot do anything important until there is a change in that underlying intangible thing which we call atmosphere and spirit. The change from acquiescent complacency to honest critical intelligence, from the fiction of a static and finished political and industrial society to the reality of a constantly shifting, altering, unstable society will not of itself enable those who go forth from our schools to forestall and prevent such crises as the present nor to cope with them when they come. But I believe that the detailed ideas and plans, which are indispensable if these results are to be brought about, cannot get a hearing, much less be adopted, unless there is a prior change in the prevailing tone and spirit of educational undertakings.

Accordingly, I shall make no apology for speaking of another general consideration that at first sight is also remote from the immediate emergency. Critics of American life have said a great deal of late about the standardization of opinion and regimentation of belief in American life. There is, I think, a much more deliberate attempt to produce this uniformity than there used to be. But it is my observation, growing out of an experience covering a good many years, that among cultivated people there were never as many truly free minds as there are now. I do not recall a time when one met so many persons mentally alert, forming their conclusions after informed inquiry and not on the basis of prejudice. There are, I feel, many more persons than there used to be emancipated from stereotyped ideas; fewer who are content to give utterance to what they regard as wise ideas or sayings merely because they have become stale with time. In my opinion, this country has never seen a time when so many persons took delight in ideas and in finding out things.

But, on the other hand, I cannot remember a time when collective thinking—the ideas that are organic to large numbers—was so stupid, so incredibly incompetent as it is today. It is a common remark that we have a surprising absence of effective leadership in this crisis, domestic and international, economic and political. Now leadership, like a bargain, has two sides. There can be leadership as there can be following only when human beings think together about a common theme with a shared purpose to a common result. Leadership is absent because this power of collective thinking in connection with solidarity of emotion and desire is lacking today. We have in its stead attempts to whip up a seeming unity of idea and sentiment by means of catchwords, slogans, and advertising devices. Few persons, however, are fooled by them except possibly those engaged in promulgating them.

Now this contrast between the alert state of the minds of cultivated individuals and the dead and impotent condition of collective thought is so paradoxical that it, too, issues a challenge to education. Why does this contrast exist? How did it come about?

One thing seems quite certain. Traditions form our collective beliefs; they are the intellectual cement of a society. Certain traditions in religion, morals, economics, and politics are still nominally held by the mass of adults, men and women. They are taught in schools. But the actual movements of social life are contrary to these traditions. They contradict and undermine them. We believe one thing in words and, to a considerable extent, in sentiment. We believe another thing in our deeds. The split prevents the older traditions from giving us real guidance, while they retain enough hold on people's minds so that they are not replaced by other collective ideas.

For example, our tradition in economics and industry is that of rugged individualism. We are taught to believe that all start equal in the economic race without any external handicaps being imposed on any persons and that reward and victory go to those of superior personal energy, ability, industry, and thrift, while, barring the exceptional cases of physical disease and accident, those who fall behind do so because of individual defects. We are taught that in this equal struggle between individuals all the great virtues of initiative, self-respect, self-help, standing on one's own feet, moral independence, and the rest are acquired.

Now these things may have been true once. They are not

true now. Industry is mainly collective and co-operative today, and economic opportunities are dependent upon collective conditions, as the condition of hundreds of unemployed men and women, graduates of colleges and technical schools, testifies at this moment. The concentrated control of finance and business is the basic and conditioning fact of industry today. But recognition of the fact goes contrary to our cherished tradition of equality of opportunity and of advancement solely through individual merit. The public clings for the most part to the nominal acceptance of the tradition, and the schools are forced to cling to it still more closely. Under these circumstances, it is practically impossible that there should be effective collective thinking regarding our economic situation in general and the depression in particular. Thinking could become effective only by being relevant to realities; in order to be related to the realities of the situation it would have to recognize that collective conditions call for collective control by the public in its own interest.

I think that teachers who led students to observe this state of things would find themselves called opprobrious names, and would be lucky if nothing worse happened to them. But unless and until we permit or rather encourage the schools to abandon the following of traditions—that is of collective ideas—which have no relation to existing social realities, our thinking in matters of the greatest public concern, including peace and war as well as industrial prosperity and depression, will continue to be thoroughly stupid and our leaders will be such only in the sense in which the blind lead the blind.

Since the schools are subject to pressure exercised by powerful forces outside the school, the challenge issuing from the present economic situation cannot be said to be primarily directed to educators. There is one aspect, however, of the challenge which comes home directly to teachers. They have been too passive, too submissive, to the dictation of these outside powers. It is our part to maintain the intellectual independence of the educative process and to strive for the right to present the defects as well as the excellencies of the existing economic order, even if by so doing some interests are offended. It is our duty as well as our right to show present society as dynamic, undergoing continuous change. To accomplish these things is the least we can do in faithfulness to the work of education itself. If we can make clear that otherwise we are failing in the operation of education, we shall also at least prepare the type of mind that can deal more effectively with economic conditions and crises than they are dealt with at present. This may not seem a very high ideal at which to aim compared with ambitious schemes which might be proposed. But those who realize the difficulties which stand in the way of securing for teachers the right to a critical and realistic consideration of existing economic realities will not despise the suggestion that the schools be emancipated from the clutches of those economic interests with their allied military and political auxiliaries which have done so much to bring the world to its present pass.

A group of educators, speaking from the standpoint of history, has recently put forth a manifesto in which they say that textbooks used in our schools still reflect more or less "the distortions of wartime propaganda" and fail to reveal that "millions of citizens in all nations were moved again and again to acts of supreme idealism and unselfishness by propaganda of interested groups controlling national interests."

Those would be naïve who assumed that the principle here stated is confined to war and the story of wars. It operates constantly in peacetime and with reference to economic matters; and until schools escape its influence through a declaration of independence by teachers, it will prevent the schools' meeting the challenge made by economic crises. The first challenge, accordingly, is to teachers to unite to inform themselves more adequately about economic and social realities and then to combine to impress upon public opinion the right and duty of intellectual freedom to deal with these realities in their teaching.

# 32

# WHY HAVE PROGRESSIVE SCHOOLS? *

ONE of the commonest charges brought against the progressive schools and schoolmasters who advocate
modern methods is that they express the aims of their kind
of education in vague and general terms. What they say
sounds well, but what does it mean?

What is any education for? Let the reader try to answer
this question. He will evolve a generalized formula much
like those of the specialists. However definite his own picture of what he means may be, the words he uses will be
capable of as many interpretations as he has listeners. This
is as true of the statements of the aims of old-fashioned education as of those of the most advanced schools. Some of the
shortest and simplest answers are: A preparation for life;
to learn to live; to give the child what he needs, or will
need, to know; to develop good citizens; to develop well-
rounded, happy, efficient individuals. Can the reader point
to any one of these and say with confidence, "This belongs
to the new," or, "This rules out the new?" No, not of these,
nor of any other definitions of the purpose of education.
He cannot because the differences of opinion about what
education should be lie, not in the purpose of education, but
in personal views about people and society.

The purpose of education has always been to everyone,
in essence, the same—to give the young the things they
need in order to develop in an orderly, sequential way into
members of society. This was the purpose of the education
given to a little aboriginal in the Australian bush before the
coming of the white man. It was the purpose of the education

* From *Current History,* July, 1933.

of youth in the golden age of Athens. It is the purpose of education today, whether this education goes on in a one-room school in the mountains of Tennessee or in the most advanced progressive school in a radical community. But to develop into a member of society in the Australian bush had nothing in common with developing into a member of society in ancient Greece, and still less with what is needed today. Any education is, in its forms and methods, an outgrowth of the needs of the society in which it exists.

No one is surprised that the educational methods in Soviet Russia are different from those here. That other methods will develop in a Hitlerized Germany is easy to understand. Yet even within two such rigid and controlled societies as these two countries are at present striving for, there is and will be experimentation, discussion and difference of opinion among teachers as to the best methods of developing members of those societies. There will be satisfied parents and dissatisfied parents. There will be happy children who like the schools and adjust to them easily, and children who do not adjust and whose difficulties are blamed on the schools.

The Australian aboriginal, the Athenian, the Soviet citizen, the Hitlerite had, or have, societies that can be defined in definite terms; the aims of which, whatever we think of them, can be recognized by any one. Accept these aims and there will be comparatively little difference of opinion about the kind of education that should be given youth in any one of the societies. In our American democracy aims have, until recently, been stated in terms of the individual, not in those of the society he is to be educated for.

In the early days of education in this country all that seemed to be necessary for the attainment of the ideals of democracy was to give every child an equal start in life by furnishing him with certain fundamentals of learning, then turn him loose and let him do the rest.

The little red schoolhouses of the country were started with a curriculum that did just this and no more. Higher schools of learning were not thought of as general educational institutions, but as strictly professional schools where ministers, lawyers, doctors and teachers learned the technical facts they needed for the pursuit of their vocations. This system of education worked, not because it was an inspired program for assuring the workings of the ideals of democracy, but because life was simple and the country offered almost unlimited opportunity for the individual. Life centered in the home. There, or in a neighborhood shop where his father worked, the child saw the industries of the country being carried on—baking, canning, dressmaking, farming, carpentry, blacksmithing, printing, wheelwrighting and so on. There, by taking part in the daily life, he learned habits of industry and perseverance and imbibed his ethical and moral standards. The small homogeneous community life of the early days enabled him to learn civics at first hand, through seeing and hearing about the running of his own town. There were space, air, fields and trees everywhere accessible, so that his play needed no specialized facilities and supervision. The only opportunities that this sharing in the life of the home and the village did not offer were for "book learning"—the Three R's. The child went to school to learn to read, write and figure. His life outside school gave him the rest of the training he needed.

Then life began to change. The things once made at home were now made in factories and the child knew nothing of them. The inventions and discoveries in science brought railroads, the telegraph and telephone, gas and electricity, farm machinery—a host of things about which one could not really know without far more training than was given by mere practice in using the finished product. Industrialization brought the big city, with its slums and palaces, its lack of play space, its sharp distinction between city and country. Finally it brought the automobile, the movies and the radio, with their enormous influence in taking the family out of the home and making even the little child much more part of the great world than had ever been dreamed of in the past.

These changes did not happen all at once. If they had,

perhaps it would have been necessary to scrap the simple curriculum of the first schools and begin afresh with one that recognized all these new and tremendously different factors at once. Instead, what happened was that gradually, as one new need was felt, a new subject was added to the course of study. The simple device of teaching reading, writing and arithmetic through the medium of the new subject did not occur to anyone. Even literature and reading, and penmanship and writing, became four separate subjects. The great increase in leisure and in the well-to-do classes made its contribution, too, to the number of subjects taught. Parents began to demand that schools teach some of the things that would enrich the use of leisure, some of the things that it would be nice to have children know, as well as the things that were necessary to enable the child to get along in the world. Thus art, music, dancing, French, and so on, were introduced into the schools. The growth of wealth and leisure also enormously increased the number of pupils in the schools of higher learning. Gradually the academy or preparatory school and the colleges ceased to be merely places for technical training and became places where one might go to go on being educated more or less regardless of what specific thing one was being educated for. And these schools, too, added more subjects to their curricula as the number of students and their demands increased.

Just as subjects were added one by one to the once-sufficient Three R's, so the methods that had been adequate for the three continued and were used unchanged. When the child's educational life, in the larger sense, was lived at home, what he needed was practice and drill in the Three R's, so that he could take them home and use them. So the new subjects were taught by drill, whether the home he would take them to offered any opportunities for their use or not. If these methods were not as successful with the new subjects, the fault lay not in the method but in the fact that because these subjects were new they were frills, lacking in the inherent disciplinary value of the old fundamentals.

The science of individual psychology began to develop after the enrichment of the curriculum was well on its way, so that the two developments went on in parallel lines touching almost not at all. The discoveries of the former about the way people learn, about individual differences and the interrelation of effort and interest, were unknown to schoolmasters, or were thought of as too newfangled for consideration. It was a little as if no one had been willing to put radios on the market because it was obviously an absurd idea that sound can be transmitted for vast distances through mountains and brick walls without special means like wires. And although these psychological discoveries are many of them as well established today as the facts of the radio, they are still temperamentally abhorrent to a great many schoolmasters and parents. A great many others are willing to admit them when stated in general terms, but feel the strongest emotional reluctance to giving children the benefit of them by applying them to teaching methods. In brief, these three discoveries may be stated as follows:

1. The human mind does not learn like a vacuum; the facts presented for learning, to be grasped, must have some relation to the previous experience of the individual or to his present needs; learning proceeds from the concrete to the general, not from the general to the particular.

2. Every individual is a little different from every other individual, not alone in his general capacity and character; the differences extend to rather minute abilities and characteristics, and no amount of discipline will eradicate them. The obvious conclusion of this is that uniform methods cannot possibly produce uniform results in education, that the more we wish to come to making every one alike the more varied and individualized must the methods be.

3. Individual effort is impossible without individual interest. There can be no such thing as a subject which in and by itself will furnish training for every mind. If work is not in itself interesting to the individual or does not have associations or by-products which make its doing interesting, the

individual cannot put his best efforts into it. However hard he may work at it, the effort does not go into the accomplishment of the work, but is largely dissipated in a moral and emotional struggle to keep the attention where it is not held.

The progressive education movement is the outgrowth of the realization by educators of the fact that our highly complex, rapid, crowded civilization demands and has been met by changes in school subjects and practice; that to make these changes effective something more is needed than simply the addition of one subject after another. The new subjects should be introduced with some relation to each other and the ways in which they operate and integrate in the world outside of school. It is also the outgrowth of the desire to put into practice in the classroom what the new science of psychology has discovered about individual learning and individual differences.

The kinds of schools, together with the methods used in them, which have developed from the desire to adjust the curriculum to society and to use the new psychology to increase the pupil's learning are numerous, almost as numerous as the schools themselves. When an individual or a group tries to adjust the curriculum to society, it immediately becomes necessary to formulate a conception of what that society is. What are its strengths that should be stressed in the schools, what its weaknesses that children should understand?

Is it a good thing to bring up the young with desires and habits that try to preserve everything just as it is today, or should they be able to meet change, to weigh the values and find good in the new? How much of the background and development of our civilization do children need to be able to understand what is in the world today? How much do they need to become cultivated individuals, able to enjoy leisure and carry on worth-while traditions? The answers to these and many other questions and the skill used in translating them into practice will determine the kind of school. Both these factors will differ according to the temperament, beliefs, background and experience of the individuals who answer them. This to the writer does not seem to be an indictment of progressive schools.

In a world changing as rapidly as ours, in a democracy with so short a history to draw on for choice of the best ways to succeed, expression of differences of opinions by different kinds of schools is a wholesome sign. In developing anything new, it is a good plan to have different methods working side by side, to experiment, to compare. This kind of difference has nothing whatever to do with whether a particular school is a good school or a bad school, with whether children learn what they are taught and are happy and successful at school and at home. Nor does this mean that all progressive schools just by the fact of being labeled "progressive" are good schools. It simply means that progressive education has not one formula, is not a fixed and finished thing about which it is legitimate and safe to make generalizations. It is as ridiculous to say that all progressive schools are good, as it is to say that the principles of progressive education are bad and unworkable because one school is poor, or because one child does not succeed in one school.

We are used to the faults of traditional schools, so used to them that when any difficulty arises we tend to lay the blame on the child or the home he comes from. There are, however, good teachers and bad teachers in traditional schools, and no curriculum, no matter how old, how cut and dried, how uniform it is, can possibly give a higher quality of output than the quality of the teacher who is using it. Probably nine-tenths of the violent criticism of progressive schools as progressive, that is so popular, would melt away like summer snows if we would look at traditional schools as we look at modern schools, or if we expected only the same amount from them. A progressive school to escape damnation has to be practically perfect, has to give each child just what his particular parents think he should have, has to succeed with every child, if he is a genius or just average, if he is nervously unstable, if he changes schools every year, however queer or unadjusted at home he may be. A traditional school is not expected to make good unless the child fits in, conforms and raises no problems. Two instances of the kind of criticism that is commonly leveled at a progressive school and practically never at an old-fashioned school are the matters of learning to read and of discipline.

Some children are backward about learning to read. They either have great difficulty learning or are so slow about it that their parents begin to think they never will. When this happens in an old-fashioned school the child either gets "left back," and has to repeat the work of the first or second grade, or the school tells the mother that she will have to teach the child to read at home if he is to go on with his class. And without any special fuss every one assumes that there is something the matter with the child. When this happens in a progressive school the chances are that parents and friends immediately assume that it is the school's fault, that the school does not even bother to teach reading, or at least does not think it important enough to "make" the child learn; the child would of course be reading fluently long ago were it not for the school's lax methods. We know today that certain children have reading difficulties, due sometimes to eye peculiarities, sometimes to left-handedness, sometimes to other more obscure causes. The only way to tell why one child does not learn to read is often a rather elaborate examination into all these possibilities. Experience has shown that if the child is mentally normal he will learn to read anyway by the time he is ten or so, and that in after life it is impossible to tell these late readers from the children who teach themselves when they are three.

In the matter of discipline the progressive school is even more subject to attack. If a child misbehaves in an old-fashioned school, he is naughty and his parents meekly undertake to see that he stops giving trouble. If he misbehaves in a modern school, the school is spoiling him, it has no standards of conduct, it sets no store by those sterling qualities obedience and orderliness. It is probably true that a progressive school seems disorderly to visitors who cannot imagine a school except as a place where rows of silent children sit quietly at desks until told to do something by a teacher. But modern education does not aim at this kind of order. Its aim is the kind of order that exists in a roomful of people, each one of whom is working at a common task. There will be talking, consulting, moving about in such a group whether the workers are adults or children. The standard for order and discipline of a group is not how silent is the room, or how few and uniform the kinds of tools and materials that are being used, but the quality and amount of work done by the individuals and the group. A different technique is required of the teacher in such a room from that required by a teacher in a room where each pupil sits at a screwed down desk and studies the same part of the same lesson from the same textbook at the same time. There are progressive teachers who have not mastered the technique. There are good teachers and poor teachers in progressive schools just as there are in traditional schools. But there is absolutely no scientific objective evidence to support the view that behavior problems are relatively more common in progressive schools than in traditional schools, or that the former are less successful in straightening out those that do arise than the latter.

Another common criticism of progressive education is that individual development and the training of special abilities or talents are stressed at the expense of learning social adjustment, good manners, how to get along with adults—that all progressive schools have a highly individualistic philosophy. If we confine ourselves to the philosophy, just the opposite seems to be the truth. It is the modern schools that have formulated their aims in definite social terms. It is they that are trying to work out some method of achieving harmony between the democratic belief in the liberty of the individual and his responsibility for the welfare of the group. A group of conservatives are already attacking them because they have expressed the belief that the schools have a responsibility to educate so that recurrence of present economic conditions will be impossible.

Individualism run riot is laid at the doors of modern schools, probably because it is these schools that first adopted teaching methods based on the new knowledge of individual psychology and on the recent findings about the growth of young bodies. To many the mere fact that children are free to move about, to seek help from others, to undertake pieces of work in small groups is taken as evidence that the aim of the methods must be to develop individualists, to let the children do as they please. These methods were, in fact, introduced because we know that physical freedom is necessary to growing bodies and because psychological investigations have proved that learning is better and faster when the learner understands his problem as a whole and does his work under his own motive power rather than under minute, piecemeal dictation from a boss.

Many others who grow up under the stern old adage, "Spare the rod and spoil the child," cannot bear, apparently, to believe that any more pleasant or congenial method of learning can possibly be good for the young. They cherish many vestiges of the old idea that children are little limbs of Satan and that the only way to bend them to the uses of civilization is force and long training in doing things just because they are told to do them, regardless of whether or not the work is of any immediate use or interest. Without this training, they claim, one will never be able to see a difficult or dull job through to completion in later life. The strong moralistic bias that colors these views seems to make it impossible for their holders to see that in giving meaning, in his own daily life, to the work a child does, there is actually a gain in the disciplinary value of the work, rather than a loss. There is gain because the work is immediately valuable and satisfactory to the child. Therefore his best effort goes into it and his critical powers and initiative are exercised and developed. Moral and intellectual powers increase in vigor when the force of the worker's spontaneous interest and desire to accomplish something are behind them. This is as true of children as of adults. It is these powers that the progressive schools seek to release. If they sometimes fail, if they sometimes make mistakes, it must be remembered that their techniques are still being developed, that they are new. We should remember, too, that the time-honored and hoary techniques of the traditional school do not always succeed in teaching every pupil to extract square roots fluently, or to be able to push every difficult and wearisome task through to a triumphant conclusion. How much shirking and bluffing goes on in old-fashioned schools?

It is also frequently said that progressive methods may work with young children, but that when the high school is reached these schools are forced to give up their methods and go back to the old so that their pupils can pass college entrance examinations. It is true that college entrance examinations require the accumulation of such a vast number of specific facts that a great deal of drill and cramming is necessary if a pupil is to know enough answers to pass. This does not mean, however, that as children grow older the only way they can learn is by drill and cramming, or that progressive methods applied at the high-school age fail to educate. It simply means that to get into college a young person has to spend a great deal of time memorizing details so that he can answer a great many detailed questions.

Some colleges have for a great number of years made exceptions in entrance requirements for the graduates of a few progressive schools. Reports are that these pupils have been able to carry on college work with records as good as, if not better than, pupils from conventional high schools. At present nearly twenty progressive schools have completed arrangements with almost all the accredited colleges and universities to begin, in 1936, admitting their graduates on other bases than the passing of the regular entrance examinations. The school will furnish a recommendation to the effect that the graduate has the necessary intelligence to do college work, has serious interests and purposes, and has demonstrated ability to work in one or more fields in which the college gives instruction. It will also furnish a careful record of the student's school life, including his records in the school examinations and his scores in various kinds of diagnostic tests. This will allow these schools to develop the curricula and teaching methods they believe best suited to the education of their students while they are in school, instead of forcing them to train for one special event in the child's future. After a reasonable number of pupils, whose high-school studies were carried on under this system, have graduated from college we shall have an authoritative answer as to whether progressive methods can be used in high schools with pupils who are going to college. If the plan works it will probably do more than any other one thing to reconcile the public to the fact that change and experimentation are needed in education.

Meantime, change and experimentation will go on anyway because life outside the school is changing, because scientific knowledge of the nature of growth is developing, and because parents want things for their children that they did not obtain when they went to school. The real measure of the success of the progressive schools is the modifications that finally take place in conservative schools because of the experimental pioneering. Judged by that standard alone, the progressive movement is making good.

I have emphasized the movement rather than schools as schools. For by the nature of the case, the various progressive schools differ widely from one another, more widely than traditional schools that have only to adhere to well-recognized standards. But also by the nature of the case, the progressive schools have something in common. They all aim at greater attention to distinctively individual needs and characteristics. Hence they are pervaded by a great degree of freedom of action and discussion. Secondly, they all utilize the outgoing activities of students to a much larger degree than does the traditional school. In other countries, especially in Latin countries, their popular name is "schools of action." Thirdly, they aim at an unwonted amount of co-operation of pupils with one another and of pupils with teachers. The latter function as fellow-workers in the activities that are going on rather than as rulers set on high. This fact determines the distinctive character of discipline in progressive schools. It is meant to be self-discipline as far as is possible, gained through sharing in work and play in which all have a common interest.

Within the limits of these three principles, there remain great possibilities of variation. But in spite of differences, their like elements sum up in the conviction that every worth-while education is a direct enrichment of the life of the young and not merely a more or less repellent preparation for the duties of adult life. They all believe that life is growth, that growth, while it involves meeting and overcoming obstacles, and hence has hard and trying spots, is essentially something to be enjoyed now. That learning is not necessarily a disagreeable process is the discovery, or rediscovery, of modern progressive education.

## 33

## THE SUPREME INTELLECTUAL
## OBLIGATION *

THE scientific worker faces a dilemma. The nature of
his calling necessitates a very considerable remoteness
from immediate social activities and interests. His vocation
is absorbing in its demands upon time, energy and thought.
As men were told to enter their closets to pray, so the scientific man has to enter the seclusion of the laboratory, museum
and study. He has, as it is, more than enough distractions to
contend with, especially if, as so often happens, he is also a
teacher and has administrative and committee duties. Moreover, the field of knowledge cannot be attacked en masse. It
must be broken up into problems, and as a rule, detailed aspects and phases of these problems must be discriminated
into still lesser elements. A certain degree of specialization is
a necessity of scientific advance. With every increase of specialization, remoteness from common and public affairs also
increases. Division of labor is as much a necessity of investigation into the secrets of nature and of man as it is of industry.

Nor does aloofness reach an end in this point. The language in use for common communication does not fit the
needs of statement of scientific inquiries and results. It was
developed for other purposes than that of accurate and precise exposition of science, and is totally unfitted to set forth
comprehensive generalizations in exact form. The result is
that the scientist speaks what for the mass of men is an un-

* Address delivered at the dinner held in honor of James McKeen Cattell
at the University Club, Boston, Wednesday, December 27, 1933. From
*Science Education*, February, 1934.

known tongue, one that requires much more training to acquire than any living speech or than any dead language. He can speak directly about his own affairs and problems only to a comparatively small circle of the initiated.

These considerations define one horn of the dilemma. The other horn is constituted by the fact that the scientist lives in the same world with others, and a world that is being made over by the fruits of his labors. There is hardly a single detail of our common and collective life, whether in transportation of persons and goods, in modes of communication, in household appliances and conveniences, in medicine, in agriculture and all the varied forms of productive industry, that is not what it is today because of what science has discovered. The scientist may be aloof in his work and language, but the results of his work pervade and permeate, they determine, every aspect of social life. The inventor, the engineer and the business man are unremittingly occupied with translating what is discovered in the laboratory into applications of utensil, device, tool and machine, which have largely revolutionized the conduct of life in the home, the farm and amusement as well as industry.

These consequences of science extend their influence far beyond what anthropologists call material culture. They affect institutions and great modes of interest and activity. We have broken with the intellectual traditions of the past and the mass of men have not had the nature of the change interpreted to them, although science set the terms on which men associate together. They transform life in ways that have created social problems of such vastness and complexity that the human mind stands bewildered. The intellect is at present subdued by the results of its own intellectual victories. It has become a common place to refer to consequences of chemistry in its application to warfare. High explosives, with their allies of steel and airplane derived from physics, are capable of destroying every city on the face of the earth, and we are even threatened with bacterial warfare. If the problems of peace and war have assumed a new and unprecedented form—which, alas, the nations are meeting for the most part only by increased expenditure for armament—it is because of applications of scientific knowledge.

I have selected but one aspect of the question. The economic problem which weighs so heavily upon us today affords another illustration of the new social impact of science. Here too it is a commonplace that mankind in advanced industrial countries and especially in the United States confronts the paradox of want in the midst of plenty. It is science, which through technological applications has produced the potentiality of plenty, of ease and security for all, while lagging legal and political institutions, unaffected as yet by the advance of science into their domain, explain the want, insecurity and suffering that are the other term of the paradox.

My title is the supreme intellectual obligation. But every obligation is moral, and in its ultimate consequences social. The demands of the situation cannot be met, as some reactionaries urge, by going backward in science, by putting restrictions upon its productive activities. They cannot be met by putting a gloss of humanistic culture over the brute realities of the situation. They can be met only by human activity exercised in human directions. The wounds made by applications of science can be healed only by a further extension of applications of knowledge and intelligence; like the purpose of all modern healing the application must be preventive as well as curative. This is the supreme obligation of intellectual activity at the present time. The moral consequences of science in life impose a corresponding responsibility.

As with almost everything in contemporary life, it is easier to diagnose the ill than to indicate the remedy. But there are some suggestions that occur to all who reflect upon the problem. The field of education is immense and it has hardly been touched by the application of science. There are, indeed, courses in science installed in high schools and colleges. That much of the educational battle has been won, and we owe a great debt to those who waged the battle against the obstacles of tradition and the inertia of institutional habit. But the scientific attitude, the will to use scientific method and the equipment necessary to put the will into effect, is still, speaking for the mass of people, inchoate and unformed. The obligations incumbent upon science cannot be met until its representatives cease to be contented with having a multiplicity of courses in various sciences represented in the schools, and devote even more energy than was spent in getting a place for science in the curriculum to seeing to it that the sciences which are taught are themselves more concerned about creating a certain mental attitude than they are about purveying a fixed body of information, or about preparing a small number of persons for the further specialized pursuit of some particular science.

I do not mean of course that every opportunity should not be afforded the comparatively small number of selected minds that have both taste and capacity for advanced work in a chosen field of science. But I do mean that the responsibility of science cannot be fulfilled by educational methods that are chiefly concerned with the self-perpetuation of specialized science to the neglect of influencing the much larger number to adopt into the very make-up of their minds those attitudes of open-mindedness, intellectual integrity, observation and interest in testing their opinions and beliefs that are characteristic of the scientific attitude.

The problem is of course much broader than the remaking of courses in science which is nevertheless requisite. Every course in every subject should have as its chief end the cultivation of these attitudes of mind. As long as acquisition of items of information, whether they be particular facts or broad generalizations, is the chief concern of instruction, the appropriation of method into the working constitution of personality will continue to come off a bad second. Information is necessary, yes, more than is now usually obtained. But it should not stand as an end in itself. It should be an integral part of the operations of learning that construct the scientific attitude; that are, indeed, a part of that attitude since the scientific inquirer is above all else a continuing and persistent learner. As long as intellectual docility is the chief aim, as long as it is esteemed more important for the young to acquire correct beliefs than to be alert about the methods by which beliefs are formed, the influence of science will be confined to those departments in which it has won its victories in the past. I cannot refrain from saying that one great obstacle is that many scientific men still hold, implicitly if not expressly, that there is region of beliefs, social, religious, and political, which is reserved for sheer acceptance and where unbiased inquiry should not intrude.

There is, moreover, a virgin field practically untouched by the influence of science. Elementary education is still a place for acquiring skills and passively absorbing facts. It is generally now admitted that the most fundamental attitudes are formed in childhood, many of them in the early years. The greatest indictment that can be brought against present civilization, in its intellectual phase, is that so little attention is given to instilling, as a part of organic habit, trust in intelligence and eager interest in its active manifestation. I take little interest in demonstrations of the average low level of native intelligence as long as I am aware how little is done to secure full operation of what native intellectual capacity there is, however limited it may be. Speaking generally, it is now everywhere subordinated to acquisition of special skills and the retention of more or less irrelevant masses of facts and principles—irrelevant, that is, to the formation of the inquiring mind that explores and tests. Yet childhood is the time of the most active curiosity and highest interest in continual experimentation. The chief responsibility for the attainment of a system of education in which the groundwork of a habit and attitude inspired and directed by something akin to the method of science lies with those who already enjoy the benefits of special scientific training.

I have spoken chiefly with respect to the education of the schools. But the problem and the responsibility of education go deeper. There are some signs of a rebirth of the educational interest that marked the Greeks who thought of it, as far as we can gather from the records, chiefly in terms of adults. The theme of adult education is in the air. There was never a time in the history of the world in which power to think with respect to conduct of social life and the remaking of traditional institutions is as important as it is today in our own country. There is an immense amount of knowledge available, knowledge economic, historical, psychological, as well as physical. The chief obstacle lies not in lack of the information that might be brought to bear, experimentally, upon our problems. It lies on the one hand in the fact that this knowledge is laid away in cold storage for safekeeping, and on the other hand in the fact that the public is not yet habituated to desire the knowledge nor even to belief in the necessity for it. Hunger is lacking and the material with which to feed it is not accessible. Yet appetite grows with eating. The trouble with much of what is called popularization of knowledge is that it is content with diffusion of information, in diluted form, merely as information. It needs to be organized and presented in its bearing upon action. Here is a most significant phase of the obligation incumbent upon the scientifically trained men and women of our age. When there is the same energy displayed in applying knowledge to large human problems as there is today in applying it to physical inventions and to industry and commerce, many of our present problems will be well on their way to solution.

# 34

# THE NEED FOR A PHILOSOPHY OF EDUCATION *

THE phrase "progressive education" is one, if not of protest, at least of contrast, of contrast with an education which was predominantly static in subject-matter, authoritarian in methods, and mainly passive and receptive from the side of the young. But the philosophy of education must go beyond any idea of education that is formed by way of contrast, reaction and protest. For it is an attempt to discover what education *is* and how it takes place. Only when we identify education with schooling does it seem to be a simple thing to tell what education actually is, and yet a clear idea of what it *is* gives us our only criterion for judging and directing what goes on in schools.

It is sometimes supposed that it is the business of the philosophy of education to tell what education *should* be. But the only way of deciding what education should be, at least, the only way which does not lead us into the clouds, is discovery of what actually takes place when education really occurs. And before we can formulate a philosophy of education we must know how human nature is constituted in the concrete; we must know about the working of actual social forces; we must know about the operations through which basic raw materials are modified into something of greater value. The need for a philosophy of education is thus fundamentally the need for finding out what education really *is*. We have to take those cases in which we find there is a real development of desirable powers, and then find out how this development took place. Then we can project what has

* From *The New Era,* November, 1934.

taken place in these instances as a guide for directing our other efforts. The need for this discovery and this projection is the need for a philosophy of education.

What then is education when we find actual satisfactory specimens of it in existence? In the first place, it is a process of development, of growth. And it is the *process* and not merely the result that is important. A truly healthy person is not something fixed and completed. He is a person whose processes and activities go on in such a way that he will continue to be healthy. Similarly, an educated person is the person who has the power to go on and get more education. Just what do we mean by growth, by development? Some of the early educational philosophers, like Rousseau and his followers, made much use of the analogy of the development of a seed into the full-grown plant. They used this analogy to draw the conclusion that in human beings there are latent capacities which, if they are only left to themselves, will ultimately flower and bear fruit. So they framed the notion of *natural* development as opposed to a directed growth which they regarded as artificial.

But in the first place the growth of a seed is limited as compared with that of a human being; its future is largely prescribed by its antecedent nature. It has not got the capacities for growth in different directions toward different outcomes that are characteristic of the more flexible and richly endowed human young. The latter is also, if you please, a seed, a collection of germinal powers, but he may become a sturdy oak, a willow that bends with every wind, a thorny cactus or a poisonous weed.

This fact suggests a second fallacy. Even the seed of a plant does not grow simply of itself. It must have light, air and moisture in order to grow. Its development is after all controlled by conditions and forces that are outside of it. Native inherent forces must interact with those of its surroundings if there is to be life and development. In fact, development, even with a plant, is a matter of the *kind of interaction* that goes on between itself and the conditions and forces that form its environment. A stunted oak, a stalk of maize that bears few ears with only a few scattered grains, exhibit so-called natural development as truly as does the noble tree with expanding branches or the ear of maize that wins the prize at an exhibition. The difference in result may in part be due to native stock, but it is also due in part to what the environment has provided. And even the finest native stock would come to an untimely end or result in a miserable product if its own energies could not interact with favorable conditions of light, moisture, air, etc.

Since there are two factors involved in the existence of any interaction, the idea and ideal of education must take account of both. Traditional school methods and subject-matter failed to take into account the *diversity* of capacities and needs that exists in different human beings. It virtually assumed that, for purposes of education at least, all human beings are as much alike as peas in a pod, and it therefore provided a uniform curriculum for all.

In the second place, it failed to recognize that the *initiative* in growth comes from the needs and powers of the pupil. The *first* step in the interaction that results in growth comes from the reaching out of the tentacles of the individual, from an effort, at first blind, to procure the materials that his potentialities demand in order that they may come into action and find satisfaction. As with the body, hunger and power of taking and assimilating nourishment are the first necessities. Without them, the food that is theoretically most nutritious is offered in vain. Nothing would be more extraordinary if we had a proper system of education than the assumption, now so commonly made, that the mind of the individual is naturally averse to learning, and has to be either browbeaten or coaxed into action. Every mind, even of the youngest, is naturally or inherently seeking for those modes of active operation that are within the limits of its capacities—precisely as the body of the baby is constantly active as long as the infant is awake. The problem, a difficult and delicate one, is to discover what tendencies are especially seeking expression at a particular time and just what materials and methods will serve to evoke and direct a truly educative development.

The practical counterpart of the failure of traditional education to see that the initiative in learning and growth is with the individual learner lay in the method of imposition from the side of the teacher and reception, absorption, from the side of the pupil. Unwillingness to learn naturally follows when there is failure to take into account tendencies that are urgent in the existing make-up of an individual. All sorts of external devices then have to be resorted to in order to achieve absorption and retention of imposed subject-matter and skills. This method of teaching may be compared to inscribing records upon a passive phonographic disc to result in giving back what has been inscribed when the proper button is pressed in recitation or examination.

It is impossible, of course, for any teacher not to observe that there *are* real differences among pupils. But because these differences are not carried back to concrete differences in individuality, to differences in needs, in desires, in direction of native interest, they are too often generalized by being summed up under two main heads. Some pupils are just naturally bright while others are dull and stupid! Some are docile and obedient and others are unruly and troublesome! Conformity then becomes the criterion by which the pupil is judged in spite of the fact that initiative, originality and independence are precious qualities in life.

While the raw material and the starting-point of growth are found in native capacities, the environing conditions which it is the duty of the educator to furnish are the indispensable means by which intrinsic possibilities are developed. Native capacities are the beginning, the starting-point. They are not the end and they do not of themselves decide the end. A gardener, a worker of metals, will not get far in his work if he does not observe and pay attention to the properties of the material he deals with. But if he permits these properties to dictate what he does, he will not get *any-*

*where*. Development will be arrested, not promoted. He must bring to his consideration of what he finds an ideal of possibilities not realized. This idea and ideal must be in line with the constitution of the raw material; it must not do violence to them; it must express *their* possibilities. But, nevertheless, it cannot be extracted from any study of them as they now exist. It must come from seeing them imaginatively, reflectively; and hence it must come from a source other than what is already at hand.

In the case of the educator the demand for imaginative insight into possibilities is greater. The gardener and worker in metals may take as their measure of the end to be accomplished the things that have already been done with plants and ores, although if they are original or inventive they will introduce some variation. But human individuals vary in their structure and possibilities as plants and metals do not. While the educator must use results that have already been accomplished he cannot, if he is truly an educator, make them his final and complete standard. Like the artist he has the problem of creating something that is not the exact duplicate of anything that has been wrought and achieved previously.

In any case, development, growth, involve change, modification, and modification in definite directions. It is quite possible for a teacher, under the supposed sanction of the idea of cultivating individuality, to fixate a pupil more or less at his existing level. Respect for individuality is primarily *intellectual*. It signifies studying the individual to see what is there to work with. Having this sympathetic understanding, the *practical* work then begins, for the practical work is one of modification, of changing, of reconstruction continued without end. The change must at least be towards more effective techniques, towards greater self-reliance, towards a more thoughtful and inquiring disposition, one more capable of persistent effort in meeting obstacles.

The weakness of some schools and teachers that would like to claim the name of progressive is that in reaction from the traditional method of external and authoritative imposition, they stop short with the recognition of the importance of giving free scope to native capacities and interests. They do not, in the first place, examine closely enough and long enough to find out what these actually may be. In the second place, they are inclined to take the individual traits that are showing themselves as finalities, instead of possibilities which by suitable direction can be transformed into something of greater significance, value and effectiveness. There is still current in many quarters the idea that evolution and development are simply matters of unfolding from within and that the unfolding will take place almost automatically if hands are kept off.

This point of view is natural as a reaction from the manifest evils of external imposition. But there is an alternative; and this alternative is not just a middle course or compromise between the two procedures. It is something radically different from either. Existing likes and powers are to be treated as possibilities, as starting-points, that are absolutely necessary for any healthy development. But development involves a point *towards* which as well as one *from* which; it involves constant movement in a given direction. Then when the point that is for the time being the goal and end is reached, it is in its turn but the starting-point of further reconstruction. The great problems of the adult who has to deal with the young is to see, and to feel deeply as well as merely to see intellectually, the forces that are moving in the young; but it is to see them as possibilities, as signs and promises; to interpret them, in short, in the light of what they may come to be. Nor does the task end there. It is bound up with the further problem of judging and devising the conditions, the materials, both physical, such as tools of work, and moral and social, which will, once more, so *interact* with existing powers and preferences as to bring about transformation in the desired direction.

The essential weakness of the old and traditional education was not just that it emphasized the necessity for provision of definite subject-matter and activities. These things *are* necessities for anything that can rightly be called education. The weakness and evil was that the imagination of educators did not go beyond provision of a fixed and rigid environment of subject-matter, one drawn moreover from sources altogether too remote from the experiences of the pupil. What is needed in the new education is more attention, not less, to subject-matter and to progress in technique. But when I say more, I do not mean more in quantity of the same old kind. I mean an imaginative vision which sees that no prescribed and ready-made scheme can possibly determine the exact subject-matter that will best promote the educative growth of every individual young person; that every new individual sets a new problem; that he calls for at least a somewhat different emphasis in subject-matter presented. There is nothing more blindly obtuse than the convention which supposes that the matter actually contained in textbooks of arithmetic, history, geography, etc., is just what will further the educational development of all children.

But withdrawal from the hard and fast and narrow contents of the old curriculum is only the negative side of the matter. If we do not go on and go far in the positive direction of providing a body of subject-matter much richer, more varied and flexible, and also in truth more definite, judged in terms of the experience of those being educated, than traditional education supplied, we shall tend to leave an educational vacuum in which anything may happen. Complete isolation is impossible in nature. The young live in some environment whether we intend it or not, and this environment is constantly interacting with what children and youth bring to it, and the result is the shaping of their interests, minds and character—either educatively or mis-educatively. If the professed educator abdicates his responsibility for judging and selecting the kind of environment that his best understanding leads him to think will be conducive to growth, then the young are left at the mercy of all the unorganized and casual forces of the modern social environment that inevitably play upon them as long as they live. In the educative environment the knowledge, judgment and experience of the teacher is a greater, not a smaller factor, than it is in the traditional school. The difference is that the teacher operates not as a magistrate set on high and marked by arbitrary authority but as a friendly co-partner and guide in a common enterprise.

Development, however, is a *continuous* process, and continuity signifies consecutiveness of action. Here was the strong point of the traditional education at its best. The subject-matter of the classics and mathematics involved of necessity, for those who mastered it, a consecutive and orderly development along definite lines. Here lies perhaps the greatest problem of the newer efforts in education. It is comparatively easy to improvise, to try a little of this today and this week and then something else tomorrow and next week. Things are done on the basis of some immediate interest and stimulation but without sufficient regard to what it leads to, as to whether or not something more difficult, setting new demands for information, need for acquisition of greater adequacy in technique and for new modes of skill, is led up to and grows naturally out of what is started. The need for taking account of spontaneous and uncoerced interest and activity is a genuine need; but without care and thought it results, all too readily, in a detached multiplicity of isolated short-time activities or projects, and the continuity necessary for growth is lost. Indeed, the new education processes require much more planning ahead on the part of teachers than did the old—for there the planning was all done in advance by the fixed curriculum.

I have spoken of the importance of environment, but a sound philosophy of education requires that the general term environment be specified. It must be seen to be dominantly human and its values as social. Through the influence of the social environment each person becomes saturated with the customs, the beliefs, the purposes, skills, hopes and fears of the cultural group to which he belongs. The features of even his physical surroundings come to him through the eyes and ears of the community. Hills and plains, plants and animals, climate and change of seasons, are clothed with the memories and traditions, and characteristic occupations and interests, of the society of which he is part. In the earlier years of education, it is particularly important that subject-matter be presented in its human context and setting. Here is one of the commonest failures of the school. We are told that instruction must proceed from the concrete to the abstract, but it is forgotten that in the experience of the child only that which has a human value and function is concrete. In his nature study and geography, physical things are presented to him as if they were independent and complete in themselves. But in the actual experience of a child, these things have a meaning for him only as they enter into human life. Even those distinctively human products, reading and writing, which have developed for the purposes of furthering human association, of making human contacts closer and richer, are treated as if they were subjects in themselves. They are not used as friendly speech is used in ordinary life, and so for the child they become abstract, a kind of mystery that belongs to the school but not to life outside the school.

As the material of genuine development is that of human contacts and associations, so the end, the value that is the criterion and directing guide of educational work, is social. The acquisition of skills is not an end in itself. They are things to be put to use, and that use is their contribution to a common and shared life. They are intended, indeed, to make an individual more capable of self-support and of self-respecting independence. But unless this end is placed in the context of services rendered to others, skills gained will be put to an egoistic and selfish use, and may be employed as means of a trained shrewdness in which one person gets the better of others. Too often, indeed, the schools, through reliance upon the spur of competition and the bestowing of special honors and prizes, only build up and strengthen the disposition that makes an individual when he leaves school employ his special talents and superior skill to outwit his fellows without respect for the welfare of others.

What is true of the skills acquired in school, is true also of the knowledge gained there. The educational end and the ultimate test of the value of what is learned is its use and application in carrying on and improving the common life of all. It should never be forgotten that the background of the traditional educational system is a class society and that opportunity for instruction in certain subjects, especially literary ones and in mathematics beyond the rudiments of simple arithmetical subjects, was reserved for the wellborn and the well-to-do. Because of this fact, knowledge of these subjects became a badge of cultural superiority and social status. For many persons the possession of knowledge was a means of display, almost of showing off. Useful knowledge, on the other hand, was necessary only for those who were compelled by their class status to work for a living. A class stigma attached to it, and the uselessness of knowledge for all purposes save purely personal culture was proof of its higher quality.

Even after education in many countries was made universal, these standards of value persisted. There is no greater egoism than that of learning when it is treated simply as a mark of personal distinction to be held and cherished for its own sake. Yet the only way of eliminating this quality of exclusiveness is that all conditions of the school environment should tend in actual practice to develop in individuals the realization that knowledge is a possession held in trust for the furthering of the well-being of all.

Perhaps the greatest need of and for a philosophy of education at the present time is the urgent need that exists for making clear in idea and effective in practice that its end is social, and that the criterion to be applied in estimating the value of the practices that exist in schools is also social. It is true that the aim of education is development of individuals to the utmost of their potentialities. But this statement in isolation leaves unanswered the question as to what is the measure of the development. A society of free individuals in which all, through their own work, contribute to the liberation and enrichment of the lives of others, is the only environment in which any individual can really grow normally to his full stature. An environment in which some are practically enslaved, degraded, limited, will always react to create conditions that prevent the full development even of those who fancy they enjoy complete freedom for unhindered growth.

There are two outstanding reasons why in the conditions of the world at present a philosophy of education must make the social aim of education the central article in its creed. The world is rapidly industrialized. Individual groups, tribes and races, once living completely untouched by the economic regime of modern capitalistic industry, now find almost every phase of their lives affected for better or worse—and often for worse—by the expansion of that system. What the Geneva Commission reported after a study of natives in the mining districts of South Africa, holds of peoples all over the world, with proper change of some of the terms used: "The investment of Western capital in African industries has made the Native dependent upon the demand of the world markets for the products of his labor and the resources of his continent." In a world that has so largely engaged in a mad and often brutally harsh race for material gain by means of ruthless competition, it behooves the school to make ceaseless and intelligently organized effort to develop above all else the will for co-operation and the spirit which sees in every other individual one who has an equal right to share in the cultural and material fruits of collective human invention, industry, skill and knowledge. The supremacy of this aim in mind and character is necessary for other reasons than as an offset to the spirit of inhumanity bred by economic competition and exploitation. It is necessary to prepare the coming generation for a new and more just and humane society which is sure to come, and which, unless hearts and minds are prepared by education, is likely to come attended with all the evils that result from social changes effected by violence.

The other need especially urgent at the present time is connected with the unprecedented wave of nationalistic sentiment, of racial and national prejudice, of readiness to resort to the ordeal of arms to settle questions, that animates the world at the present time. The schools of the world must have somehow failed grievously or the rise of this evil spirit on so vast a scale would not have been possible. The best excuse, probably, that can be made is that schools and educators were caught unawares. Who could have dreamed that the demon of fear, suspicion, prejudice and hatred, would take possession of men's minds in the way it has done? But that excuse is no longer available. We now know the enemy; it is out in the open. Unless the schools of the world can engage in a common effort to rebuild the spirit of common understanding, of mutual sympathy and goodwill among all peoples and races, to exorcise the demon of prejudice, isolation and hatred, the schools themselves are likely to be submerged by the general return to barbarism, which is the sure outcome of present tendencies if they go on unchecked by the forces which education alone can evoke and fortify.

# 35

# THE TEACHER AND HIS WORLD *

SHOULD teachers be ahead of or behind their times? Perhaps some one with a logical turn of mind will object to the question. He will point out that there is another alternative—teachers might keep even with their times, neither ahead nor behind. One might ask whether this middle course is not the wisest course for teachers to steer? The idea seems plausible. But it suffers from a fatal defect: our time is not consistent with itself. It is a medley of opposed tendencies. It is enough to point out two or three familiar matters. One hears on every hand of the economy of scarcity and the economy of abundance. We are living in times in which both are present and they are fighting each other. Unless there were abundance, the banks would not be congested with money; factories would not be idle; cotton would not be plowed under; cattle would not be destroyed. But unless there were scarcity, millions would not be idle; twenty millions or more would not be living on charity, public and private; schools would not be closed, the size of classes increased, valuable social services eliminated.

We are also living in times when private and public aims and policies are at strife with each other. What I mean by "private" may be indicated by reference to Mr. Hoover's rugged individualism. What I mean by "public" may be indicated by the fact that Mr. Hoover himself, while President, organized the Reconstruction Finance Corporation and other agencies of public action in an effort to stem the tide of depression. He and those who agreed with him in his emphasis upon private initiative and management in business assumed

* From *The Social Frontier*, January, 1935.

that it is the business of Government to help restore national prosperity. These contradictions in an individual are typical of the state of the times. Let me give one more illustration that comes close to the occupation of teachers. Our country is committed to the policy of public education. In pursuit of this policy we have increased five or six fold the number of students in high schools and colleges during hardly more than a generation. On the other hand, the young people whom we have trained in these institutions now find themselves to a very large degree without the opportunity to use their training. They cannot find jobs. Does this state of affairs look like consistency or evenness in the times in which teachers live?

The sum of the matter is that the times are out of joint, and that teachers cannot escape, even if they would, some responsibility for a share in putting them right. They may regard it, like Hamlet, as a cursed spite, or as an opportunity. But they cannot avoid the responsibility. Drifting is merely a cowardly mode of choice. I am not trying here to tell teachers with which of the antagonistic tendencies of our own time they should align themselves—although I have my own convictions on that subject. I am trying only to point out that the conflict is here, and that as matter of fact they are strengthening one set of forces or the other. The question is whether they are doing so blindly, evasively, or intelligently and courageously. If a teacher is conservative and wishes to throw in his lot with forces that seem to me reactionary and that will in the end, from my point of view, increase present chaos, at all events let him do it intelligently, after a study of the situation and a conscious choice made on the basis of intelligent study. The same thing holds for the liberal and radical.

This intelligent understanding of the social forces and movements of our own times, and the role that educational institutions have to play, cannot be accomplished save as teachers are aware of a social goal. I suppose some teachers are impatient at general discussion. Teachers are unfortunately somewhat given to wanting to be told what to do, something specific. But is it not true that understanding of forces at work, of their direction and the goal to which they point, is the first prerequisite of intelligent decision and action? What will it profit a man to do this, that, and the other specific thing, if he has no clear idea of why he is doing them, no clear idea of the way they bear upon actual conditions and of the end to be reached? The most specific thing that educators can first do is something general. The first need is to become aware of the kind of world in which we live; to survey its forces; to see the opposition in forces that are contending for mastery; to make up one's mind which of these forces come from a past that the world in its potential powers has outlived and which are indicative of a better and happier future. The teacher who has made up his mind on these points will have little difficulty in discovering for himself what specific things are needed in order to put into execution the decisions that he has arrived at. Justice Holmes once said that theory was the most practical thing in the world. This statement is pre-eminently true of social theory of which educational theory is a part.

# 36

# THE TEACHER AND THE PUBLIC *

WHO is a worker? Are teachers workers? Do workers have common ties to unite them? Should these ties be expressed in action? These are some of the questions I want to discuss with you for a few moments.

Who is a worker? I answer this question by saying that all who engage in productive activity are workers. It is customary to speak of a certain class of criminals as "second-story workers." The appellation is obviously humorous, and so it is when we speak of one person "working" another to get something out of him. Not every form of activity, even if it brings in some return to the person engaged in it, is work. It is work only when it is productive of things that are of value to others, and of value not simply in a particular case but when that *kind* of activity is generally of service. Those who live upon the work of others without rendering a return are parasites of one kind or another. The man who lives upon interest, dividends, or rent is, so far as that includes what he does, a parasite. There is something intellectually and morally, as well as economically, topsy-turvy when honor, esteem, and admiration go to a section of society because its members are relieved from the necessity of work. To believe otherwise is to believe that those who subtract from the real wealth of society instead of adding to it are the highest type. Everybody assents to this statement in theory, but in fact the attention given in this country to the rich just because they are rich, proves that we do not live up to our theoretical belief.

---

* An address in the WEVD University of the Air, Wednesday, January 16th, 1935. From *The American Teacher*, March-April, 1935.

Are teachers workers? The basis for answering this question has been given. Are they engaged in productive activity? Are only those persons who turn out material products producers?

Physicians who maintain the health of the community are certainly producers of a fundamental social good. The business of the teacher is to produce a higher standard of intelligence in the community, and the object of the public school system is to make as large as possible the number of those who possess this intelligence. Skill, ability to act wisely and effectively in a great variety of occupations and situations, is a sign and a criterion of the degree of civilization that a society has reached. It is the business of teachers to help in producing the many kinds of skill needed in contemporary life. If teachers are up to their work, they also aid in production of character, and I hope I do not need to say anything about the social value of character.

Are teachers producers, workers? If intelligence, skill, and character are social goods, the question answers itself. What is really important is to see how the production of material things depends finally upon production of intellectual and moral goods. I do not mean that material production depends upon these things in quantity alone, though that is true. The quality of material production depends also upon moral and intellectual production. What is equally true and finally even more important is that the distribution and consumption of material goods depends also upon the intellectual and moral level that prevails. I do not need to remind you that we have in this country all the means necessary for production of material goods in sufficient quantity, and also, in spite of the low grade often produced because of desire for profit, that we have all the resources, natural and technical, for production of sufficient quantities of good quality. Nevertheless, we all know without my telling you that millions have no work, no security, and no opportunity either to produce or to enjoy what is produced. Ultimately, the state of affairs goes back to lack of sufficient production of intelligence, skill, and character.

Why do I say these things which are, or should be, commonplace? I say them because of their bearing on the third question I raised. Do teachers as workers, as producers of one special kind of goods, have close and necessary ties with other workers, and if they do, how shall these ties be made effective in action?

Some of the facts that indicate the answer to these questions are found in the fact that schools and teachers, education generally, have been one of the chief sufferers from that vast industrial and economic dislocation we call the depression. Salary or wage cuts are almost universal. Multitudes of schools have been closed. Classes have been enlarged, reducing the capacity of teachers to do their work. Kindergartens and classes for the handicapped have been lopped off. Studies that are indispensable for the production of the skill and intelligence that society needs have been eliminated. The number of the employed has been increased in consequence, and the mass consuming power necessary for recovery has been contracted. But along with these consequences, there has been a greater injury. The productive work that is the special business of teachers has been greatly impaired, and impaired at just the time when its products of intelligence, skill, and character are most needed.

The cause is well known. It is in part the inability of large numbers to pay taxes, combined, however, with the desire of those able to pay taxes to escape what they regard as a burden. In other words, it is due to the depression on one side and on the other side to the control exercised by the small class that represents the more parasitical section of the community and nation, those who live upon rent, interest, and dividends.

If something striking, striking home, was necessary to demonstrate to teachers that they are workers in the same sense in which farmers, factory employees, clerks, engineers, etc., are workers, that demonstration has been provided. The same causes that have created the troubles of one group have created those of the other group. Teachers are in the same boat with farmers, manual and white-collar workers. Whatever affects the power of the latter to produce, affects the power of teachers to do their work. By the same token whatever measures will improve the security and opportunity of one, will do the same thing for the other. In both the causes that produce the trouble and the remedies that will better and prevent the recurrence, teachers are bound by necessity to workers in all fields.

Teachers have been slow to recognize this fact. They have felt that the character of their work gave them a special position, marked off from that of the persons who work with their hands. In spite of the fact that the great mass of their pupils come from those who work with their hands on farms, in shops and factories, they have maintained an aloof attitude toward the primary economic and political interests of the latter. I do not need to go into the causes of this attitude that has been so general. One phase of it, however, is definitely related to my main topic. I have said that the business of the teachers is to produce the goods of character, intelligence, and skill. I have also said that our present situation shows and is proof of lack of these goods in our present society. Is not this fact a proof, it may be asked, of a widespread failure of teachers to accomplish their task?

The frank answer to this question is, Yes. But neither the question nor the answer gives the cause of the failure. The cause goes back to the excessive control of legislation and administration exercised by the small and powerful class that is economically privileged. Position, promotion, security of the tenure of teachers has depended largely upon conformity with the desires and plans of this class. Even now teachers who show independence of thought and willingness to have fair discussion of social and economic questions in school are being dismissed, and there is a movement, sponsored by men of wealth, to label (bolsheviks, reds, and subversives) all those who wish to develop a higher standard of economic intelligence in the community.

This fact brings me to the answer of the last question asked. If teachers are workers who are bound in common ties with all other workers, what action do they need to take? The answer is short and inclusive. Ally themselves with their friends against their common foe, the privileged class, and in the alliance develop the character, skill, and intelligence that are necessary to make a democratic social order a fact. I might have taken for my text the preamble of the constitution of the national American Federation of Teachers. A part of it reads as follows: *We believe that the teacher is one of the most highly productive of workers, and that the best interests of the schools and of the people demand an intimate contact and an effective co-operation between the teachers and the other workers of the community—upon whom the future of democracy must depend.*

In union is strength, and without the strength of union and united effort, the state of servility, of undemocratic administration, adherence to tradition, and unresponsiveness to the needs of the community that are also pointed out in the same document, will persist. And in the degree in which they continue, teachers will of necessity fail in the special kind of productive work that is entrusted to them.

# 37

# YOUTH IN A CONFUSED WORLD *

I CONFESS that I do not know very well just what is the youth question today. Is it what we are going to do with and for youth? Or is it what youth is going to do to us, later? By "we" and "us," I mean society as it is controlled and managed by those exercising authority—political, economic, intellectual, educational. I suppose, however, that the issue concerns both of the questions that have just been asked. For in all human probability what we do in the next few years for and with youth will determine in later years what they do with and to the institutions in which they find themselves. We have all read a statement coming from the Office of Education in Washington that since 1929 twelve millions have reached the employable age, and that, as far as available facts enable us to judge, at least half of the number have not found steady employment. (The fact that adequate data are not at hand for a precise estimate is itself evidence that we are living in a time of undirected and haphazard drift.)

If one reads this fact with any imagination, if one surveys what it implies, it is eloquent. It tells what society is now doing to youth. It is charged with predictions, threatening ones, for the future. Moreover, it is only part of the story. Just as I was sitting down to write this article, I received a letter from a discharged junior college teacher in a public school system in this country, himself recently emerging from youth into active service. In his letter he says:

I held before students the ideal of intellectual integrity, of the scientific attitude of mind, of a social point of view, the develop-

* From *The Social Frontier*, May, 1935.

ment of a critical attitude toward modern society and its problems, but always with a suspended judgment until all the facts are available.

He was dismissed with the statement that he "was undermining the school system and ruining the students." As the end of this school year approaches, two more teachers in the same school are refused renewal of their contracts on similar grounds.

If I read such incidents aright—incidents that are multiplying all over the country—they signify that we are not only refusing to one out of two of the youth of the country opportunity to do the work for which they have been preparing themselves, but we are also deliberately refusing to give them the intellectual and moral guidance they need and that the society of the future is to need. It requires an impervious mind to assert today that what is "ruining" youth is a fair social and scientific presentation of the facts of contemporary life. One would suppose that what is ruining their standing and their chance for a useful life is the breakdown of the economic system and the probability of their being conscripted to fight in wars which they have done nothing to precipitate.

It is terrible enough that so many youths should have no opportunity to obtain employment under the conditions set by the present economic system. It is equally terrible that so many young people should be refused opportunity in what we *call* a public educational system, to find out about the causes of this tragic situation, and, in large measure, should be indoctrinated in ideas to which the realities about them give the lie. Confusion and bewilderment are sufficiently rife so that it is not necessary to add to them a deliberately cultivated blindness.

There are, of course, different phases of the situation in which youth finds itself. There is the immediate emergency to be dealt with. It is reported that one group in the Administration is ready with plans to use in behalf of youth part of the funds recently voted by Congress for relief and recovery. The newspapers carry the report that millions in money will be asked to secure an organization of the resources of local communities to provide cultural and technical training, together with recreational and artistic opportunities, for unemployed youth up to the age of about twenty-four. The immediate emergency has to be dealt with, and the plans mentioned are a move in this direction. But persons who are intelligent enough to project these plans are probably also wise enough to recognize that at best they deal with symptoms, not with causes. They should be carried into effect to salvage individuals from wreckage. But they leave intact the economic and moral forces that create the need for emergency measures.

As far as I can see, the best way to do something of permanent value for present youth and for the future of society is to take the measures that will change the social causes that have produced the present plight. The experience of the Old World, notably Italy and Germany, shows that "youth movements" when they move in isolation from basic changes in the structure of society may be directed toward reaction even more readily than toward desirable ends. Youth, made desperate by finding that society makes no provision for it, may grasp at straws if the straws float on a current that supplies some immediate outlet for pent-up energies. We may expect in this country more and more appeals addressed to youth from American congeners of European Fascism. Suppression of freedom of inquiry and discussion in schools is a first step in this direction. For the youth problem in this country I see no solution (which also will be a solution of the problem of the future of society) save one that enlists their minds and hearts in behalf of intelligent plans for social change based upon understanding of existing conditions.

# 38

# TOWARD A NATIONAL SYSTEM OF
# EDUCATION *

FROM the standpoint of any European country, except Great Britain, the American public school system is a chaos rather than a system. The British system, from the continental standpoint, is even more chaotic than ours, because public education there is superimposed upon schools carried on by religious bodies. Until the arrival of Hitler, there was a good deal of provincial educational autonomy in Germany; the larger divisions of the U.S.S.R. exercise considerable autonomy though of course within the limits of the proletarian-communist scheme. But there is no other country where local control and differentiation are carried as far as in this country.

The historical causes for our peculiar difference are fairly evident. Regions developed in the country before the nation, and localities before regions. Settlers had no choice save to go without schools or themselves to form a school for their own locality, the latter often not being even a village but a collection of farm-homesteads scattered over a considerable territory. The district school and the little red schoolhouse were the answer. As settlers moved westward and out to the frontier, the same conditions prevailed; in addition they naturally followed the precedent with which they were familiar.

Some degree of centralization has followed, by townships, by counties, and by states—but always with the limitations suggested by the word "some." The movement never extended to the nation. The "Office of Education" in Washing-

* From *The Social Frontier,* June, 1935.

ton is the expression and record of the limitation of the movement. I do not propose to discuss the concrete matter of changing the Office into a Cabinet Department, but rather to say something about a few general principles that seem to me to lie at the basis of a genuinely national system of education.

In the first place, there is a fundamental difference between a national and a nationalistic system, and we must face the issue of whether we can have one without growing sooner or later into the other. By a nationalistic system, I mean one in which the school system is controlled by the Government in power in the interest of what it takes to be the welfare of its own particular national state, and of the social-economic system the Government is concerned to maintain. The school systems of Japan, Italy, the U.S.S.R., and now Germany, define better what is meant by "nationalistic" education than will any abstract descriptions.

A national system in its distinction from a nationalistic one is not so easy to define. Roughly speaking, it is an educational system that corresponds to the spirit, the temper, the dominant habits and purposes that hold the people of a country together, so far as they *are* held together in a working unity of life. These terms are all vague, but the vagueness lies in the nature of the situation. In spite of the vagueness, it may be readily demarcated from a nationalistic system. The latter is imposed by government and maintained by government, though not of necessity in opposition to the will of the people. A national system is an outgrowth from the people. It develops from below, rather than imposed from above. The government intervenes by legislation and administratively, but it follows rather than precedes the more spontaneous and voluntary efforts of the people.

That we do not have a nationalistic system of education in this country is too obvious to require argument. Because of the historic conditions already mentioned, we have a national system only partially and somewhat amorphously. That, as time has passed, local and regional interests have tended to merge, while local boundaries have lost force in comparison with the concerns of the country as a whole, is clear in every field. The educational system could not escape this influence. Unification in economic directions has increased the importance of unity in the ideas and policies that affect national policies. Nevertheless, it was practically inevitable in so large a country and in one with so short a history that the intellectual and moral unification of the different regions of the country should lag behind economic unification.

Some undoubted advantages have accrued to offset the disadvantages of our local and dispersive system. The schools have been closer to the local communities; in many cases local responsibility has been stimulated. There has been, along with great unevenness, a stimulus to experimentation such as a closed centralized system does not afford. Meetings of teachers, emulation, and the spread of ideas by social osmosis, have had to play the part taken by ministries of education in other countries. Mechanical uniformity has not been allowed to exclude wholesome diversity.

Yet the necessity in a time of great changes, like the present, of direction in the interest of the people as a whole (unless we are to sink into deeper chaos) is a fact that cannot be escaped. It would however be a great mistake, in my opinion, to think that this urgent need settles the way in which the need should be satisfied. It rather presents a problem. The easy conversion in Europe of centralized systems into agencies of a dominant political regime is a warning. Moreover, local interests and jealousies are still so strong in this country that an administrative national system could not be brought about in this country except through something approaching class coercion of a Fascist variety or a great amount of dangerous propaganda—or both. On the other hand, as I have already said, unless we are to drift into a worse situation than that in which we now find ourselves, a strong unified intelligence and purpose must be built up in support of policies that have a definite trend toward a socialized co-operative democracy. The schools cannot remain outside this task.

Here are the two horns of our dilemma. As far as I can see, the surest as well as safest way out is for teachers themselves to work actively to establish the autonomy of education, rather than to share in *direct* attempts to establish a national system. By autonomy I do not mean, of course, something separate. Autonomy means rather the right of teachers to determine the subject-matter and methods employed in the schools. This is a right they are far from now having. Part of the confusion and the social irresponsibility of public education at present springs from the fact that it is controlled in such large measure by interests that are concerned chiefly with ends that lie outside of the educative field. If the teaching profession can educate itself and the public to the need of throwing off this incubus, genuinely educative forces will be released to do their work. In consequence, the freedom and impetus that result will enable the schools, without a centralized system, to develop a system of truly national education—by which I mean one animated by policies and methods that will help create that common purpose without which the nation cannot achieve unified movement.

What is urged is far from indoctrination in the sense of inculcation of fixed beliefs. In the first place, this end could not be accomplished without first indoctrinating teachers into a single body of beliefs, and nothing but Fascist or Communist coercion can bring about even a semblance of such unification. In the second place, any unification of the national will effected by such a method will have no firm and enduring roots. Dr. Randall has recently made the following pertinent remarks regarding the use of the method of intelligence in education:

It is implied that because intelligence does not attain final truth, it reaches no conclusion at all.... The futile debate about "indoctrination" in education illustrates this strange delusion. If you stimulate inquiry and educate, this leaves the student free to adopt any opinion or conclusion he wishes! Therefore it is necessary to indoctrinate" him with the ends you have decided upon. As though inquiry never discovered anything, and investigation never reached conclusions that force themselves upon the mind of the investigator!... Inquiry is meaningless unless you discover ideas that put other ideas at a disadvantage.

The bearing of these remarks upon my theme is that they point to the need of concentration and clarification of the methods of free mutual discussion and communication among teachers—methods that are responsible for whatever advances have been made in public education in the past. I do not say this is the final step in the development of a national education, but it is the first step. Moreover, concentration and clarification involve a good deal. They involve cutting out repetition of conventionalities, of hullabaloo, and settling down to basic issues of the relation of education to social direction. If this can be accomplished, I think the process of self-education of teachers will educate also the public, and take us on the sure road to the now distant goal of a truly national education.

# 39

## LIBERTY AND SOCIAL CONTROL *

TODAY there is no word more bandied about than liberty. Every effort at organized control of economic forces is resisted and attacked, by a certain group, in the name of liberty. The slightest observation shows that this group is made up of those who are interested, from causes that are evident, in the preservation of the economic status quo; that is to say, in the maintenance of the customary privileges and legal rights they already possess. When we look at history in the large we find that the demand for liberty and efforts to achieve it have come from those who wanted to *alter* the institutional set-up. This striking contrast is a stimulus to thoughtful inquiry. What does liberty mean anyway? Why should the cause of liberty have been identified in the past with efforts at change of laws and institutions while at the present time a certain group is using all its vast resources to convince the public that change of economic institutions is an attack upon liberty?

Well, in the first place, liberty is not just an idea, an abstract principle. It is power, effective power to do specific things. There is no such thing as liberty in general; liberty, so to speak, at large. If one wants to know what the condition of liberty is at a given time, one has to examine what persons *can* do and what they *cannot* do. The moment one examines the question from the standpoint of effective action, it becomes evident that the demand for liberty is a demand for power, either for possession of powers of action not already possessed or for retention and expansion of powers already possessed. The present ado in behalf of liberty

* From *The Social Frontier*, November, 1935.

by the managers and beneficiaries of the existing economic system is immediately explicable if one views it as a demand for preservation of the powers they already possess. Since it is the existing system that gives them these powers, liberty is thus inevitably identified with the perpetuation of that system. Translate the present hullabaloo about liberty into struggle to retain powers already possessed, and it has a meaning.

In the second place, the possession of effective power is always a matter of the *distribution* of powers that exists at the time. A physical analogy may make clear what I mean. Water runs downhill and electric currents flow because of *difference in potentials*. If the ground is level, water is stagnant. If on the level ocean, there are dashing waves, it is because there is another power operating, that of the winds, occasioned ultimately by a difference in the distribution of temperature at different points. There is no such thing physically as manifestation of energy or effective power by one thing except in relation to the energy manifested by other things. There is no such thing as the liberty or effective power of an individual, group, or class, except in relation to the liberties, the effective powers, of *other* individuals, groups, and classes.

Demand for retention of powers already possessed on the part of a particular group means, therefore, that other individuals and groups shall continue to possess only the capacities in and for activity which *they* already possess. Demand for increased power at one point means demands for change in the distribution of powers, that is, for less power somewhere else. You cannot discuss or measure the liberty of one individual or group of individuals without thereby raising the question of the effect upon the liberty of others, any more than you can measure the energy of a headwater at the head without measuring the difference of levels.

In the third place, this relativity of liberty to the existing distribution of powers of action, while meaning that there is no such thing as absolute liberty, also means necessarily that wherever there is liberty at one place there is restraint at some other place. *The system of liberties that exists at any time is always the system of restraints or controls that exists at that time.* No one can *do* anything except in relation to what others can do and cannot do.

These three points are general. But they cannot be dismissed as mere abstractions. For when they are applied either in idea or in action they mean that liberty is always a *social* question, not an individual one. For the liberties that any individual actually has depends upon the distribution of powers or liberties that exists, and this distribution is identical with actual social arrangements, legal and political—and, at the present time, economic, in a peculiarly important way.

Return now to the fact that historically the great movements for human liberation have always been movements to change institutions and not to preserve them intact. It follows from what has been said that there have been movements to bring about a changed distribution of power to do —and power to think and to express thought is a power to do—such that there would be a more balanced, a more equal, even, and equitable system of human liberties.

The present movement for organized control of industry, money and credit, is simply a part of this endless human struggle. The present attempt to define liberty in terms of the existing distribution of liberty is an attempt to maintain the existing system of control of power, of social restraints and regimentations. I cannot go here into the nature and consequences of this system. If one is satisfied with it, let him support the conception of liberty put forth by, say, the Liberty League, which represents the present economic system. But let him not be fooled into thinking that the issue is liberty versus restraint and regimentation. For the issue is simply that of one system of control of the social forces upon which the distribution of liberties depends, versus some other system of social control which would bring about another distribution of liberties. And let those who are struggling to replace the present economic system by a co-operative one also remember that in struggling for a new system of social restraints and controls they are also struggling for a more equal and equitable balance of powers that will enhance and multiply the effective liberties of the mass of individuals. Let them not be jockeyed into the position of supporting social control at the expense of liberty, when what they want is another method of social control than the one that now exists, one that will increase significant human liberties.

It is nonsense to suppose that we do not have social control *now*. The trouble is that it is exercised by the few who have economic power, at the expense of the liberties of the many and at the cost of increasing disorder, culminating in that chaos of war which the representatives of liberty for the possessive class identify with true discipline.

# 40

# THE SOCIAL SIGNIFICANCE OF ACADEMIC FREEDOM *

I AM not especially fond of the phrase academic freedom as far as the adjective *academic* is concerned. It suggests something that is rather remote and technical. Indeed, it is common to use the word as a term of disparagement. But the reality for which the phrase stands has an importance far beyond any particular expression used to convey it. Freedom of *education* is the thing at issue—I was about to say at stake. And since education is not a function that goes on in the void, but is carried on by human beings, the freedom of education means, in the concrete, the freedom of students and teachers: the freedom of the school as an agent of education.

The inclusion of students in the idea of freedom of education is even more important than the inclusion of teachers; at least it would be if it were possible to separate the two. Freedom of teachers is a necessary condition of freedom for students to learn.

The American people are historically committed to "free schools" with a devotion that probably exceeds that given to any other aim in our common life. The full significance of free schools is, however, far from realization in the public mind and in the workings of our educational system. Freedom from payment of fees, support by public taxation, is a necessary condition for schools that are to be free of access to all. This aspect of free schools has been extended to free textbooks, free libraries, and, in some public schools, to free dental and medical service and free lunches for those

* From *The Social Frontier,* March, 1936.

who cannot pay—at least it was so extended until the depression led heavy taxpayers to limit these services. But in final resort, these manifestations of freedom are tributary to freedom of education as the social enterprise in which education forms character and intelligence. There are plenty of restrictions put upon moral and intellectual freedom of education within the school system itself. It is bound, often hidebound, by hampering traditions that originated under conditions alien to the present. These traditions affect subject-matter, methods of instruction, discipline, the organization and administration of the schools. These limitations of free education, serious and weighty enough in all conscience, have been the objects of attack by educational reformers at all times. But there is another limitation added to these onerous ones that is especially dangerous at the present time. It is the attempt to close the minds, mouths, and ears of students and teachers alike to all that is not consonant with the practices and beliefs of the privileged class that represents the economic and political status quo.

The question of teachers' oaths is so familiar that I refer to it only by way of illustration. Since our Constitution provides for its own change, though by awkward and cumbrous methods, and since it expressly reserves to the people (as well as to state governments) all rights not conferred upon the Federal Government, and since this reservation of rights to the people includes the right of revolution when conditions become intolerable—as both Jefferson and Lincoln have pointed out—a teacher need have no conscientious scruples in taking an oath of loyalty to the Constitution. But the selection of teachers as the class of persons who must take the oath is socially serious because it is one phase of the general movement calculated to prevent freedom of education in all matters that relate to economic and political conditions and policies.

Liberty is a social matter and not just a claim of the private individual. Freedom is a matter of the distribution of effective power; the struggle for liberty is important because of its consequences in effecting more just, equable, and human relations of men, women, and children to one another. In no phase of social endeavor is the realization of the social content of freedom more important than in the struggle for academic freedom. Everyone who has read the pleas made in the early struggle for universal and free schools in this country knows the emphasis that was put upon education as a necessary condition for creation of the kind of citizenship indispensable to the success of democracy. Today freedom of teaching and learning on the part of instructors and students is imperatively necessary for that kind of intelligent citizenship that is genuinely free to take part in the social reconstructions without which democracy will die. The question is now whether democracy is a possible form of society when affairs are as complex and economic power is as concentrated as today.

Since freedom of mind and freedom of expression are the root of all freedom, to deny freedom in education is a crime against democracy. Because academic freedom is so essentially a social issue, since it is intimately bound up with what the future citizenship of the country is going to do in shaping our political and economic destiny, it is not surprising that those who either give only lip-service or who openly strive to restrict it, should also strive to present it to the public as a matter that concerns teachers only as individuals, and to represent those *active* in supporting its cause as more or less unbalanced individuals who want more liberty to assert their personal views. There is nothing paradoxical in saying that it is just because of the social significance of liberty of education that it is presented as something that affects only individual teachers.

It cannot be denied that there is at present an unusually large number of young people who find themselves deprived of opportunity in the present situation, who find their legitimate desires and aspirations so blocked that they have become converts to the idea that social change cannot be effected by democratic methods, but only by violent force.

The idea sedulously cultivated in the Hearst press, but not confined to it, that this attitude is the result of teachers' imposition of subversive ideas under the camouflage of academic freedom, is laughable to all those who know the facts about our schools. This attitude is the product of the restrictive and oppressive effect of the present industrial system, aided by a school system which discounts the value of social intelligence. The feeling that social change of any basic character can be brought about only by violent force is the product of lack of faith in intelligence as a method and this loss of faith is in large measure the product of a schooling that, because of its comparatively unfree condition, has not enabled youth to face intelligently the realities of our social life, political and economic.

There are ultimately but three forces that control society —habit, coercive and violent force, and action directed by intelligence. In fairly normal times, habit and custom are by far the strongest force. A social crisis like the present means that this force has in large measure ceased to operate. The other forces, therefore, come more conspicuously into play. Reactionaries who strive to prevent any change of the old order are possessed of the power that enables them to use brute force in its less overt forms: by coercion, by intimidation, and by various forms of indirect pressure. From lack of understanding of social affairs, a lack of understanding owing to faulty education, as well as to deliberate refusal to learn, reactionaries unintelligently resist change. Those who have suffered from the old order then react by appeal to direct use of force as the only means at their command. Because of the intellectual suppressions experienced in the course of their own education they have little knowledge of means of effecting social changes by any method other than force.

In short, the social significance of academic freedom lies in the fact that without freedom of inquiry and freedom on the part of teachers and students to explore the forces at work in society and the means by which they may be directed, the habits of intelligent action that are necessary to the orderly development of society cannot be created. Training for good citizenship is one thing when conditions are simple and fairly stable. It is quite another thing when conditions are confused, complicated, and unsettled, when class divisions and struggles are imminent. Every force that operates to limit the freedom of education is a premium put upon ultimate recourse to violence to effect needed change. Every force that tends to liberate educational processes is a premium placed upon intelligent and orderly methods of directing to a more just, equitable, and humane end the social changes that are going on anyway.

# 41

# CLASS STRUGGLE AND THE DEMOCRATIC WAY *

I FIND myself rather confused when it is urged that educators adopt the class concept as their intellectual guide
and practical dynamic. I do not know just what is meant
by the class concept; what its implications are, intellectual
and practical. The arguments, when boiled down, seem to
amount to the following:

A radical reconstruction of the existing social order is demanded. The needed reconstruction is opposed by the powerful
class now in control of social affairs, whose property, power, and
prestige are threatened by the reconstruction that is required.
On the other side are the workers who suffer in countless ways
from the present social order and who will be the gainers in
security, freedom, and opportunity, by basic change. Teachers
are workers and their own class interest is with fellow-workers.
Moreover, social consciousness and social conscience should lead
them to side with the workers; they belong on that side of the
struggle that is going on.

Now my confusion arises because I do not see the bearing
of these considerations, even if they are admitted, upon the
conclusion drawn; namely, that the *concept* of the class
struggle is the one which will give educators the intellectual
and practical direction they need. In fact, this conclusion
seems to me to be of the nature of a *non sequitur*. At least
it seems to be a *non sequitur* except upon the basis of an
unexpressed premise. This premise, made explicit, would be
to the effect that recognition of certain facts, namely, those
of class struggle, is sufficient to give direction to the thinking

* From *The Social Frontier,* May, 1936.

and activity that are to be brought to bear upon the facts. I can see that the empirical facts, as far as they are admitted to be facts, constitute a most serious problem. I do not see how the terms of a social problem are identical with the method of its solution, certainly not with a solution by any experimental method. I do not see how they constitute the leading ideas that will give direction to the efforts of educators. To know the empirical facts is one condition of experimental method; but the question of what to do about the facts and how to do it is another matter.

When the importance of the concept of class and class war is urged by those who have no use for the experimental point of view, I do not experience the confusion I have spoken of. For example, I do not find the gap I have mentioned in the position of communists of the current Marxist-Leninist type. For their premise is that class struggle is and always has been the source of social change; that class struggle by means of the forces of material productivity conditions the nature, the rise, and the fall of all social and cultural institutions; that at present the war is between the capitalist bourgeoisie and the proletariat; that the irrepressible conflict now going on will finally break out into overt civil war; that the end of the struggle will be the dictatorship of the proletariat as the means of final transition to a classless society. There is no ambiguity in this view. It is clear-cut and simple, for it rests upon the assumption that the class struggle determines of itself the course of events and their issue, either automatically or else because a sufficient number of persons become aware of the class struggle and become class-conscious.

If this is the point of view of those who urge upon educators the importance of the class concept, it is free from the confusion to which I have referred. But such does not seem to be the case with some writers. I mention two points of serious difference. One is that there is a subjective factor in every concept of class. This point of view is adequately stated by Dr. Childs, who says: "All classifications are tools made for a purpose." From the standpoint of current Marxian orthodoxy, this position is thoroughly heterodox. For, according to the latter, the class concept is a strictly realistic apprehension of the *existing* social reality and of that which will exist.

The further difference that follows is of even greater significance. It concerns the nature of the educational process. If the essential facts are all in, and if these facts in and of themselves decide the nature of educational policy, then, when the essential facts are said to be those of class struggle, it follows that education becomes simply a matter of inculcation—in short, of agitation and propaganda. But some at least of those who urge the importance of the class concept do not seem to draw this conclusion. Yet what is the point of the class concept as a determining factor in educational procedure unless it is to have such a controlling influence on the latter that education becomes a special form of constant indoctrination? And in that case what becomes of the plea for freedom in teaching? Is it a plea merely for freedom to inculcate a certain view of society, logically entailing lack of freedom for presentation of other views?

The point may be made clearer by supposing that one adopts the position implied in the following question of Dr. Childs: "Is it not highly probable that they [a myriad of interest groups] will merge into large classes and that American society *ultimately* will be divided into those who advocate and those who oppose this drastic reconstruction?" If one believes that this is likely to happen, what then? Shall the educator as an educator endeavor to hasten and intensify the division? And what attitude shall he take toward the problem of *how* drastic social reconstruction is to be affected? Does education have anything to do with development of the attitudes and convictions that influence the *manner* of the transition? Putting the question in an extreme form, is it the task of educators, because of acceptance of the class concept, to intensify a consciousness of class division and class war, or is it to help determine the kind of social awareness that is to exist so that the transformation may be accomplished, as far as possible, by educational means instead of by conflict? What kind of "classes" are we to have, as far as education has anything to say on that matter, whether its influence be light or great? Is it enough, for the purpose of effecting the needed social transformation, that the exploited class become conscious that it is an exploited group and then try to gain the physical or even the political power to become the dominant class? From the standpoint of those who put their faith in the idea that a violent revolution is the solution, and that subsequent dictatorship by a class is the best or only means to effect the transformation, it is quite possible that this *is* enough, that anything else would tend to hinder the day of reconstruction. But I have difficulty in imagining any educator taking this point of view unless he has abandoned in advance all faith in education.

I hope the point of these questions is clear. What does the acceptance of the class concept *mean* for the work of the educators? I cannot but think that the acceptance of a *social* point of view rather than that of a special class has led those who have advocated the class concept to adopt the convictions they hold about the place of education in social transformation. If this is so, it would seem as if this broader and more inclusive point of view is the one from which they should carry on their educational work. The acceptance of this point of view does not mean that they should close their minds to the injustices and inequities of the present order, to their effects—impoverishment and insecurity—or to the disastrous effect of these tragic evils upon the culture of all groups in society. But certainly those who believe that education in the schools has some part to play in bringing about social transformation have a greater responsibility than any others to consider the *means* by which the transformation is to be brought about and the especial place of educational means among the total means. Except as educators accept the current Marxian view of the means that are alone necessary, I can but conclude that my confusion in reading what has been said is a result of a confusion on the part of the writers. They seem to convert a just plea that educators should become aware of the existence of social injustice, oppression, and disorder into the idea that this recognition suffices of itself to determine educational policies and methods. I repeat that such recognition forms a significant part of the *problem* of education, but it does not provide a key to its solution.

For an American, at least, the acceptance of a social instead of an exclusive class point of view, means acceptance of the democratic idea as the frame of reference and the source of the directive ideas of educational action. The issue of whether educators shall stay out of the process of social transformation or shall participate in it is quite another question from that of whether their participation shall be controlled by the class concept. To see this point seems to me the beginning of clarity of thought upon the whole matter. And there need be no fear that honest adoption of the democratic idea and criterion will lead to apathy and complacency —save in the case of those so intellectually dishonest that they would find some evasion in any case. The democratic frame of reference is capable of energizing action as well as of directing critical reflection and educational thought.

As far as I can see, the ambiguity in the concept of class orientation arises from confusing orientation *toward* a class, the class of workers, with orientation *by* a class interest. One's sympathies and, as occasion presents itself, one's efforts may well be with workers as against an exploiting class. But one's frame of values and one's controlling framework of ideas may nevertheless be derived from a sense of a comprehensive social interest. As I read those to whom reference has been made, this larger sense is in fact their animating spirit. The writers urge teachers to recognize that they too are workers and that their function and their success in performing it are bound up with the struggle in which workers are engaged. I am not taking exception to this point of view nor am I urging that teachers should be "neutral"—an impossibility in any case. It is possible to be alert and active in the struggle for social reorganization and yet recognize that it is *social* reorganization that is required, and that it must be undertaken in the social, rather than a class interest. Because I am persuaded the writers recognize that educational means and methods, rather than those of brute force, should play as large a part as possible in bringing about the reorganization, I am concerned lest they urge their plea from the standpoint of a class rather than from that of our democratic tradition and its methods.

## 42

## RATIONALITY IN EDUCATION *

LANCELOT HOGBEN'S *The Retreat from Reason* and President Hutchins' *The Higher Learning in America* are superficially extraordinarily similar and fundamentally extraordinarily different. Both deal with basic educational problems in relation to contemporary conditions. Both are troubled deeply about education as it now exists and about contemporary life. Both are concerned with the place of reason and understanding in education and in life, Professor Hogben being profoundly affected by the eclipse of intelligence characteristic of present society and President Hutchins saying that the "most important job that can be performed in the United States is first to establish higher education on a rational basis, and second, to make our people understand it." Both books deserve the most serious attention and study on the part of educators.

At this point similarity ceases, save that there is some degree of agreement in spirit, if not in words, as to the causes that have occasioned our present ills. The profound difference between the two books, a difference which leads them to opposite conclusions, lies in the conceptions respectively entertained by the two men as to the nature of what both call by the same name—Reason. Mr. Hutchins looks to Plato, Aristotle, and St. Thomas Aquinas in order to discover the nature of Reason and its modes of operation; Mr. Hogben looks to the activities of experimental science as the place in which to discover its real nature. To Mr. Hutchins the sciences represent in the main the unmitigated empiricism which is a great curse of modern life, while to

* From *The Social Frontier*, December, 1936.

331

Mr. Hogben the conceptions and methods which Mr. Hutchins takes to be the true and final definition of rationality are obscurantist and fatally reactionary, while their survival in economic theory and other branches of social "science" is the source of intellectual irrelevance of the latter to the fundamental problems of our present culture. Indeed, these disciplines are more than irrelevant and futile. They are literally terrible in their distraction of social intelligence and activity from genuine social problems and from the only methods by which the problems can be met.

This basic difference reflects itself in the authors' treatment of every aspect of education and social culture, both in themselves and in their connection with one another. Of these aspects I select three for special consideration: the constitution of human nature, the relation of theory and action, and the method of the working and development of "reason."

President Hutchins is quite sure that the elements of human nature are fixed and constant. They "are the same in any time and place." One great business of education is "to draw out the elements of our common human nature." "The truth is everywhere the same." Hence, omitting details, "the heart of education will be, if education is rightly understood, the same at any time, in any place, under any political, social, or economic conditions." Mr. Hogben emphasizes equally common elements in human nature. But these elements are *needs*, and therefore the first questions to be considered "are whether the common needs of men as members of the same species, phylum, and type of matter, are at present satisfied, what resources for satisfying them exist, and how far these resources are used." Moreover, the needs in question are growing, not fixed; the needs for food, for protection, for reproduction, for example, are always the same in the abstract, but in the concrete they and the means of satisfying them change their content with every change in science, technology, and social institutions.

The bearing of this difference upon the relation of theory

and social practice is close and direct. President Hutchins feels strongly that the invasion of vocationalism is the great curse of contemporary education. Mr. Hogben would agree as far as by vocational "we usually mean that [which] helps us gain a livelihood irrespective of the social usefulness of the occupation chosen." But the isolation of existing education, taken generally, from connection with social usefulness in distinction from personal pecuniary advancement, is the chief ground of his criticism of that education. The exaltation of knowledge as something too "pure" to be contaminated by contact with human needs and the resources available for satisfying them, he puts on the same level as the prostitution of learning to serve those needs of individuals that are due to the existence of competitive, acquisitive, pecuniary economic-social institutions and ideals—if they can be called ideals. He quotes with approval the saying of Bacon that "the true and lawful goal of science is to endow life with new powers and inventions"; that of Boyle to value "knowledge save as it tends to use," and of Thomas Huxley, "the great end of life is not knowledge but action."

The educational implications of this position contrast with the conclusion which President Hutchins logically draws from his conception of the nature of knowledge and action in their relations to one another. Higher education is to be purified and reformed according to him by complete separation of general and "liberal" education from professional and technical education. The student having exclusively acquired in the liberal college the basic principles of knowledge in a purely theoretical way and having thereby learned "correct thinking," will later proceed to studies that prepare him exclusively for some line of practical activity.* More-

* The completeness of the separation set up is indicated by such passages as the following: "I concede the probable necessity in some fields of practical training which the young man or woman should have before being permitted to engage in the independent practice of a profession. *Since by definition this training cannot be intellectual,* and since by definition a university must be intellectual, this type of specific training for specific jobs cannot be conducted as part of the university's work."

over, even in the latter there will be as little connection with "experience" as possible, later practical life supplying the factor of experience, which Aristotle and St. Thomas have already shown to be merely empirical, to be non-rational save as parts of it may be deductively derived from the eternal first principles of rational knowledge.

Mr. Hogben is himself a scientist of standing as well as a humanist in the only sense in which I can attach meaning to that much abused word. I should give a totally wrong impression if what I have quoted from him indicates that he has a low conception of the value of knowledge and the search for it. On the contrary, the idea of the intimate connection that exists between the very nature of knowledge and such action as is socially useful (rather than socially harmful) carries with it the conclusion that students would obtain more knowledge in a more significant way and have a deeper and more enduring apprehension of the meaning of truth, if the facts and ideas acquired in school had some vital connection with basic social needs, with the resources available for common satisfaction of them, and with an understanding of the forces that now prevent these resources from being used. The methods of getting knowledge are to him best exemplified in the natural sciences and most badly represented in the present methods of the so-called social sciences. He calls, therefore, for more science, taught very differently from the way in which it is now taught; for the necessity of science in the education of those who are to control, directly and indirectly, political life; and for the closest association between the teaching of human history and the course of scientific advance. While he does not discuss the question of "truth," I take it that he would agree that "truth is the same everywhere," though he might well be chary of speaking of the truth. But just because truth is so important, the methods of arriving at it are the things of primary importance in education and in life.

To President Hutchins on the contrary truth only needs to be taught and learned. Somehow or other it is there, and there is something in existence called the Intellect that is ready to apprehend it. *The* truth is embodied in "permanent studies" as distinct from progressive studies. As with the great masters, Plato, Aristotle, and St. Thomas, the eternal and the changing are in sharp opposition to each other. And there is no doubt as to what are the permanent studies with permanent content. They are the three arts, grammar, rhetoric, and logic, which constituted the *trivia* of the university in those medieval days when knowledge was organized and universities *were* universities—though the historian might say that they were most of all professional schools. Then there are the classics, though not necessarily taught in the original language, and mathematics; and "of the mathematical studies chiefly those that use the type of exposition that Euclid employed"—a somewhat curious statement in view of the fact that contemporary logicians recognize the many logical defects in the Euclidean exposition, while working scientists would agree, I think, that of all branches of mathematics it is the one that is of least importance in their pursuits. As for science, "the Physics of Aristotle, which deals with change and motion in nature, is fundamental to the natural sciences and to medicine." In contrast with these permanent studies, what is now called the "scientific spirit" consists in gathering facts indiscriminately and hoping for the best. The basis and keystone of the entire educational arch is metaphysics, which it would appear, though no specimens are given, is also an established system of permanent truths. It is concerned in any case with "things highest by nature, first principles, and first causes."

It is not to be inferred that all "empirical" studies are excluded by President Hutchins. Information, historical and current, may be introduced in the degree that "such data illustrate or confirm principles or assist in their development." But all other studies including the natural and social sciences are to be pursued in "subordination" to the "hierarchy of truths." These empirical studies would proceed, in accord with the classic logic of antiquity and the Middle

Ages, "from first principles to whatever recent observations are significant in understanding them." *

I agree with both of the writers in holding that present education is disordered and confused. The problem as to the direction in which we shall seek for order and clarity is the most important question facing education and educators today. Teachers and administrators are not given to asking what the nature of knowledge is, as distinct from the subject-matter that is taken to be known, nor by what methods knowledge is genuinely attained—as distinct from the methods by which the facts and ideas that are taken to be known shall be taught and learned. These two books taken together serve to present the problem in its two aspects with extraordinary clarity. Until educators have faced the problem and made an intelligent choice between the contrasting conceptions represented in these two books, I see no great hope for unified progress in the reorganization of studies and methods in the schools.

* Mr. Hogben's idea about such methods may be gathered from the following quotation, which in its context refers to economics as deduced from "rational" first principles: "We can only conclude that economics, as studied in our universities, is the astrology of the Machine Age; it provides the same kind of intellectual relief as chess, in which success depends entirely on knowing the initial definition of moves and processes of checking, casting, etc. . . . In science the final arbiter is not the self-evidence of the initial statement, nor the façade of flawless logic that conceals it. A scientific law embodies a recipe for doing something, and its final validation rests in the domain of action."

# 43

# DEMOCRACY AND EDUCATIONAL
## ADMINISTRATION *

**M**Y EXPERIENCE in educational administration is limited. I should not venture to address a body of those widely experienced and continuously engaged in school administration about the details of the management of schools. But the topic suggested to me has to do with the relation of school administration to democratic ideals and methods, and to the general subject of the relation of education and democracy I have given considerable thought over many years. The topic suggested concerns a special phase of this general subject. I shall begin, then, with some remarks on the broad theme of democratic aims and methods. Much of what I shall say on this subject is necessarily old and familiar. But it seems necessary to rehearse some old ideas in order to have a criterion for dealing with the special subject.

In the first place, democracy is much broader than a special political form, a method of conducting government, of making laws and carrying on governmental administration by means of popular suffrage and elected officers. It is that, of course. But it is something broader and deeper than that. The political and governmental phase of democracy is a means, the best means so far found, for realizing ends that lie in the wide domain of human relationships and the development of human personality. It is, as we often say, though perhaps without appreciating all that is involved in the saying, a way of life, social and individual. The keynote

* Read at the General Session of the Department of Superintendence of the National Education Association, New Orleans, February 22, 1937. From *School and Society*, April 3, 1937.

of democracy as a way of life may be expressed, it seems to me, as the necessity for the participation of every mature human being in formation of the values that regulate the living of men together: which is necessary from the standpoint of both the general social welfare and the full development of human beings as individuals.

Universal suffrage, recurring elections, responsibility of those who are in political power to the voters, and the other factors of democratic government are means that have been found expedient for realizing democracy as the truly human way of living. They are not a final end and a final value. They are to be judged on the basis of their contribution to end. It is a form of idolatry to erect means into the end which they serve. Democratic political forms are simply the best means that human wit has devised up to a special time in history. But they rest back upon the idea that no man or limited set of men is wise enough or good enough to rule others without their consent; the positive meaning of this statement is that all those who are affected by social institutions must have a share in producing and managing them. The two facts that each one is influenced in what he does and enjoys and in what he becomes by the institutions under which he lives, and that therefore he shall have, in a democracy, a voice in shaping them, are the passive and active sides of the same fact.

The development of political democracy came about through substitution of the method of mutual consultation and voluntary agreement for the method of subordination of the many to the few enforced from above. Social arrangements which involve fixed subordination are maintained by coercion. The coercion need not be physical. There have existed, for short periods, benevolent despotisms. But coercion of some sort there has been; perhaps economic, certainly psychological and moral. The very fact of exclusion from participation is a subtle form of suppression. It gives individuals no opportunity to reflect and decide upon what is good for them. Others who are supposed to be wiser and who in any case have more power decide the question for them and also decide the methods and means by which subjects may arrive at the enjoyment of what is good for them. This form of coercion and suppression is more subtle and more effective than is overt intimidation and restraint. When it is habitual and embodied in social institutions, it seems the normal and natural state of affairs. The mass usually become unaware that they have a claim to a development of their own powers. Their experience is so restricted that they are not conscious of restriction. It is part of the democratic conception that they as individuals are not the only sufferers, but that the whole social body is deprived of the potential resources that should be at its service. The individuals of the submerged mass may not be very wise. But there is one thing they are wiser about than anybody else can be, and that is where the shoe pinches, the troubles they suffer from. The foundation of democracy is faith in the capacities of human nature; faith in human intelligence and in the power of pooled and co-operative experience. It is not belief that these things are complete but that if given a show they will grow and be able to generate progressively the knowledge and wisdom needed to guide collective action. Every autocratic and authoritarian scheme of social action rests on a belief that the needed intelligence is confined to a superior few, who because of inherent natural gifts are endowed with the ability and the right to control the conduct of others; laying down principles and rules and and directing the ways in which they are carried out. It would be foolish to deny that much can be said for this point of view. It is that which controlled human relations in social groups for much the greater part of human history. The democratic faith has emerged very, very recently in the history of mankind. Even where democracies now exist, men's minds and feelings are still permeated with ideas about leadership imposed from above, ideas that developed in the long early history of mankind. After democratic political institutions were nominally established, beliefs and ways of looking at life and of acting that originated when men and women were externally controlled and subjected to arbitrary power, persisted in the family, the church, business and the school, and experience shows that as long as they persist there, political democracy is not secure.

Belief in equality is an element of the democratic credo. It is not, however, belief in equality of natural endowments. Those who proclaimed the idea of equality did not suppose they were enunciating a psychological doctrine, but a legal and political one. All individuals are entitled to equality of treatment by law and in its administration. Each one is affected equally in quality if not in quantity by the institutions under which he lives and has an equal right to express his judgment, although the weight of his judgment may not be equal in amount when it enters into the pooled result to that of others. In short, each one is equally an individual and entitled to equal opportunity of development of his own capacities, be they large or small in range. Moreover, each has needs of his own, as significant to him as those of others are to them. The very fact of natural and psychological inequality is all the more reason for establishment by law of equality of opportunity, since otherwise the former becomes a means of oppression of the less gifted.

While what we call intelligence be distributed in unequal amounts, it is the democratic faith that it is sufficiently general so that each individual has something to contribute, whose value can be assessed only as it enters into the final pooled intelligence constituted by the contributions of all. Every authoritarian scheme, on the contrary, assumes that its value may be assessed by some *prior* principle, if not of family and birth or race and color or possession of material wealth, then by the position and rank a person occupies in the existing social scheme. The democratic faith in equality is the faith that each individual shall have the chance and opportunity to contribute whatever he is capable of contributing and that the value of his contribution be decided by its place and function in the organized total of similar contributions, not on the basis of prior status of any kind whatever.

I have emphasized in what precedes the importance of the effective release of intelligence in connection with personal experience in the democratic way of living. I have done so purposely because democracy is so often and so naturally associated in our minds with freedom of *action,* forgetting the importance of freed intelligence which is necessary to direct and to warrant freedom of action. Unless freedom of individual action has intelligence and informed conviction back of it, its manifestation is almost sure to result in confusion and disorder. The democratic idea of freedom is not the right of each individual to *do* as he pleases, even if it be qualified by adding "provided he does not interfere with the same freedom on the part of others." While the idea is not always, not often enough, expressed in words, the basic freedom is that of freedom of *mind* and of whatever degree of freedom of action and experience is necessary to produce freedom of intelligence. The modes of freedom guaranteed in the Bill of Rights are all of this nature: Freedom of belief and conscience, of expression of opinion, of assembly for discussion and conference, of the press as an organ of communication. They are guaranteed because without them individuals are not free to develop and society is deprived of what they might contribute.

What, it may be asked, have these things to do with school administration? There is some kind of government, of control, wherever affairs that concern a number of persons who act together are engaged in. It is a superficial view that holds government is located in Washington and Albany. There is government in the family, in business, in the church, in every social group. There are regulations, due to custom if not to enactment, that settle how individuals in a group act in connection with one another.

It is a disputed question of theory and practice just how far a democratic political government should go in control of the conditions of action within special groups. At the present time, for example, there are those who think the federal and state governments leave too much freedom of independent action to industrial and financial groups, and there are others who think the government is going altogether too far at the present time. I do not need to discuss this phase of the problem, much less to try to settle it. But it must be pointed out that if the methods of regulation and administration in vogue in the conduct of secondary social groups are non-democratic, whether directly or indirectly or both, there is bound to be an unfavorable reaction back into the habits of feeling, thought and action of citizenship in the broadest sense of that word. The way in which any organized social interest is controlled necessarily plays an important part in forming the dispositions and tastes, the attitudes, interests, purposes and desires, of those engaged in carrying on the activities of the group. For illustration, I do not need to do more than point to the moral, emotional and intellectual effect upon both employers and laborers of the existing industrial system. Just what the effects specifically are is a matter about which we know very little. But I suppose that every one who reflects upon the subject admits that it is impossible that the ways in which activities are carried on for the greater part of the waking hours of the day, and the way in which the share of individuals is involved in the management of affairs in such a matter as gaining a livelihood and attaining material and social security, can not but be a highly important factor in shaping personal dispositions; in short, forming character and intelligence.

In the broad and final sense all institutions are educational in the sense that they operate to form the attitudes, dispositions, abilities and disabilities that constitute a concrete personality. The principle applies with special force to the school. For it is the main business of the family and the school to influence directly the formation and growth of attitudes and dispositions, emotional, intellectual and moral. Whether this educative process is carried on in a predominantly democratic or non-democratic way becomes, therefore, a question of transcendent importance not only for education itself but for its final effect upon all the interests and activities of a society that is committed to the democratic way of life. Hence, if the general tenor of what I have said about the democratic ideal and method is anywhere near the truth, it must be said that the democratic principle requires that every teacher should have some regular and organic way in which he can, directly or through representatives democratically chosen, participate in the formation of the controlling aims, methods and materials of the school of which he is a part. Something over thirty years ago, I wrote: "If there is a single public-school system in the United States where there is official and constitutional provision made for submitting questions of methods of discipline and teaching, and the questions of the curriculum, text-books, etc., to the discussion and decision of those actually engaged in the work of teaching, that fact has escaped my notice." I could not make that statement today. There has been in some places a great advance in the democratic direction. As I noted in my earlier article there were always in actual fact school systems where the practice was much better than the theory of external control from above: for even if there were no authorized regular way in which the intelligence and experience of the teaching corps was consulted and utilized, administrative officers accomplished that end in informal ways. We may hope this extension of democratic methods has not only endured but has expanded. Nevertheless, the issue of authoritarian versus democratic methods in administration remains with us and demands serious recognition.

It is my impression that even up to the present democratic methods of dealing with pupils have made more progress than have similar methods of dealing with members of the teaching staff of the classroom. At all events, there has been an organized and vital movement in the first matter while that in the second is still in its early stage. All schools that pride themselves upon being up-to-date utilize methods of instruction that draw upon and utilize the life-experience of students and strive to individualize treatment of pupils. Whatever reasons hold for adopting this course with respect to the young certainly more strongly hold for teachers, since the latter are more mature and have more experience. Hence the question is in place: What are the ways by which can be secured more organic participation of teachers in the formation of the educational policies of the school?

Since, as I have already said, it is the problem I wish to present rather than to lay down the express ways in which it is to be solved, I might stop at this point. But there are certain corollaries which clarify the meaning of the issue. Absence of participation tends to produce lack of interest and concern on the part of those shut out. The result is a corresponding lack of effective responsibility. Automatically and unconsciously, if not consciously, the feeling develops, "This is none of our affair; it is the business of those at the top; let that particular set of Georges do what needs to be done." The countries in which autocratic government prevails are just those in which there is least public spirit and the greatest indifference to matters of general as distinct from personal concern. Can we expect a different kind of psychology to actuate teachers? Where there is little power, there is correspondingly little sense of positive responsibility. It is enough to do what one is told to do sufficiently well to escape flagrant unfavorable notice. About larger matters, a spirit of passivity is engendered. In some cases, indifference passes into evasion of duties when not directly under the eye of a supervisor; in other cases, a carping, rebellious spirit is engendered. A sort of game is instituted between teacher and supervisor like that which went on in the old-fashioned schools between teacher and pupil. Other teachers pass on, perhaps unconsciously, what they feel to be arbitrary treatment received by them to their pupils.

The argument that teachers are not prepared to assume the responsibility of participation deserves attention, with its accompanying belief that natural selection has operated to put those best prepared to carry the load in the positions of authority. Whatever the truth in this contention, it still is also true that incapacity to assume the responsibilities involved in having a voice in shaping policies is bred and increased by conditions in which that responsibility is denied. I suppose there has never been an autocrat, big or little, who did not justify his conduct on the ground of the unfitness of his subjects to take part in government. I would not compare administrators to political autocrats. Upon the whole, what exists in the schools is more a matter of habit and custom than it is of any deliberate autocracy. But, as was said earlier, habitual exclusion has the effect of reducing a sense of responsibility for what is done and its consequences. What the argument for democracy implies is that the best way to produce initiative and constructive power is to exercise it. Power, as well as interest, comes by use and practice. Moreover, the argument from incapacity proves too much. If it is so great as to be a permanent bar, then teachers can not be expected to have the intelligence and skill that are necessary to execute the directions given them. The delicate and difficult task of developing character and good judgment in the young needs every stimulus and inspiration possible. It is impossible that the work should not be better done when teachers have that understanding of what they are doing that comes from having shared in forming its guiding ideas.

Classroom teachers are those who are in continuous direct contact with those taught. The position of administrators is at best indirect by comparison. If there is any work in the world that requires the conservation of what is good in experience so that it may become an integral part of further experience, it is that of teaching. I often wonder how much waste there is in the traditional system. There is some loss even at the best of the potential capital acquired by successful teachers. It does not get freely transmitted to other teachers who might profit by it. Is not the waste very considerably increased when teachers are not called upon to communicate their successful methods and results in a form by which it would have organic effect upon general school policies? Add to this waste that results when teachers are called upon to give effect in the classroom to courses of study they do not understand the reasons for, and the total loss mounts up so that it is a fair estimate that the absence of democratic methods is the greatest single cause of educational waste.

I conclude by saying that the present subject is one of peculiar importance at the present time. The fundamental beliefs and practices of democracy are now challenged as they never have been before. In some nations they are more than challenged. They are ruthlessly and systematically destroyed. Everywhere there are waves of criticism and doubt as to whether democracy can meet pressing problems of order and security. The causes for the destruction of political democracy in countries where it was nominally established are complex. But of one thing I think we may be sure. Wherever it has fallen it was too exclusively political in nature. It had not become part of the bone and blood of the people in daily conduct of its life. Democratic forms were limited to Parliament, elections and combats between parties. What is happening proves conclusively, I think, that unless democratic habits of thought and action are part of the fiber of a people, political democracy is insecure. It can not stand in isolation. It must be buttressed by the presence of democratic methods in all social relationships. The relations that exist in educational institutions are second only in importance in this respect to those which exist in industry and business, perhaps not even to them.

I recur then to the idea that the particular question discussed is one phase of a wide and deep problem. I can think of nothing so important in this country at present as a rethinking of the whole problem of democracy and its implications. Neither the rethinking nor the action it should produce can be brought into being in a day or year. The democratic idea itself demands that the thinking and activity proceed co-operatively. My utmost hope will be fulfilled if anything I have said plays any part, however small, in promoting co-operative inquiry and experimentation in this field of democratic administration of our schools.

## 44

## EDUCATION AND SOCIAL CHANGE *

UPON certain aspects of my theme there is nothing new to be said. Attention has been continually called of late to the fact that society is in process of change, and that the schools tend to lag behind. We are all familiar with the pleas that are urged to bring education in the schools into closer relation with the forces that are producing social change and with the needs that arise from these changes. Probably no question has received so much attention in educational discussion during the last few years as the problem of integration of the schools with social life. Upon these general matters, I could hardly do more than reiterate what has often been said.

Nevertheless, there is as yet little consensus of opinion as to what the schools can do in relation to the forces of social change and how they should do it. There are those who assert in effect that the schools must simply reflect social changes that have already occurred, as best they may. Some would go so far as to make the work of schools virtually parasitic. Others hold that the schools should take an active part in *directing* social change, and share in the construction of a new social order. Even among the latter there is, however, marked difference of attitude. Some think the schools should assume this directive role by means of indoctrination; others oppose this method. Even if there were more unity of thought than exists, there would still be the practical problem of overcoming institutional inertia so as to realize in fact an agreed-upon program.

There is, accordingly, no need to justify further discussion

* From *The Social Frontier*, May, 1937.

of the problem of the relation of education to social change. I shall do what I can, then, to indicate the factors that seem to me to enter into the problem, together with some of the reasons that prove that the schools do have a role—and an important one—in *production* of social change.

One factor inherent in the situation is that schools *do* follow and reflect the social "order" that exists. I do not make this statement as a grudging admission, nor yet in order to argue that they should *not* do so. I make it rather as a statement of a *conditioning* factor which supports the conclusion that the schools thereby do take part in the determination of a future social order; and that, accordingly, the problem is not whether the schools *should* participate in the production of a future society (since they do so anyway) but whether they should do it blindly and irresponsibly or with the maximum possible of courageous intelligence and responsibility.

The grounds that lead me to make this statement are as follows: The existing state of society, which the schools reflect, is not something fixed and uniform. The idea that such is the case is a self-imposed hallucination. Social conditions are not only in process of change, but the changes going on are in different directions, so different as to produce social confusion and conflict. There is no single and clear-cut pattern that pervades and holds together in a unified way the social conditions and forces that operate. It would be easy to cite highly respectable authorities who have stated, as matter of historic fact and not on account of some doctrinal conclusion to be drawn, that social conditions in all that affects the relations of human beings to one another have changed more in the last one hundred and fifty years than in all previous time, and that the process of change is still going on. It requires a good deal of either ignorance or intellectual naïveté to suppose that these changes have all been tending to one coherent social outcome. The plaint of the conservative about the imperiling of old and time-tried values and truths, and the efforts of reactionaries to stem the tide of changes that occur, are sufficient evidence, if evidence be needed to the contrary.

Of course the schools have mirrored the social changes that take place. The efforts of Horace Mann and others a century ago to establish a public, free, common school system were a reflection primarily of the social conditions that followed the war by the colonies for political independence and the establishment of republican institutions. The evidential force of this outstanding instance would be confirmed in detail if we went through the list of changes that have taken place in (1) the kind of schools that have been established, (2) the new courses that have been introduced, (3) the shifts in subject-matter that have occurred, and (4) the changes in methods of instruction and discipline that have occurred in intervening years. The notion that the educational system has been static is too absurd for notice; it has been and still is in a state of flux.

The fact that it is possible to argue about the desirability of many of the changes that have occurred, and to give valid reasons for deploring aspects of the flux, is not relevant to the main point. For the stronger the arguments brought forth on these points, and the greater the amount of evidence produced to show that the educational system is in a state of disorder and confusion, the greater is the proof that the schools have responded to, and have reflected, social conditions which are themselves in a state of confusion and conflict.

Do those who hold the idea that the schools should not attempt to give direction to social change accept complacently the confusion that exists, because the schools *have* followed in the track of one social change after another? They certainly do not, although the logic of their position demands it. For the most part they are severe critics of the existing state of education. They are as a rule opposed to the studies called modern and the methods called progressive. They tend to favor return to older types of studies and to strenuous "disciplinary" methods. What does this attitude mean? Does it not show that its advocates in reality adopt the position that the schools can do something to affect positively and constructively social conditions? For they hold in effect that the school should discriminate with respect to the social forces that play upon it; that instead of accepting the latter *in toto,* education should select and organize in a given direction. The adherents of this view can hardly believe that the effect of selection and organization will stop at the doors of schoolrooms. They must expect some ordering and healing influence to be exerted sooner or later upon the structure and movement of life outside. What they are really doing when they deny directive social effect to education is to express their opposition to some of the directions social change is actually taking, and their choice of other social forces as those with which education should throw in its lot so as to promote as far as may be their victory in the strife of forces. They are conservatives in education because they are socially conservative and vice versa.

This is as it should be in the interest of clearness and consistency of thought and action. If these conservatives in education were more aware of what is involved in their position, and franker in stating its implications, they would help bring out the real issue. It is not whether the schools shall or shall not influence the course of future social life, but in what direction they shall do so and how. In some fashion or other, the schools will influence social life anyway. But they can exercise such influence in different ways and to different ends, and the important thing is to become conscious of these different ways and ends, so that an intelligent choice may be made, and so that if opposed choices are made, the further conflict may at least be carried on with understanding of what is at stake, and not in the dark.

There are three possible directions of choice. Educators may act so as to perpetuate the present confusion and possibly increase it. That will be the result of drift, and under present conditions to drift is in the end to make a choice. Or they may select the newer scientific, technological, and cultural forces that are producing change in the old order; may estimate the direction in which they are moving and their outcome if they are given freer play, and see what can be done to make the schools their ally. Or, educators may become intelligently conservative and strive to make the schools a force in maintaining the old order intact against the impact of new forces.

If the second course is chosen—as of course I believe it should be—the problem will be other than merely that of accelerating the rate of the change that is going on. The problem will be to develop the insight and understanding that will enable the youth who go forth from the schools to take part in the great work of construction and organization that will have to be done, and to equip them with the attitudes and habits of action that will make their understanding and insight practically effective.

There is much that can be said for an intelligent conservatism. I do not know anything that can be said for perpetuation of a wavering, uncertain, confused condition of social life and education. Nevertheless, the easiest thing is to refrain from fundamental thinking and let things go on drifting. Upon the basis of any other policy than drift—which after all is a policy, though a blind one—every special issue and problem, whether that of selection and organization of subject-matter of study, of methods of teaching, of school buildings and equipment, of school administration, is a special phase of the inclusive and fundamental problem: What movement of social forces, economic, political, religious, cultural, shall the school take to be controlling in its aims and methods, and with which forces shall the school align itself?

Failure to discuss educational problems from this point of view but intensifies the existing confusion. Apart from this background, and outside of this perspective, educational questions have to be settled *ad hoc* and are speedily unsettled. What is suggested does not mean that the schools shall throw themselves into the political and economic arena and take sides with some party there. I am not talking about parties; I am talking about social forces and their movement. In spite of absolute claims that are made for this party or that, it is altogether probable that existing parties and sects themselves suffer from existing confusions and conflicts, so that the understanding, the ideas, and attitudes that control their policies need re-education and re-orientation. I know that there are some who think that the implications of what I have said point to abstinence and futility; that they negate the stand first taken. But I am surprised when educators adopt this position, for it shows a profound lack of faith in their own calling. It assumes that education as education has nothing or next to nothing to contribute; that formation of understanding and disposition counts for nothing; that only immediate overt action counts and that it can count equally whether or not it has been modified by education.

Before leaving this aspect of the subject, I wish to recur to the utopian nature of the idea that the schools can be completely neutral. This idea sets up an end incapable of accomplishment. So far as it is acted upon, it has a definite social effect, but that effect is, as I have said, perpetuation of disorder and increase of blind because unintelligent conflict. Practically, moreover, the weight of such action falls upon the reactionary side. Perhaps the most effective way of reinforcing reaction under the name of neutrality consists in keeping the oncoming generation ignorant of the conditions in which they live and the issues they have to face. This effect is the more pronounced because it is subtle and indirect; because neither teachers nor those taught are aware of what they are doing and what is being done to them. Clarity can develop only in the extent to which there is frank acknowledgment of the basic issue: Where shall the social emphasis of school life and work fall, and what are the educational policies which correspond to this emphasis?

So far I have spoken of those who assert, in terms of the views of a conservative group, the doctrine of complete impotence of education. But it is an old story that politics makes strange bedfellows. There is another group which holds the schools are completely impotent; that they so necessarily reflect the dominant economic and political regime, that they are committed, root and branch, to its support. This conclusion is based upon the belief that the organization of a given society is fixed by the control exercised by a particular economic class, so that the school, like every other social institution, is of necessity the subservient tool of a dominant class. This viewpoint takes literally the doctrine that the school can only reflect the existing social order. Hence the conclusion in effect that it is a waste of energy and time to bother with the schools. The only way, according to advocates of this theory, to change education in any important respect is first to overthrow the existing class-order of society and transfer power to another class. Then the needed change in education will follow automatically and will be genuine and thoroughgoing.

This point of view serves to call attention to another factor in the general issue being discussed. I shall not here take up in detail the basic premise of this school of social thought, namely the doctrine of domination of social organization by a single rather solidly unified class; a domination so complete and pervasive that it can be thrown off only by the violent revolutionary action of another distinct unified class. It will be gathered, however, from what has been said that I believe the existing situation is so composite and so marked by conflicting criss-cross tendencies that this premise represents an exaggeration of actual conditions so extreme as to be a caricature. Yet I do recognize that so far as any general characterization of the situation can be made, it is on the basis of a conflict of older and newer forces—forces cultural, religious, scientific, philosophic, economic, and political.

But suppose it is admitted for the sake of argument that a social revolution is going on, and that it will culminate in a transfer of power effected by violent action. The notion that schools are completely impotent under existing conditions then has disastrous consequences. The schools, according to the theory, are engaged in shaping as far as in them lies a mentality, a type of belief, desire, and purpose that is consonant with the present class-capitalist system. It is evident that if such be the case, any revolution that is brought about is going to be badly compromised and even undermined. It will carry with it the seeds, the vital seeds, of counter-revolutions. There is no basis whatever, save doctrinaire absolutism, for the belief that a complete economic change will produce of itself the mental, moral, and cultural changes that are necessary for its enduring success. The fact is practically recognized by the school of thought under discussion in that part of their doctrine which asserts that no genuine revolution can occur until the old system has passed away in everything but external political power, while within its shell a new economic system has grown to maturity. What is ignored is that the new system cannot grow to maturity without an accompanying widespread change of habits of belief, desire, and purpose.

It is unrealistic, in my opinion, to suppose that the schools can be a *main* agency in producing the intellectual and moral changes, the changes in attitudes and disposition of thought and purpose, which are necessary for the creation of a new social order. Any such view ignores the constant operation of powerful forces outside the school which shape mind and character. It ignores the fact that school education is but one educational agency out of many, and at the best is in some respects a minor educational force. Nevertheless, while the school is not a sufficient condition, it is a necessary condition of forming the understanding and the dispositions that are required to maintain a genuinely changed social order. No social change is more than external unless it is attended by and rooted in the attitudes of those who bring it about and of those who are affected by it. In a genuine sense, social change is accidental unless it has also a psychological and moral foundation. For it is then at the mercy of currents that veer and shift. The utmost that can be meant by those who hold that schools are impotent is that education in the form of *systematic indoctrination* can only come about when some government is sufficiently established to make schools undertake the task of single-minded inculcation in a single direction.

The discussion has thus reached the point in which it is advisable to say a few words about indoctrination. The word is not free from ambiguity. One definition of the dictionary makes it a synonym for teaching. In order that there may be a definite point to consider, I shall take indoctrination to mean the systematic use of every possible means to impress upon the minds of pupils a particular set of political and economic views to the exclusion of every other. This meaning is suggested by the word "inculcation," whose original signification was "to stamp in with the heel." This signification is too physical to be carried over literally. But the idea of stamping in is involved, and upon occasion does include physical measures. I shall discuss this view only as far as to state, in the first place, that indoctrination so conceived is something very different from education, for the latter involves, as I understand it, the active participation of students in reaching conclusions and forming attitudes. Even in the case of something as settled and agreed upon as the multiplication table, I should say if it is taught educatively, and not as a form of animal training, the active participation, the interest, reflection, and understanding of those taught are necessary.

The upholders of indoctrination rest their adherence to the theory in part upon the fact that there is a great deal of indoctrination now going on in the schools, especially with reference to narrow nationalism under the name of patriotism, and with reference to the dominant economic regime. These facts unfortunately *are* facts. But they do not prove that the right course is to seize upon the method of indoctrination and reverse its objective.

A much stronger argument is that unless education has some frame of reference it is bound to be aimless, lacking a unified objective. The necessity for a frame of reference must be admitted. There exists in this country such a unified frame. It is called democracy. I do not claim for a moment that the significance of democracy as a mode of life is so settled that there can be no disagreement as to its significance. The moment we leave glittering generalities and come to concrete details, there is great divergence. I certainly do not mean either that our political institutions as they have come to be, our parties, legislatures, laws, and courts constitute a model upon which a clear idea of democracy can be based. But there is a tradition and an idea which we can put in opposition to the very much that is undemocratic in our institutions. The idea and ideal involve at least the necessity of personal and voluntary participation in reaching decisions and executing them—in so far it is the contrary of the idea of indoctrination. And I, for one, am profoundly skeptical of the notion that because we now have a rather poor embodiment of democracy we can ultimately produce a genuine democracy by sweeping away what we have left of one.

The positive point, however, is that the democratic ideal, in its human significance, provides us with a frame of reference. The frame is not filled in, either in society at large or in its significance for education. I am not implying that it is so clear and definite that we can look at it as a traveler can look at a map and tell where to go from hour to hour. Rather the point I would make is that the *problem* of education in its relation to direction of social change is all one with the *problem* of finding out what democracy means in its total range of concrete applications: economic, domestic, international, religious, cultural, economic, *and* political.

I cannot wish for anything better to happen for, and in, our schools than that this problem should become the chief theme for consideration until we have attained clarity concerning the concrete significance of democracy—which like everything concrete means its application in living action, individual and collective. The trouble, at least one great trouble, is that we have taken democracy for granted; we have thought and acted as if our forefathers had founded it once for all. We have forgotten that it has to be enacted anew in every generation, in every year and day, in the living relations of person to person in all social forms and institutions. Forgetting this, we have allowed our economic and hence our political institutions to drift away from democracy; we have been negligent even in creating a school that should be the constant nurse of democracy.

I conclude by saying that there is at least one thing in which the idea of democracy is not dim, however far short we have come from striving to make it reality. Our public school system was founded in the name of equality of opportunity for all, independent of birth, economic status, race, creed, or color. The school can not by itself alone create or embody this idea. But the least it can do is to create individuals who understand the concrete meaning of the idea with their minds, who cherish it warmly in their hearts, and who are equipped to battle in its behalf in their actions.

Democracy also means voluntary choice, based on an intelligence that is the outcome of free association and communication with others. It means a way of living together in which mutual and free consultation rule instead of force, and in which co-operation instead of brutal competition is the law of life; a social order in which all the forces that make for friendship, beauty, and knowledge are cherished in order that each individual may become what he, and he alone, is capable of becoming. These things at least give a point of departure for the filling in of the democratic idea and aim as a frame of reference. If a sufficient number of educators devote themselves to striving courageously and with full sincerity to find the answers to the concrete questions which the idea and the aim put to us, I believe that the question of the relation of the schools to direction of social change will cease to be a question, and will become a moving answer in action.

45

# DEMOCRACY AND EDUCATION IN THE
# WORLD OF TODAY *

I SUPPOSE there was no one in this country or elsewhere who insisted with greater emphasis and clarity that democracy is a moral idea than did Dr. Adler. In his appreciation, his emphasis upon the dignity of the human personality, the individual personality, and consequently the possibilities that are in the human personality which demand all those conditions that we call democracy, and in his emphasis upon this conception of democracy and its relation to the individual, he never made the mistake of insisting simply upon democracy as a matter of the rights and claims of the individual, but he emphasized equally the duty and the responsibility of every individual to draw out not just what was best in himself, but to conduct himself so in all his human relations that he could do everything in his power to bring out, develop and realize whatever was significant and important in the individuality of others. I think we needed in his time and we still need this emphasis upon the reciprocity of the rights and claims and duties of human beings with reference to helping each other, not merely materially, though materially when that is needed, but even more—helping to realize whatever is significant and important in others.

Coming back directly to my subject, it is obvious that the relation between democracy and education is a reciprocal one, a mutual one, and vitally so. Democracy is itself an

* The first annual lecture in honor of Felix Adler, founder of the Society for Ethical Culture and the Ethical Culture Schools, delivered on Monday evening, October 24, 1938, at the Society for Ethical Culture as the first of a series of events in celebration of the 60th Anniversary of the Ethical Culture Schools.

359

educational principle, an educational measure and policy. There is nothing novel in saying that even an election campaign has a greater value in educating the citizens of the country who take any part in it than it has in its immediate external results. Our campaigns are certainly not always as educational as they might be, but by and large they certainly do serve the purpose of making the citizens of the country aware of what is going on in society, what the problems are and the various measures and policies that are proposed to deal with the issues of the day.

Mussolini remarked that democracy was passé, done with, because people are tired of liberty. There is a certain truth in that remark, not about democracy being done with, at least we hope not, but in the fact that human beings do get tired of liberty, of political liberty and of the responsibilities, the duties, the burden that the acceptance of political liberty involves. There is an educational principle and policy in a deeper sense than that which I have just mentioned in that it proposes in effect, if not in words, to every member of society just that question: Do you want to be a free human being standing on your own feet, accepting the responsibilities, the duties that go with that position as an effective member of society?

The meaning of democracy, especially of political democracy which, of course, is far from covering the whole scope of democracy, as over against every aristocratic form of social control and political authority, was expressed by Abraham Lincoln when he said that no man was good enough or wise enough to govern others without their consent; that is, without some expression on their part of their own needs, their own desires and their own conception of how social affairs should go on and social problems be handled.

A woman told me once that she asked a very well known American statesman what he would do for the people of this country if he were God. He said, "Well, that is quite a question. I should look people over and decide what it was that they needed and then try and give it to them."

She said, "Well, you know, I expected that to be the answer that you would give. There are people that would *ask* other people what they wanted before they tried to give it to them."

That asking other people what they would like, what they need, what their ideas are, is an essential part of the democratic idea. We are so familiar with it as a matter of democratic political practice that perhaps we don't always think about it even when we exercise the privilege of giving an answer. That practice is an educational matter because it puts upon us as individual members of a democracy the responsibility of considering what it is that we as individuals want, what our needs and troubles are.

Dr. Adler expressed very much the same idea. I am not quoting his words, but this was what he said, that "no matter how ignorant any person is there is one thing that he knows better than anybody else and that is where the shoes pinch on his own feet"; and because it is the individual that knows his own troubles, even if he is not literate or sophisticated in other respects, the idea of democracy over against any conception of aristocracy is that every individual must be consulted in such a way, actively not passively, that he himself becomes a part of the process of authority, of the process of social control; that his needs and wants have a chance to be registered in a way where they count in determining social policy. Along with that goes, of course, the other feature which is necessary for the realization of democracy, as it is educational, and that is mutual conference and mutual consultation and arriving ultimately at social control by pooling, by putting together all of these individual expressions of ideas and wants.

The ballot box and majority rule are external and very largely mechanical symbols and expressions of this. They are expedients, the best devices that at a certain time have been found, but beneath them there are the two ideas: first, of the opportunity, the right and the duty of every individual to form some conviction and to express some conviction regarding his own place in the social order, and the relations of that social order to his own welfare; second, the fact that each individual counts as one and one only on an equality with others, so that the final social will comes about as the co-operative expression of the ideas of many people. And I think it is perhaps only recently that we are realizing that that idea is the essence of all sound education.

Even in the classroom we are beginning to learn that learning that develops intelligence and character does not come about when only the textbook and the teacher have a say, that every individual becomes educated only as he has an opportunity to contribute something from his own experience, no matter how meager or slender that background of experience may be at a given time, and finally that enlightenment comes from the give and take, from the exchange of experiences and ideas.

The realization of that principle in the schoolroom, it seems to me, is an expression of the significance of democracy as an educational process without which individuals cannot come either into the full possession of themselves or make a contribution, if they have it in them to make, to the social wellbeing of others, to the welfare of the whole of which they are a part.

I said that democracy and education bore a reciprocal relation. It is not merely then that democracy is itself an educational principle, but that democracy cannot endure, much less develop, without education in that narrower sense in which we ordinarily think of it, the education that is given in the family, and especially as we think of it in the school. The school is the essential distributing agency for whatever values and purposes any social group cherishes. It is not the only means, but it is the first means, the primary means and the most deliberate means by which the values that any social group cherishes, the purposes that it wishes to realize, are distributed and brought home to the thought, the observation, judgment and choice of the individual.

What would a powerful dynamo in a big power house

amount to if there were no line of distribution leading into shops and factories to give power, leading into the home to give light? No matter what fine ideals or fine resources, the products of past experience, past human culture, exist somewhere at the center, they become significant only as they are carried out, or are distributed. That is true of any society, not simply of a democratic society; but what is true of a democratic society is, of course, that its special values and its special purposes and aims must receive such distribution that they become part of the mind and the will of the members of society. So that the school in a democracy is contributing, if it is true to itself as an educational agency, to the democratic idea of making knowledge and understanding, in short the power of action, a part of the intrinsic intelligence and character of the individual.

I think we have one thing to learn from the anti-democratic states of Europe today, and that is that we should take as seriously the preparation of the members of our society for the duties and responsibilities of democracy, as they take seriously the formation of the thoughts and minds and characters of their population for their particular aims and ideals.

Instead of meaning that we should imitate their universal propaganda, that we should prostitute the schools, the radio and the press to the inculcation of one single point of view and the suppression of everything else, it does mean that we should take seriously, energetically and vigorously the use of democratic schools and democratic methods in the schools; that we should educate the young and the youth of the country in freedom for participation in a free society. It may be that with the advantage of great distance from these troubled scenes in Europe we may learn something from the terrible tragedies that are occurring there, in taking the idea of democracy more seriously, asking ourselves what it means, and taking steps to make our schools more completely the agents for preparation of free individuals for intelligent participation in a free society.

Our free public school system was founded, promoted, just

about 100 years ago by its early prophets, because of the realization of men like Horace Mann and Henry Barnard and others that citizens needed to participate in what they called a republican form of government; that they needed enlightenment, and that that could come about only through a system of free education.

If you have read the writings of men of those times, you know how few schools existed, how poor they were, how short their terms were, how poorly most of the teachers were prepared, and, judging from what Horace Mann said, how general was the indifference of the average well-to-do citizen to the education of anybody except his own children.

You may recall the terrible indictment that he drew of the well-to-do classes because of their indifference to the education of the masses, and the vigor with which he pointed out that they were pursuing a dangerous course; that no matter how much they educated their own children, if they left the masses ignorant they would be corrupted and that they themselves and their children would be the sufferers in the end. As he said, "We did not mean to exchange a single tyrant across the sea for a hydra-headed tyrant here at home"; yet that is what we will get unless we educate our citizens.

I referred to that particularly because to such a very large extent the ideas, the ideals which Horace Mann and the others held have been so largely realized. I think even Horace Mann could hardly have anticipated a finer, more magnificent school plan, school building and school equipment than we have in some parts of our country. On the side of the mechanical and the external, the things that these educational statesmen 100 years ago strove for have been to a considerable extent realized. I should have to qualify that. We know how poor many of the rural schools are, especially in backward states of the country, how poorly they are equipped, how short their school years are; but in a certain sense, taking what has been done at the best, the immediate ideals of Horace Mann and the others have been realized.

Yet the problem we have today of the relation of education and democracy is as acute and as serious a problem as the problem of providing school buildings, school equipment, school teachers and school monies was a hundred years ago.

If, as we all know, democracy is in a more or less precarious position throughout the world, and has even in our own country enemies of growing strength, we cannot take it for granted as something that is sure to endure. If this is the situation, I think one reason for it is that we have been so complacent about the idea of democracy that we have more or less unconsciously assumed that the work of establishing a democracy was completed by the founding fathers or when the Civil War abolished slavery. We tend to think of it as something that has been established and that remains for us simply to enjoy.

We have had, without formulating it, a conception of democracy as something static, as something that is like an inheritance that could be bequeathed, a kind of lump sum that we could live off and upon. The crisis that we are undergoing will turn out, I think, to be worth-while if we learn through it that every generation has to accomplish democracy over again for itself; that its very nature, its essence, is something that cannot be handed on from one person or one generation to another, but has to be worked out in terms of needs, problems and conditions of the social life of which, as the years go by, we are a part, a social life that is changing with extreme rapidity from year to year.

I find myself resentful and really feeling sad when, in relation to present social, economic and political problems, people point simply backward as if somewhere in the past there were a model for what we should do today. I hope I yield to none in appreciation of the great American tradition, for tradition is something that is capable of being transmitted as an emotion and as an idea from generation to generation. We have a great and precious heritage from the past, but to be realized, to be translated from an idea and an emotion, this tradition has to be imbedded and embodied by active effort in the relations which we as human beings bear to each other under present conditions. It is because the conditions of life change, that the problem of maintaining a democracy becomes new, and the burden that is put upon the school, upon the educational system, is not that of stating merely the ideas of the men who made this country, their hopes and their intentions, but of teaching what a democratic society means under existing conditions.

The other day I read a statement to the effect that more than half of the working people in shops and factories in this country today are working in industries that didn't even exist forty years ago. It would seem to mean that, as far as the working population is concerned, half of the old industries have gone into obsolescence and been replaced by new ones. The man who made that statement, a working scientist, pointed out that every worker in every industry today is doing what he is doing either directly or indirectly because of the progress that has been made in the last half century in the physical sciences. In other words, in the material world, in the world of production, of material commodities and material entities, the progress of knowledge, of science, has revolutionized activity in the form of putting forth of human energy (revolutionized is not too strong a word) in the last fifty years.

How can we under these circumstances think that we can live from an inheritance, noble and fine as it is, that was formed in earlier days—one might as well say pre-scientific and pre-industrial days—except as we deliberately translate that tradition and that inheritance into the terms of the realities of present society, which means simply our relations to one another.

To go back to Horace Mann and the efforts of the other educators 100 years ago, the United States was essentially agricultural. The things with which we are most familiar that enter into the formation of a material part of our life didn't exist. Railways were just beginning, but all the other great inventions that we take for granted were hidden in the darkness of the future time. Even then in those earlier days, Thomas Jefferson predicted evils that might come to man with the too-rapid development of manufacturing industries, because, as he saw it, the backbone of any democratic society was the farmer who owned and cultivated his own land. He saw the farmer as a man who could control his own economic destiny, a man who, therefore, could stand on his own feet and be really a free citizen of a free country. What he feared was what might happen when men lost the security of economic independence and became dependent upon others.

Even Alexander Hamilton, who belonged to the other school of thought, when he was speaking of judges, said that those who controlled a man's subsistence controlled his will. If that is true of judges on the bench it is certainly true to a considerable extent of all people; and now we have economic conditions, because of the rapid change in industry and in finance, where there are thousands and millions of people who have the minimum of control over the conditions of their own subsistence. That is a problem, of course, that will need public and private consideration, but it is a deeper problem than that; it is a problem of the future of democracy, of how political democracy can be made secure if there is economic insecurity and economic dependence of great sections of the population if not upon the direct will of others, at least upon the conditions under which the employing sections of society operate.

I mention this simply as one of the respects in which the relation of education and democracy assumes a very different form than it did in the time when these great men thought, "If we can only have schools enough, only have school buildings and good school equipment and prepared teachers, the necessary enlightenment to take care of republican institutions will follow almost as a matter of course."

The educational problem today is deeper, it is more acute, it is infinitely more difficult because it has to face all of the problems of the modern world. Recently we have been reading in some quarters about the necessity of coalition, whether in arms or not, at least some kind of a coalition of democratic nations to oppose and resist the advance of Fascist, totalitarian, authoritarian states. I am not going to discuss the merits of that issue, but I do want to ask a few questions. What do we mean when we assume that we, in common with certain other nations, are really democratic, that we have already so accomplished the ends and purposes of democracy that all we have to do is to stand up and resist the encroachments of non-democratic states?

We are unfortunately familiar with the tragic racial intolerance of Germany and now of Italy. Are we entirely free from that racial intolerance, so that we can pride ourselves upon having achieved a complete democracy? Our treatment of the Negroes, anti-Semitism, the growing (at least I fear it is growing) serious opposition to the alien immigrant within our gates, is, I think, a sufficient answer to that question. Here, in relation to education, we have a problem: what are our schools doing to cultivate not merely passive toleration that will put up with people of different racial birth or different colored skin, but what are our schools doing positively and aggressively and constructively to cultivate understanding and goodwill which is certainly an essential part of any real democratic society?

We object, and object very properly, to the constant stream of false propaganda that is put forth in the states for the suppression of all free inquiry and freedom, but how again do we stand in those respects? I know we have in many schools a wonderful school pledge where the children six years old and up properly arise and pledge allegiance to a flag and to what that stands for—one indivisible nation, justice and liberty. How far are we permitting a symbol to become a substitute for the reality? How far are our citizens, legislators and educators salving their conscience with the idea that genuine patriotism is being instilled in these children because they recite the words of that pledge? Do they know what allegiance and loyalty mean? What do they mean by an indivisible nation when we have a nation that is still more or less torn by factional strife and class division? Is that an indivisible nation and is the reciting of a verbal pledge any educational guarantee of the existence of an indivisible nation?

And so I might go on about liberty and justice. What are we doing to translate those great ideas of liberty and justice out of a formal ceremonial ritual into the realities of the understanding, the insight and the genuine loyalty of the boys and girls in our schools?

We say we object, and rightly so, to this exaggerated, one-sided nationalism inculcated under the name of devotion to country, but until our schools have themselves become clear upon what public spirit and good citizenship mean in all the relations of life, they cannot meet the great responsibilities that rest upon them.

We deplore, also, and deplore rightly, the dependence of the authoritarian states in Europe upon the use of force. What are we doing to cultivate the idea of the supremacy of the method of intelligence, of understanding, the method of goodwill and of mutual sympathy over and above force? I know that in many respects our public schools have and deserve a good reputation for what they have done in breaking down class division, creating a feeling of greater humanity and of membership in a single family, but I do not believe that we have as yet done what can be done and what needs to be done in breaking down even the ordinary snobbishness and prejudices that divide people from each other, and that our schools have done what they can and should do in this respect.

And when it comes to this matter of force as a method of settling social issues, we have unfortunately only to look at our own scene, both domestic and international. In the present state of the world apparently a great and increasing number of people feel that the only way we can make ourselves secure is by increasing our army and navy and making our factories ready now to manufacture munitions. In other words, somehow we too have a belief that force, physical and brute force, after all is the best final reliance.

With our fortunate position in the world I think that if we used our resources, including our financial resources, to build up among ourselves a genuine, true and effective democratic society, we would find that we have a surer, a more enduring and a more powerful defense of democratic institutions both within ourselves and with relation to the rest of the world than the surrender to the belief in force, violence and war can ever give. I know that our schools are doing a great deal to inculcate ideas of peace, but I sometimes wonder how far this goes beyond a certain sentimental attachment to a realization of what peace would actually mean in the world in the way of co-operation, goodwill and mutual understanding.

I have only endeavored to call your attention first to the inherent, the vital and organic relation that there is between democracy and education from both sides, from the side of education, the schools, and from the side of the very meaning of democracy. I have simply tried to give a certain number of more or less random illustrations of what the problems of the schools are today with reference to preparing the youth of the country for active, intelligent participation in the building and the rebuilding and the eternal rebuilding—because, as I have said, it never can be done once for all—of a genuinely democratic society, and, I wish to close (as I began) with saying, that after all the cause of democracy is the moral cause of the dignity and the worth of the individual. Mutual respect, mutual toleration, give and take, the pooling of experiences, is ultimately the only method by which human beings can succeed in carrying on this experiment in which we are all engaged, the greatest experiment of humanity—that of living together in ways in which the life of each of us is at once profitable in the deepest sense of the word, profitable to himself and profitable and helpful in the building up of the individuality of others.

Psychology, 5, 159, 273-274
Public opinion, 248
Public school, 63, 113, 243, 363-364

Randall, J. H., 314
Reading, 26f., 276
Reason, 331-336
Recapitulation theory, 56-57
Religion, Ch. 6
Rockefeller School, 125
Romanticism, 69
Roosevelt, Theodore, 95
Rousseau, 68, 174

Science, 21-22, 77, 142, 149, 152, 155-156, 283-284, 334
Sense-perception, 58
Sentimentalism, 15
Social change, 348-358
Social control, 142, 146, 316-319
Social democracy, 71, 143
Social problems, 255-256
Social reform, 68
Sociology, 141-144
Sophists, 83
Soviet Union, 312
Specialism, 25, 194
Spirituality, 81

State, 78, 79, 190, 191
State-consciousness, 78f.
Superiority, 172f.
Supernatural, 76, 85
Symbols, 25-26

Teachers, 63-68, 344-345
Teachers College, Columbia University, 200-201
Teachers Union, 303-307
Torquemada, 134
Training schools, 154
Truth, 85, 334

Veblen, Thorstein, 139
Vocational education, 126f. See Industrial education
Voltaire, 191

War Department, 262
Washington, George, 231
Wilson, Woodrow, 103
Wood, Major General, 93
World War, 261
Writing, 24

Young, Ella Flagg, 212

Federal Bureau of Education, 95
Feudalism, 172-173
Fiske, John, 25
Freedom, *see* Liberty
Free will, 146
French Revolution, 134
Froebel, 58
Frontier, 108

Geneva Commission, 298
Germany, 88-89
Goals, 251-252
God, 17, 75, 134, 145, 191, 360
Goodrich, Rear Admiral, 96
Government, 158
Greek, 18, 47, 148
Growth, 71-73, 22, 289, 291-292, 295

Habit, 131. *See* Discipline
Hamilton, Alexander, 367
Hamlet, 301
Hearst, 323
Higher education, 39-40
High school, 51-52
History, 10, 33, 103
Hitler, 270, 311
Hogben, L., 331-336
Holmes, Justice, 302
Hoover, H., 252, 300
Humanism, 90
Humanities, 43
Human nature, 332-333
Hutchins, M., 331-336

Idealism, 118, 141, 146, 162, 251
Individualism, 69, 98, 164, 166, 266, 278
Individuality, 67-68, 170, 361-370
Indoctrination, 356-357
Industrial control, 319
Industrial education, 22f., 129-131
Industrialism, 110
Industrial revolution, 42-43, 158, 236, 366
Inferiority, 172f.
Initiative, 290
Instincts, 74, 87
Integration, 140
Intellectual freedom, 187
Intelligence, 69, 95-97, 132, 369
Intelligence tests, 167-168
Interaction, 210, 293
Inventions, 152, 158

James, William, 151
Jefferson, Thomas, 175, 321, 367
Jowett, Benjamin, 26

Knowledge, 79-81. *See* Science

Language training, 11f., 231-233
Latin, 28, 47, 148
Lenin, 134
Liberalism, 185-186, 193
Liberty, 68, 186, 196, 316-319
Liberty League, 318
Lincoln, 321
Lippmann, W., 95, 158, 159, 166
Literature, 10-11, 33
Loyalty, 133-134, 137

Magic, 97, 122
Magna Charta, 148
Mann, Horace, 63, 350, 364, 366
Manual training, Ch. 4
Measurement, 60
Mediocrity, 169-170
Merriam, C. E., 264
Militarism, 93
Miller, Professor, 244
Modern school, 122
Mort, Professor, 252
Motivation, 155
Motor activity, 55, 58
Mussolini, 360

National Education Association, 106
National system of education, 88, 95f., 311-315
Nationalism, 114-116
Nature study, 32-33
Newton, 176
Neutrality in education, 353

Parker, F. W., 217, 218
Pasteur, 176
Patriotism, 161
Perry, Arthur, 135
Plato, 79, 80, 83, 331, 335
Political democracy, 338-339, 346, 361
Preachers, 83
Preparedness, 101f.
Printing, 158
Progressive education, 216, 219-22, 273-281, 288f.
Propaganda, 122, 159, 268, 327
Provincialism, 103-104

# INDEX

Abstraction, 26
Academic freedom, 192, 320-324
Adams, John, 175
Addams, Jane, 262
Administration, problems of, 149, 192, 337-347
Americanism, 114
Americanization, 97-98
American Association of University Professors, 247
American Chemical Society, 246
American Federation of Labor, 254
Antin, Mary, 93
Anti-Semitism, 368
Aquinas, St. Thomas, 331, 335
Aristocracy, 173-175
Aristotle, 164, 175, 176, 331, 335
Arnold, Matthew, 157
Art, 145, 153
Association of American Medical Colleges, 246
Association of American Universities, 246
Austin, Mary, 150
Authoritarianism, 136-38
Authority, 155
Autocracy, 64-66
Averages, 166

Barnard, Henry, 63, 364
Bates, Professor, 247
Beard, C. A., 104
Belgium, 90
Board of Education, 135, 136
Books, 29-30, 70

Capitalism, 354-355
Carlyle, 136, 158
Chamber of Commerce, 254
Character, 45-46, 148-149
Child-centered school, 218-219
Childs, J. L., 326, 327
Christianity, 78-80
Church, 76, 78, 79, 190, 191

Civics, 104
Civil War, 365
Classes, 120, 179, 327-329
Classification, 167, 173
Class struggle, 325-330
Committee of Fifteen, 27
Committee on Social Trends, 257
Communism, 314
Consciousness, 12
Conservatism, 351-352
Culture, 46-49, 107-108, 131
Culture-epoch theory, 56
Custom, 142
Cutten, G. B., 165, 166, 168, 169
Curriculum, 11-12, 20, 44-45, 186, 208-210, 238-239

Democracy, 32-33, 62, 68, 73, 76-77, 86, 119, 158, 174, 225, 275, 322, 341-342, 359-370
Discipline, 8, 46-47, 55, 140, 155, 350
Dogberry, 140
Drift, 301, 313

Economic factors, 129f., 252-254, 261-266, 285, 307-310
Education, *see passim*
Einstein, 176
Elementary school, 38f.
Emerson, 230
Emotions, 14
England, 90
Environment, 295-297
Equality, 176-177, 340
Euclid, 335
Europeanism, 98, 120
Evolution, 43
Experience, 69, 76, 151-152, 170
Experimentation, 123-124, 152, 239-242, 280. *See* Science

Faith, 63
Fascism, 310, 314

371